Good luck + happiness Dee.
With love from everyone on S.C.B.U. xx.

Good luck + happiness Dee.
With love from everyone on S.C.B.U. xx.

# Red Sea
# Reef Fishes

# Red Sea Reef Fishes

## Dr JOHN E. RANDALL

IMMEL
Publishing

*Dedicated to my parents*

**Red Sea Reef Fishes**
Designed and produced by Cigale Limited
for IMMEL Publishing, a division of
International Marketing Middle East Limited
Ely House 37 Dover Street London W1 X 3RB
First published 1983
Reprinted 1986
© 1983 John E. Randall

Phototypeset in Monophoto Plantin Light by
MS Filmsetting Limited, Frome,
Somerset, England
Printed and bound in Japan by
Dai Nippon Printing Co, Tokyo

*House Editor*: Janet MacLennan
*Map artwork*: Ian Stephen


British Library Cataloguing in Publication Data

Randall, John E.
   Red Sea reef fishes.
   1. Coral reef fauna – Red Sea – Identification
   2. Marine fishes – Red Sea – Identification
   I. Title
   597.092′733      QL622.34

ISBN 0 907151 04 3


PUBLISHERS' NOTE: Every effort has been made to
ensure that the most widely accepted nomenclature is
included in this work.

# Contents

# Foreword

Twenty-six years ago my wife and I looked at a coral reef through face masks for the first time, and were so moved and excited by what we saw that we became committed snorkellers and, later, scuba divers. We get even more enjoyment and interest from both these activities now than we did on that very first experience at Michaelmas Cay on the Great Barrier Reef. But that was the day of revelation, and never-to-be-forgotten.

Ornithology had been my special interest before that, and, of course, it still is, but I found that fishes are, in many respects, underwater birds. Just as a 'field guide' is essential for the maximum enjoyment of any aspiring birdwatcher, so an underwater guide performs the same indispensable function for a fishwatcher. From the beginning I wanted to know the names of the fishes I saw, and I found that the available books in those days were, for the most part, poorly illustrated and covered only limited areas. It was not long before I found myself tapping the expertise of that most distinguished of fish taxonomists – the author of this book. It has been for me a most rewarding friendship, and Jack Randall's knowledge has been responsible for a great increase in my enjoyment of the underwater world. Having swum many times in the Red Sea without the assistance of a fish identification guide, and having myself illustrated the *Fishwatchers Guide to West Atlantic Coral Reefs* (which was the first such book to be printed in waterproof form), I greatly welcome this latest of Jack Randall's many publications and wish it all success. When next my wife and I go to the Red Sea, it will most certainly accompany us.

**Sir Peter Scott**
CHAIRMAN OF THE WORLD WILDLIFE
FUND INTERNATIONAL
Slimbridge
*July 1982*

# Introduction

The purpose of this book is to provide the means for the identification of the most common reef fishes that a snorkeler or diver might encounter in the Red Sea. The objective has been to present the minimum information required to identify each species positively. The maximum total length for each is given in centimetres (cm); anyone wishing to convert these lengths to inches should divide the centimetre length by 2.54. The greatest length attained by each species is not precisely known for most fishes; for some discussed below the length is given from sources that may have recorded estimates rather than actual measurements of specimens.

In their research, ichthyologists use the standard length of fishes as their primary measurement to express body proportions. This is the straight-line length from the tip of the snout (not the lower jaw in case it projects forward of the snout) to the base of caudal fin (=tail fin); this place on the fish is also the end of the vertebral column. The caudal fin of preserved specimens is often broken or distorted, hence the reason for using this length instead of total length. An example of such a proportion which the reader will often find in the species accounts herein: the depth of body 'X' in standard length. This tells exactly how high-bodied or elongate a fish is. If the depth is 1.5 in the standard length (meaning the depth measurement is contained $1\frac{1}{2}$ times in the standard length), the fish is a high-bodied species; if the proportion is 5, the fish is elongate. Since the depth of the body of a fish, and other proportional measurements as well, may vary from individual to individual, a range is generally given for these characteristics. Proportional measurements are based on fishes of adult size. If they were given for small juveniles as well, the ranges would at times be too great to be of diagnostic value in separating species.

Ichthyologists are fortunate because most fishes have many things that can be counted, such as the spines and soft rays of the various fins, the scales in the lateral line, the gill rakers, and the vertebrae (usually determined by X-rays). Collectively, these counts alone often provide positive identification of a species. Counts of the spines and soft rays of the dorsal, anal, and pelvic fins are differentiated by Roman and Arabic numerals, respectively. Thus, dorsal rays X,9 would mean the fin has ten spines and nine soft rays. When a dash (-) separates two numbers for the dorsal ray count, it indicates complete division into two fins.

The listing of characteristics whereby a fish can be identified requires the use of some technical terms for which there are no comparable words in everyday English. The reader is referred to the section following this introduction for labelled drawings showing the principal external parts of fishes. Also at the back of the book (in front of the index) there is a Glossary of ichthyological and other biological terms.

The colour of fishes is, of course, very important in the identification of most species. Although all the fishes in this book are portrayed in colour, a summary of the colour pattern is given in order to emphasize the salient features and to document variation. Often juveniles are different in colour from adults, and for a few families (particularly the wrasses and parrotfishes) males and females may be dramatically different in colour. In the colour descriptions, a bar is a vertical marking, a stripe horizontal, and a band oblique or irregular.

The geographical distribution of each species is also expressed in the briefest possible terms. If a fish is known only from the Red Sea, only the locality Red Sea will appear. If it occurs in the Red Sea and in enough localities in the western Indian Ocean (west of the southern tip of India) to suggest a broad distribution, the range is listed merely as western Indian Ocean. If a fish is known to range from the Red Sea through Indonesia to Pacific shores but not to Oceanic islands of the central and western Pacific, the distribution is given as East Africa to the western Pacific. If it extends eastward to French Polynesia (sometimes to the Pitcairn Group and rarely to Easter Island), the range is summarized simply as Indo-Pacific. When an Indo-Pacific pattern is indicated, this does not imply that the species is known throughout the entire region. There may be gaps (often the Hawaiian Islands is one) which may be real or may be due to inadequate collecting. But Indo-Pacific does indicate a very broad distribution within this vast tropical and subtropical region. More properly it is called the Indo-West Pacific to emphasize that such a distribution does not extend to the tropical eastern Pacific (western shores of the Americas and associated islands such as the Galapagos). Very few species of reef and shore fishes have crossed the broad expanse of ocean called the East Pacific Barrier which separates the easternmost islands of Polynesia from the Americas. Reef and shore fishes are dependent for their distribution on passive transport in ocean currents. As might be expected, those few that are common to both the eastern Pacific and Indo-Pacific have large larval stages and hence a presumed long period of pelagic development.

The marine fauna of the Red Sea is unique in the Indian Ocean region in that it has many native species. More than 10 per cent of the fishes are confined as species or subspecies to the Red Sea and Gulf of Aden. The percentage of endemism varies greatly from family to family. Of the 10 little fishes of the family Pseudochromidae, all but one are endemic (and that one ranges only to the Arabian Gulf). Of the 14 butterflyfishes (Chaetodontidae) seven are not found outside the Red Sea or Gulf of Aden. Still other families have no native Red Sea species.

Other remarks in species accounts may include comments on habitat (particularly if fishes are found in other environments than coral reefs), depth of occurrence in metres (m), and something of their natural history and habits when known.

Readers are encouraged to refer to the general discussions of the different families of fishes as there are remarks here which apply to all the species of these groups.

Fishes fall into two major classes, the bony fishes (Osteichthyes) and the sharks and rays (Chondrichthyes). These, in turn, are divisible into subclasses, such as the Teleostei, the major group of bony fishes considered in this book. Beneath this category we have orders, the largest of the teleosts being the Perciformes (note the 'iformes' ending which is common to all ordinal names). The principal classification below the order (and the one for which group common names are often given, such as damselfishes, wrasses, and parrotfishes) is the family. The names for these all end in 'idae', hence Chaetodontidae (butterflyfishes). Some families are divided into subfamilies (with an 'inae' ending). The final two categories are the genus and species which together comprise the scientific name given to all recorded animals and plants. The name for modern man is well known, *Homo sapiens*. It is customary to

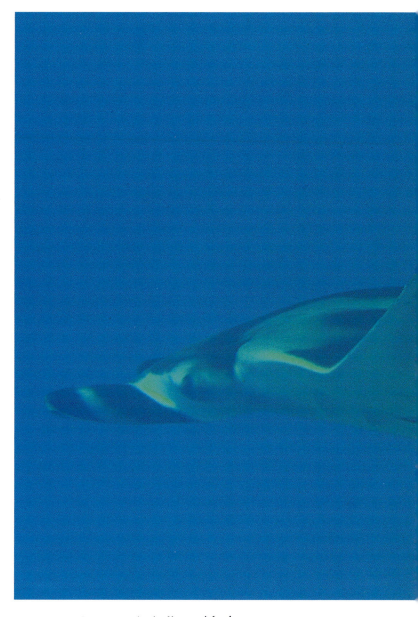

print scientific names in italics, with the generic part capitalized. A genus may consist of one species (in which case it is called monotypic) or two or more closely related species. Scientific names are derived from the Latin or Greek; often they depict some salient feature of the organism, but they can refer to the place where it was found, or the man who first collected it, or something of its habits.

It is customary after the species name to identify the person who gave the animal its scientific name and described its characteristics; often this is followed by the date of the publication in which the name and description appeared. If the author of the species used a different generic name from that given, his name is placed in parentheses.

Many animals and plants have been described as new species more than once. This is particularly true of wide-ranging fishes. One early naturalist might name a fish unaware that it had already been

described by someone else in another part of the species' range. The earliest scientific name (providing it appeared in print with adequate description in the year 1758 or thereafter) becomes the valid name for the species; those published later are called junior synonyms (here shortened to synonyms). Some synonyms have been used for many years in the belief they were the correct names. Those that have been commonly used in recent publications on fishes (and hence invalidated only within the last few years) are mentioned in the species accounts below.

Our system of classification of life began with the tenth edition of *Systema Naturae* written by the Swedish naturalist Carl Linnaeus in 1758. Some of the fishes in this book were named by him. Of the 325 species in this book, 58 were described by Peter Forsskål, also Swedish. He was one of a six-man Danish expedition to the Red Sea in 1762. Five of the men died during the expedition, among them Forsskål. The survivor, Carsten Niebuhr, brought back Forsskål's notes which were published in 1775 as his *Descriptiones Animalium*. This included 151 fishes, most of which were new to science. Forsskål preserved the Red Sea fish specimens by drying skins. Ninety-nine of these remain in the Zoological Museum in Copenhagen, of which 58 are type specimens of the species named by Forsskål.

In 1822 Dr Eduard Rüppell, representing the Senckenberg Museum in Frankfurt, collected fishes in the Red Sea. During the period 1828–30 he published *Fische des rothen Meeres* in his *Atlas zu der Reise im nordischen Afrika*; of the 161 species described, 75 were regarded as new. After more field work in the Red Sea in 1831, his *Fische des rothen Meeres* in *Neue Wirbelthiere zu der Fauna van Abyssinien Gehorig* was published in four parts (1835–38); of 164 species described, 100 were named as new.

At the same time Rüppell was in the Red Sea, C. G. Ehrenberg and F. G. Hemprich, also Germans, were obtaining fishes. Hemprich died in Massawa; Ehrenberg brought back to Berlin a large collection of plants and animals. He made the fishes available to the famous Baron Georges Cuvier and Achille Valenciennes for their monumental 22-volume *Histoire naturelles des poissons* (1828–47). They described a number of new Red Sea fishes, attributing the authorship to Ehrenberg. They also described other species extralimital to the Red Sea which were later found to range into the sea. In the present work the authorship of all species named in *Histoire naturelle des poissons* is given as Cuvier and Valenciennes even though it has been shown that one or the other should be sole author depending on which volume or part thereof he wrote.

Beginning in 1864 another German, the physician Carl Klunzinger, commenced a five-year study of Red Sea fishes in Egypt, which culminated in 1870–71 in his *Synopsis der Fische des Rothen Meeres*; this contained 520 species. Three more years of field work in Egypt commencing in 1872 and subsequent study of his specimens resulted in the first part of his *Die Fische des Rothen Meeres* (1884) with 261 fishes; the second part never appeared.

Since Klunzinger, many people have collected fishes in the Red Sea, and numerous scientific papers dealing with them have been published; no one, however, has attempted a full compilation except for two checklists (Botros, 1971; Dor, 1982). Approximately one thousand species of fishes are now recorded from the Red Sea.

The author has made eight trips to the Red Sea to collect and photograph fishes, the first in 1972. He has described 18 fishes as new from the sea, mostly with colleagues; still others remain to be named in the Apogonidae, Gobiidae, and Pseudogrammatidae.

Thanks are due the following people who have assisted in the preparation of this book in some significant way: Gerald R. Allen, William D. Anderson, Jr., Marjorie Awai, Avi Baranes, Christine Baer, Nathan A. Bartlett, Marie-Louise Bauchot, Loreen R. Bauman, Adam Ben-Tuvia, Kent E. Carpenter, Eugenie Clark, Bruce B. Collette, Jan Copeland, Roger F. Cressey, Garth Davis, Charles E. Dawson, Donald P. de Sylva, M. Dor, William N. Eschmeyer, Walter Fischer, Lev FisShelson, Thomas H. Fraser, David Fridman, J. A. F. Garrick, Janet R. Gomon, Ofer Gon, Paul Guézé, Graham S. Hardy, Adel Ali Hassan, Douglass F. Hoese, J. Barry Hutchins, Ilan Karplus, Wolfgang Klausewitz, Leslie W. Knapp, Katsuzo Kuronuma, Eitan Levy, Keiichi Matsuura, L. A. Maugé, John E. McCosker, R. J. McKay, E. O. Murdy, Rupert F. G. Ormond, Theodore W. Pietsch, Dan Popper, Dov F. Por, Helen A. Randall, Jean Michel Rose, Adrian P. L. Sanders, Torao Sato, Yukio Sawada, Hagen Schmid, Johannes H. Schroeder, William F. Smith-Vaniz, Victor G. Springer, Arnold Y. Suzumoto, Peter J. and Paula Vine, Robin S. Waples, Alwyne C. Wheeler, A. W. White, Jeffrey T. Williams, Thosaporn Wongratana and David J. Woodland.

# Morphology of Fishes

## *Cartilaginous Fishes (sharks and rays)*

The two illustrations below and the four on the facing page are labelled to show the principal external parts of fishes. These terms are also defined in the Glossary at the back of the book.

### Tiger Shark
(*Galeocerdo cuvier*)

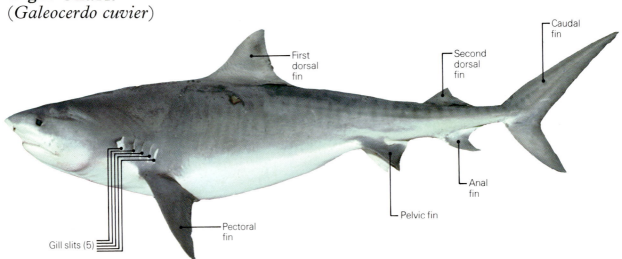

First dorsal fin

Second dorsal fin

Caudal fin

Anal fin

Pelvic fin

Pectoral fin

Gill slits (5)

### Stingray
(*Himantura uarnak*)

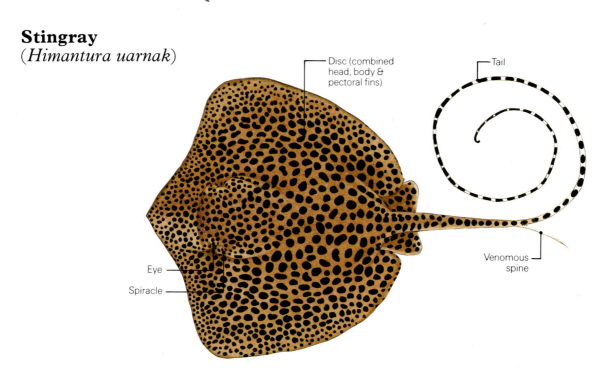

Disc (combined head, body & pectoral fins)

Tail

Venomous spine

Eye

Spiracle

# Bony Fishes

## Bluestripe Snapper
(*Lutjanus kasmira*)

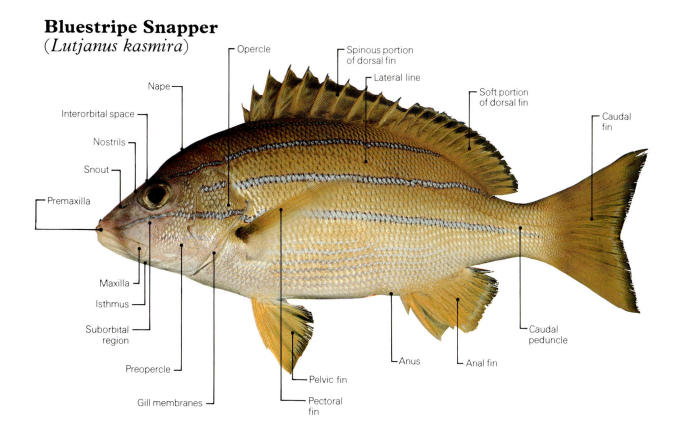

A

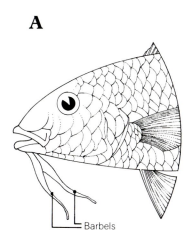

The drawing labelled **A** is the head of a goatfish (Mullidae) and shows the pair of barbels on the chin. These are moved over the bottom or thrust into the sediment during feeding to assist the fish in finding its food.

**B** shows the tail of a trevally (Carangidae) which has a falcate caudal fin; this shape is often found on fishes capable of swimming very rapidly. Because of the stress placed on the narrow caudal peduncle, fishes such as jacks and tunas usually reinforce it with scutes and/or keels.

B

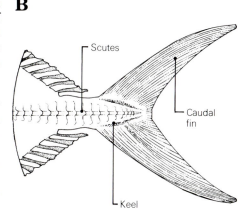

C

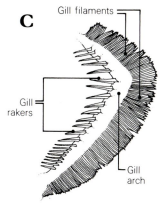

**C** depicts one of the gills (respiratory organ of fishes). The gill arch is the structural part. Gaseous exchange takes place in the gill filaments and the gill rakers keep food items from passing out of the gill opening along with expired water.

**D** is the roof of the mouth of a percomorph fish and shows the typical dentition of the premaxilla, vomer and palatine bones.

D

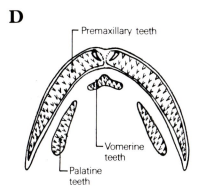

# Habitat

Above: *the coral reef is an assemblage of animals and plants which constitutes the most complex community in the sea. Many species of fishes make their home in reefs, taking advantage of the abundance and variety of food organisms and the shelter it affords from predators. The little blenny in the centre of the picture is* Ecsenius gravieri, *a mimic of another blenny which possesses venomous fangs.*

Right: *the coral reef community interacts with the organisms of other habitats. Some fishes such as grunts (Haemulidae) and snappers (Lutjanidae) use reefs for shelter by day, moving out into seagrass beds or sand flats at night to feed. Many small reef fishes, such as these bluegreen chromis (Chromis caerulea) rise from the bottom to pick individual animals from the plankton in the passing water mass; with the approach of danger, the fishes quickly descend to hide among the branches of coral.*

Below: *the water column above coral reefs is an important source of food, not only for some reef fishes but to pelagic species like these striped mackerel* (Rastrelliger kanagurta) *which are feeding on tiny crustaceans and other animals of the plankton by straining them from the sea on their numerous slender gill rakers.*

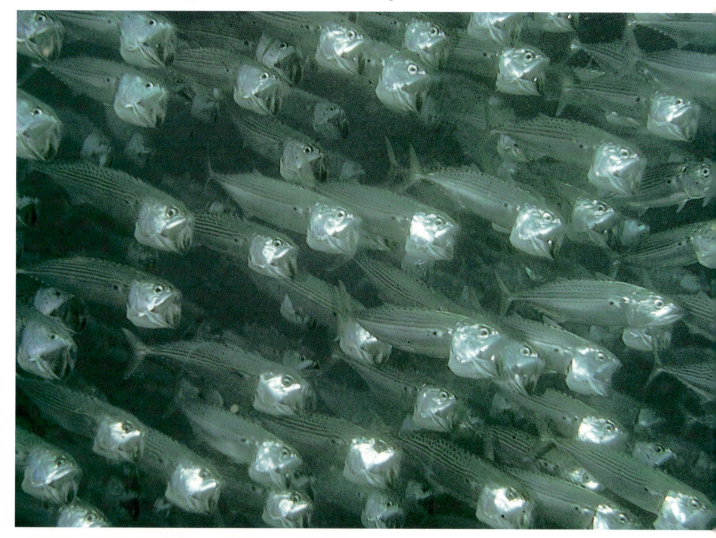

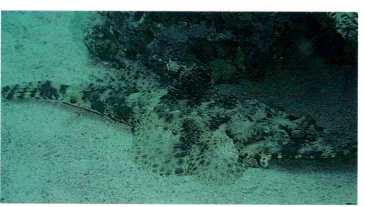

Left: *the seagrass habitat, often adjacent to or near a coral reef, is important as a nursery ground for many reef fishes. Some species live there as adults such as this parrotfish* (Leptoscarus vaigiensis). *Other adult residents are the garden eel* Gorgasia sillneri, *the filefish* Paramonacanthus barnadi, *the wrasse* Novaculichthys macrolepidotus, *and some pipefishes and seahorses.*

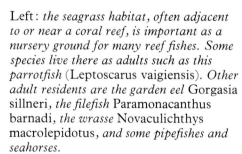

Left: *sand flats are the usual habitat next to coral reefs. Fishes which live here are either protectively coloured to look like sand, or bury partially or completely in the sand, or both. Examples are flatheads* (Platycephalidae) *like this large* Cociella crocodila *lurking on the sand in the shadow of a reef, dragonets* (Callionymidae), *snake eels* (Ophichthidae), *sanddivers* (Trichonotidae), *razorfishes (genus* Xyrichtys *of the wrasse family Labridae), and various flatfishes and gobies.*

17

# Cartilaginous Fishes (Chondrichthyes)

This class of fishes consists of the subclass Elasmobranchii, which includes the sharks (Squaliformes) and rays and skates (Rajiformes), and subclass Holocephali, which includes the Chimaeriformes, a small, bizarre, deep water group. The shark and rays are characterized by having a cartilaginous skeleton, five to seven gill slits on each side, no gas bladder, a spiral-valve intestine, and internal fertilization (accomplished by the development in the male of a pair of elongate organs called claspers, one on the inner edge of each pelvic fin). Most sharks and rays give birth to living young. These fishes have evolved separately from the bony fishes for a very long time. The presence of their distinctive teeth in fossil deposits has revealed that most recent genera existed in the Cretaceous Period which began 135 million years ago. Among the families of sharks represented in the Red Sea are the nurse sharks (Orectolobidae), the whale shark (Rhincodontidae), thresher sharks (Alopiidae), mackerel sharks (Isuridae), requiem sharks (Carcharhinidae), and hammerheads (Sphyrnidae). The Red Sea rays include the sawfishes (Pristidae), guitarfishes (Rhinobatidae), electric rays (Torpedinidae; see *Torpedo* on the half-title page), stingrays (Dasyatididae), eagle rays (Myliobatidae; see *Aetobatis* on page 11), and the mantas (Mobulidae; see *Manta* on page 11). In the present book we will consider only the requiem sharks and stingrays.

# Requiem Sharks (Carcharhinidae)

This family of sharks is represented by more species in the world than any other. Nearly all of the sharks dangerous to man are members of the Carcharhinidae, the Isuridae (includes the makos and the great white shark, the latter not known in the Red Sea), and the Sphyrnidae. The requiem sharks may be characterized as follows: five gill slits, the fifth over or posterior to origin of pectoral fin; no gill rakers; nostrils separate from mouth, without a barbel; labial furrows present; eye with a well developed nictitating membrane; teeth in one functional row and with only one cusp (except *Triaenodon* with two rows and small basal cusps); caudal fin with an expanded lower lobe (but much shorter than upper lobe); upper caudal lobe distinctly less than half total length; most species with an obvious precaudal pit above and below origin of caudal fin; second dorsal fin of most much smaller than first. Development is either ovoviviparous or viviparous with yolk sac placenta. Nineteen carcharhinids have been recorded in the Red Sea, including the tiger shark, *Galeocerdo cuvier* (Peron and Lesueur), the lemon shark, *Negaprion acutidens* (Rüppell), two dogfishes (*Mustelus*), and ten species of *Carcharhinus*. Accounts are given below to the four species of the family most often encountered on Red Sea reefs.

# 1 Blacktip Reef Shark

*Carcharhinus melanopterus* (Quoy and Gaimard), 1824

No median longitudinal ridge on back between dorsal fins; snout relatively blunt and rounded, its length before mouth about 3.5 in head (to fifth gill opening); all fins prominently tipped with black, the broad black apical end of the first dorsal fin often set off by a pale band below it. Penetrates shallow reef and sand flats more readily than other sharks, the first dorsal fin frequently breaking the surface. A relatively small species, probably not exceeding 180 cm (6 feet). Wide-ranging in the Indo-Pacific. Feeds mainly on fishes, sometimes on octopuses. Generally frightened away when approached by divers. The few attacks on man have been mainly on feet or legs of persons wading in the shallows.

# 2 Shortnose Blacktail Shark

*Carcharhinus wheeleri* (Garrick), 1982

No median longitudinal ridge on back between dorsal fins; snout short, its length before mouth slightly less than one-third head length (to fifth gill opening); posterior margin of caudal fin blackish; tip and outer half of trailing edge of first dorsal fin narrowly pale [but not as conspicuously and broadly white as in *C. albimarginatus* (Rüppell), the other fins of which are white-tipped]. May occur at depths of only a few metres, but usually not far from deeper water where generally found. Maximum length about 175 cm. Western Indian Ocean. Seems not as aggressive as its counterpart in the eastern Indo-Pacific, the grey reef shark, *C. amblyrhynchos* (Bleeker), from which it was distinguished as a distinct species only recently. Previously this shark has been misidentified as *C. amblyrhynchos*, *C. menisorrah* (Müller and Henle), and *C. spallanzani* (Leseur).

# 3 Sandbar Shark
*Carcharhinus plumbeus* (Nardo), 1827

A low median longitudinal ridge on back between dorsal fins; dorsal fin extremely large, the height as much as 18 per cent total length, its origin directly above rear end of pectoral fin base; length of snout in front of mouth about one-third head length (to fifth gill opening); dermal denticles (scales) wider than long and not overlapping; grey-brown dorsally, whitish ventrally, without distinct fin markings. Largest recorded, 240 cm. Atlantic and Indo-Pacific in tropical and warm temperate seas. Feeds mainly on small bottom fishes and invertebrates such as octopuses and crabs. Has not been implicated in attacks on man; this may be related to its preference for small prey. Nevertheless, potentially dangerous. *C. milberti* (Müller and Henle) is a synonym.

# 4 Whitetip Reef Shark
*Triaenodon obesus* (Rüppell), 1835

No ridge on back; body slender; snout very blunt, its length before mouth about 5 in head; teeth small, each with a large central cusp and a small basal cusp (sometimes two) on each side (teeth of other carcharhinids without small basal cusps), and in at least two functional rows; dorsal fins and upper lobe of caudal fin conspicuously white-tipped. Attains 170 cm. East Africa to the eastern Pacific. Truly a reef-dwelling species; often seen at rest in caves by day. Feeds mainly on reef fishes, occasionally on octopuses. The few attacks on man have involved spearfishermen with bleeding fish. A tagging study of subadults by the author at Johnston Island revealed slow growth, about 2.5 cm per year.

# Stingrays (Dasyatididae)

Like other rays, the head, body and pectoral fins of stingrays are joined as one ovate to subquadrangular flattened form termed the disc. The elongate tapering tail, usually bearing one or two venomous spines extends from the midposterior part of the disc; there are no rayed dorsal or caudal fins; the pelvic fins are joined to the disc to each side of the base of the tail. The teeth are small, close-set, in numerous rows, rhomboid in outline; the surface of the teeth sometimes has cusps. The gill slits are on the ventral side. Water for respiration is drawn into a small hole behind each eye called the spiracle and expelled through the gill slits. When at rest on the seabed bottom, rays are often partially buried in the sand or mud. They generally feed by excavating the sediment for molluscs, worms, and crustaceans; crater-like depressions in the bottom are indicative of sites where rays have fed. The stingrays are ovoviviparous, the embryos lying free within the uterus without any direct physical contact with the mother; nutrition for development comes initially from the yolk of the egg and later from

# 5 Reef Stingray

*Taeniura lymma* (Forsskål), 1775

Disc broadly ovate, slightly longer than wide, somewhat pointed at the front; tail longer than disc with one or two venomous spines posterior to midpoint; anal fin a long fold posteriorly on underside of tail; spiracles about as large as eye; teeth small, rhomboid, with a backward-projecting cusp on posterior corner; dorsal surface of disc orangish brown to olive-brown with numerous bright blue spots, those near margins smaller; tail with a blue stripe on each side. Reaches a total length of about 100 cm. East Africa to the western Pacific. Hides on sand patches in small caves or beneath ledges in reefs.

albuminous fluid secreted from vascular filaments which line the uterine wall. The venomous spines have a series of recurved barbs along each edge; the glandular tissue secreting the venom lies in a longitudinal groove on each side of the top of the spine. Wounds from these spines are very painful and may be serious. Of the eight dasyatidid rays recorded from the Red Sea, only *Taeniura lymma* can be regarded as a reef fish. The large *Himantura uarnak* (Forsskål) (see painting of this species on page 14) may be found close inshore.

# Bony Fishes (Osteichthyes)

In contrast to sharks and rays, this class of fishes has a bony skeleton and there is a single gill opening on each side. Most species lay numerous eggs; only a few are live-bearing. There are two subclasses, the Choanichthyes (lobefin fishes – the lungfishes and *Latimeria*) and the Actinopterygii (rayfin fishes). The latter subclass is divisible into three super-orders, of which only members of the Teleostei occur in the Red Sea.

## Herrings & Sardines (Clupeidae)

These are small schooling fishes which feed on plankton. They are not reef fishes in the strict sense, but may range over shallow reefs and be preyed upon by resident carnivorous species. They are characterized by a single dorsal fin, no spines in fins, pectoral fins low on the body, pelvic fins in a posterior abdominal position, a forked caudal fin, and no lateral line (or at most a very short one). Usually there is a series of sharp midventral scales (called scutes) on the chest and abdomen. The related anchovies (Engraulididae) are readily distinguished by their blunt overhanging snout and huge ventral mouth. One representative of the 11 clupeid fishes known from the Red Sea is discussed below.

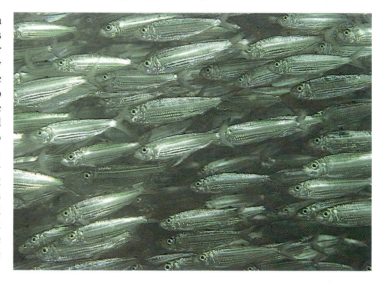

### 6 Fourspot Sardine

*Herklotsichthys quadrimaculatus* (Rüppell), 1837

Dorsal rays 17 to 20; anal rays 17 to 19; pectoral rays 15 or 16; depth of body 3.3 to 5.5 in standard length; eye 2.3 to 3.7 in standard length; wing-shaped median predorsal scales hidden under the normal paired and overlapping median scales; no prominent ridge of teeth on palatines; scales toothed posteriorly; silvery blue-green on back, silvery below, with a yellow stripe on body at level of eye and a small yellowish spot above and below it just behind the gill opening. Attains 15 cm. East Africa to Samoa. Unlike many clupeids, this one does not live in brackish environments. *Harengula bipunctata* Cuvier and Valenciennes is a synonym.

# Lizardfishes (Synodontidae)

Lizardfishes are named for their reptile-like heads. They have a large mouth and numerous slender sharp teeth, a cylindrical body, no spines in the fins, a high dorsal fin with 10 to 13 rays, an adipose fin (small fleshy fin between the dorsal and caudal fins) and large pelvic fins of 8 or 9 rays. Typically they lie in wait on sedimentary bottoms (they are able to partially bury in sand), darting upward with great rapidity to seize prey (usually small fishes) that venture near. The two underwater photos show *Synodus variegatus* eating a smaller member of its own species (this was a natural-occurring event photographed by the author in the Gulf of Aqaba). Nine species of synodontid fishes occur in the Red Sea. The most common representative of each of the two principal genera that may be seen in or around shallow Red Sea reefs is discussed below.

## 7 Common Lizardfish

*Synodus variegatus* (Fowler), 1912

Dorsal rays 10 to 13 (usually 12); anal rays 8 to 10 (usually 9); lateral-line scales 56 to 61 (modally 59); this and other *Synodus* are separated from *Saurida* by having a single series of teeth on the palatines (each side of roof of mouth), and the lips largely covering the small teeth along side of jaws; light tan with eight or nine dark brown saddle-like bars which narrow as they pass ventrally on back and expand at lateral line to an approximate diamond shape; lesser brown blotches between the dark bars, fins except anal usually with cross bands. Attains about 25 cm. Indo-Pacific, generally in less than 20 m.

## 8 Slender Lizardfish

*Saurida gracilis* (Quoy and Gaimard), 1824

Dorsal rays 11 or 12 (usually 11); anal rays 9 or 10 (usually 10); pectoral rays 12 to 14 (usually 13); lateral-line scales 50 to 52; a second short inner series of teeth on palatines; numerous small teeth exposed on side of jaws; pectoral fins 12 per cent or more of standard length; pale greenish to light brown dorsally, whitish ventrally, with a series of about ten indistinct vertically elongate blackish blotches on body, the two darkest tending to merge dorsally beneath posterior half of dorsal fin; lesser dark blotches among the large ones; dark bars on side of mouth and dark spots forming bands in fins. Reaches about 30 cm. Indo-Pacific.

# Morays (Muraenidae)

Moray eels are unmistakable with their elongate, muscular, somewhat compressed bodies, no paired fins and large mouths. Most species have long sharp canine teeth, but some such as *Gymnomuraena zebra* (Shaw) and the species of *Echidna*, have low nodular teeth. The gill opening is small, there are no spines, and the caudal fin is not distinct (confluent at the tip of the tail with the dorsal and anal fins). The ribbon-like, transparent, leptocephalus larval stage is long-lived, resulting in broad distributions for most species. Those with canine teeth tend to feed on fishes and not infrequently on octopuses, while those with nodular teeth take mostly crabs. The moray is feared by most novice divers, but they soon learn that it is not ordinarily aggressive. Most bites from these eels are the result of provocation (such as by spearing) or the misidentification of a hand as prey. Some authors prefer the generic name *Lycodontis* for the species listed below in *Gymnothorax*. Much systematic research remains to be done on this family at both the generic and species level.

## 9 Snowflake Moray

*Echidna nebulosa* (Ahl), 1789

Depth of body 14 to 20 in total length; anus slightly posterior to middle of total length; origin of dorsal fin just anterior to a vertical through gill opening; upper jaw with stout conical teeth anteriorly and a row of small compressed teeth with sharp edges on side; lower jaw with two rows of teeth, the inner anterior row stout and conical, the remaining teeth nodular; vomerine teeth nodular, in two rows; whitish with large dendritic black blotches containing yellow spots; small black spots or short irregular lines among the black blotches. Attains 75 cm. Indo-Pacific. Typically found in shallow water under rocks or in crevices in reefs; sometimes ventures into seagrass or algal flats. *E. polyzona* (Richardson) differs in having 23 to 30 broad brown rings encircling head and body.

## 10 Grey Moray

*Siderea grisea* (Lacepède), 1803

Depth of body 17 to 22 in total length; anus well in front of middle of length, the snout to anus distance about 2.4 in total length; origin of dorsal fin closer to eye than gill opening; relatively short conical teeth in two rows on side of upper jaw, front of lower jaw and on vomer (in one row elsewhere); body yellowish, densely mottled with small light brown spots; head anterior to dorsal fin brownish grey; pores on head and lateral line in small black spots, thus forming dotted lines. Maximum length about 65 cm. Western Indian Ocean. The most common moray in the Red Sea. Sometimes classified in the genus *Gymnothorax*; *Muraena geometricus* Rüppell is a synonym.

## 11 Yellowmargin Moray

*Gymnothorax flavimarginatus* (Rüppell), 1830

Depth of body 11 to 18 in total length; snout to anus distance 2.2 to 2.5 in total length; snout short, its length less than distance from front of eye to corner of mouth; origin of dorsal fin slightly anterior to gill opening; canine teeth in one row in jaws, compressed with sharp edges, particularly those on side of jaws; teeth at front of jaws long and fang-like; the two longest in a median row on intermaxilla at front of upper jaw; vomerine teeth in one irregular row; yellowish brown, densely mottled with small dark brown spots; gill opening in a black blotch; fins edged with yellow-green posteriorly. Attains at least 120 cm. Indo-Pacific and the eastern Pacific.

## 12 Yellowmouth Moray

*Gymnothorax nudivomer* (Playfair and Günther), 1867

Depth of body 11 to 16 in total length; snout to anus distance 2.1 to 2.3 in total length; snout short, shorter than distance from front edge of eye to corner of mouth; compressed canine teeth in a single row in jaws, the edges sharp and finely serrate; anterior six pairs of teeth in upper jaw enlarged; no teeth on vomer; light brown, darker posteriorly, with very small irregular white spots anteriorly, becoming large and dark-edged on tail; edge of gill opening dusky; inside of mouth bright yellow. Reaches 100 cm. East Africa to the Hawaiian Islands; *Gymnothorax xanthostomus* is a synonym. Red Sea specimens have fewer and smaller white spots posteriorly on body and a more systematic study of this form is needed. Frequently makes a threat display to intruders by broadly opening its mouth, the effect of which is accentuated by the yellow colour. The author and Japanese colleagues discovered that the mucus of this eel possesses a toxin, the function of which remains unknown.

27

## 13 Giant Moray

*Gymnothorax javanicus* (Bleeker), 1859

Depth of body 11 to 18 in total length (small individuals more slender); snout to anus distance 2.1 to 2.2 in total length; snout short, shorter than distance from hind edge of eye to corner of mouth; origin of dorsal fin about equidistant to corner of mouth and gill opening; canine teeth in one row in jaws, compressed with sharp edges, particularly those on side of jaws; teeth at front of jaws long and fang-like, the two longest in a median row on intermaxillary bone; vomerine teeth in one irregular row; brown with large dark brown blotches (which may contain spots of lighter brown) and numerous small dark brown spots; gill opening in a large black spot. The largest Indo-Pacific *Gymnothorax*; attains at least 220 cm (unverified reports to 300 cm or more). Feeds mainly on a wide variety of reef fishes.

# Conger Eels (Congridae)

The Congridae is one of 23 families of eels of the order Anguilliformes. Like the morays, congers have elongate bodies, large mouths, a small gill opening, and the caudal fin confluent with the dorsal and anal fins. They differ notably in having pectoral fins, and their body is nearly round anteriorly. The family is divisible into two subfamilies, the Congrinae (most occur in deep-water; the most common shallow-water species is discussed below), and the Heterocongrinae, popularly known as garden eels. An underwater photo of the Red Sea species, *Gorgasia sillneri* Klausewitz, is shown to the right.

## 14 Mustache Conger

*Conger cinereus* Rüppell, 1830

Pectoral fins with 16 to 18 rays; lateral-line pores anterior to anus 37 to 41; depth of body 16 to 22 in total length; origin of dorsal fins anterior to tip of pectoral fins; teeth at edge of jaws compressed, close-set, forming a shearing edge; brownish grey with black margins on median fins; a blackish streak above upper lip; a blackish area on pectoral fins of adults. Reaches 130 cm. Indo-Pacific. Hides in reefs by day and forages for food (mainly fishes, sometimes crustaceans) by night at which time it assumes a colour pattern of broad, dark, encircling rings.

# Eel Catfishes (Plotosidae)

The Plotosidae is one of 30 families of catfishes (order Siluriformes), most of which are characterized by having barbels around the mouth. Only two have truly marine species, this family and the Ariidae; each is represented in the Red Sea by one species. The plotosid catfishes are elongate, hence the common name, eel catfishes. They have two dorsal fins (the second dorsal fin is actually a forward extension of the caudal fin) and no adipose fin. The long second 'dorsal' and anal fins are joined with the caudal fin around the tip of the tail. The single dorsal and pectoral spines are serrate and venomous. Wounds from these spines may be dangerous (deaths have been reported in older literature). Plotosids are confined to the Indo-Pacific region; about half occur in the marine environment.

## 15 Striped Eel Catfish

*Plotosus lineatus* (Thunberg), 1787

First dorsal fin with a stout serrate spine at the front and 5 rays; pectoral fin with a comparable spine at upper end and 11 rays; pelvic fins with 12 rays; four pairs of barbels around mouth; brown with two narrow pale stripes, shading to white ventrally. The young, which are darker with yellowish stripes, are often seen in dense schools moving over shallow reefs and seagrass beds. Maximum length about 30 cm (reports of greater length probably apply to other species). East Africa to the western Pacific. *P. anguillaris* (Bloch) and *P. arab* (Bleeker) (after

Forsskål) are synonyms. The dorsal and pelvic spines are venomous and can inflict painful wounds.

# Needlefishes (Belonidae)

The needlefishes have very slender bodies and extremely elongate jaws with numerous needle-like teeth. The fins lack spines; the dorsal and anal fins are posterior in position, and the pelvics occur towards the end of the abdomen and six-rayed. The lateral line is low on the body, and the scales are small. These fishes live at the surface and are protectively coloured for this mode of life – green or blue on the back and silvery white on the sides and ventrally. When frightened (for example, by a light at night), they may leap from the water and skip at the surface. They have been known to injure people who lie in their path at this time, and fatalities have resulted. Needlefishes feed mainly on small pelagic fishes. Their eggs are large and have adhesive filaments with which they attach themselves to floating objects. Six species are recorded from the Red Sea. Two species of *Tylosurus* and *Platybelone argalus* (Lesueur) (underwater photo shows one individual in centre of field; the other fish are half-beaks) are the ones most apt to be seen inshore over reefs.

## 16 Red Sea Houndfish

*Tylosurus choram* (Rüppell), 1837

Dorsal rays usually 21; anal rays 20 or 21; pectoral rays 13 or 14 (including rudimentary upper ray); body very elongate (more so in juveniles than adults); jaws extremely long and pointed (becoming relatively shorter with age), teeth slender, needle-sharp, and perpendicular in jaws; caudal peduncle about as deep as wide (much wider than deep in *Platybelone argalus*); keel posteriorly on caudal peduncle and base of caudal fin poorly developed, receiving lateral line (keel very well developed in *P. argalus*, the lateral line passing below); caudal fin deeply emarginate, the lower lobe distinctly longer than upper; dorsal fin commencing posterior to origin of anal fin; green on back, silvery on sides and ventrally. Reaches 65 cm. Appears to be confined to the Red Sea and Mediterranean (by way of the Suez Canal). Very closely related to the circumtropical *T. crocodilus* (Peron and Lesueur) which also occurs in the Red Sea. *T. choram* has a longer head, its length 1.6 to 2.0 in body length compared to 2.0 to 2.6 for *crocodilus*.

# Halfbeaks (Hemiramphidae)

The halfbeaks are grouped with the needlefishes and flyingfishes in the order Beloniformes; they share many of the general characters with these two families. Some authors prefer to classify the hemiramphids in the same family as the flyingfishes (Exocoetidae). With few exceptions, the halfbeaks have a very long lower jaw (often tipped with red) and a very short upper jaw (triangular when viewed from above); they have larger scales than the needlefishes. They also tend to leap and skitter at the surface, and two offshore species which occur in the Red Sea are able to glide in the air on out-stretched pectoral fins like flyingfishes. Seven species of halfbeaks are known from the Red Sea; one of each of the two largest genera, *Hemiramphus* and *Hyporhamphus*, is discussed below.

A second species of *Hemiramphus*, *H. marginatus* (Forsskål), is shown in an underwater photo with the needlefish *Platybelone argalus* (see belonid family discussion).

## 17 Spotted Halfbeak

*Hemiramphus far* (Forsskål), 1775

Dorsal rays 12 to 14; anal rays 10 to 12; lateral-line scales 50 to 55; no scales on upper jaw; green dorsally, shading to silvery white on side and ventrally, with a longitudinal row of four to nine blackish blotches on upper side, anterior dorsal fin and upper lobe of caudal fin suffused with orange-yellow; tip of lower jaw light red. Attains 45 cm. East Africa to Samoa. Has become established in the Mediterranean Sea via the Suez Canal. The author observed this species feeding on floating pieces of seagrass over shallow reefs and seagrass beds in Kenya.

## 18 Red Sea Halfbeak

*Hyporhamphus gambarur* (Lacepède), 1803

Dorsal rays 14 or 15; anal rays 13 to 16 (usually 14 or 15); lateral-line scales 49 to 53; scales dorsally on upper jaw; origin of pelvic fins closer to pectoral-fin base than caudal-fin base; lateral line (low on body) weakly pigmented with black dots; blue-green on the back, silvery on the lower side and ventrally; lower jaw tipped with red. Closest to *H. acutus* (Günther), also found in the Red Sea, which usually has 16 to 18 anal rays. Reaches 20 cm. Apparently endemic to the Red Sea and the Gulf of Aden.

31

# Silversides (Atherinidae)

These are small schooling fishes, usually found inshore and sometimes over reefs. They have two dorsal fins, the first consisting of a few slender spines; the pelvic fins, which have one spine and five rays, are usually abdominal in position; there is no lateral line. Atherinid fishes have a broad silvery stripe on the side. They are heavily preyed upon by other fishes such as jacks. Although usually classified in the older literature with the mullets and barracudas, recent studies now suggest that the silversides are allied to the halfbeaks.

## 19 Robust Silverside

*Atherinomorus lacunosus* (Bloch and Schneider), 1801

Dorsal rays IV to VII–I,8 to 11; anal rays I,12 to 16; pectoral rays 15 to 19; body robust, the depth 4.1 to 5.6 in standard length; eye large, 2.4 to 3.1 in head length; origin of first dorsal fin posterior to middle of standard length; caudal fin forked; greenish grey on back, the scale edges dusky; a broad silvery stripe on side, its upper edge with an iridescent blue line. Reaches 13 cm. Indo-Pacific. A schooling species which feeds on zooplankton. Often classified in

*Pranesus. Atherina pinguis* Lacepède and *A. forskalii* Rüppell are synonyms.

# Cornetfishes (Fistulariidae)

These extremely elongate fishes have a depressed body, a very long tubular snout with a short oblique mouth at the end, minute teeth, no spines in fins, a single dorsal fin posteriorly on the body directly over the anal fin, and a forked caudal fin with a long median filament. They feed by sucking in prey animals in pipette fashion. Four species are known in the world, one of which ranges into the

Red Sea. The related trumpetfish family (Aulostomidae) has not been reported from the Red Sea.

## 20 Cornetfish

*Fistularia commersonii* (Rüppell), 1838

Dorsal rays 15 to 17; anal rays 14 to 16; pectoral rays usually 15; greenish dorsally, shading to silvery white below, with two blue stripes or rows of blue spots on back. Attains 150 cm (including the long median caudal filament). Circumtropical. A free-swimming carnivore over reefs and seagrass beds. Near the bottom it can adopt a dark-barred pattern (see underwater photo). Feeds mainly on fishes (including bottom-dwelling species such as blennies and moray eels), occasionally on shrimps. Sometimes misidentified as *F. petimba* Lacepède, but this name applies to a deep-water species with a row of narrow bony plates along the side of its body; those occurring posteriorly bear a recurved spine.

# Pipefishes & Seahorses
## (Syngnathidae)

This family consists of small fishes whose bodies are encased in bony rings. The rings anterior to the anus are called trunk rings, and those posterior to the anus tail rings. Like their distant relatives, the cornetfishes, they have tubular snouts, small mouths, and feed by a rapid intake of water. Their usual prey is tiny crustaceans. They have a very small gill opening, no spines in the fins, no pelvic fins, a single dorsal fin, and a very small anal fin (dorsal, anal, and/or pectoral fins absent on a few species). The seahorses and some of the pipefishes have lost the caudal fin; the tail of seahorses serves as a prehensile organ. Seahorses are unique in the vertical orientation of the body but horizontal position of the head.

Syngnathids are remarkable in that the eggs are reared by the male in a ventral brood area or pouch after being laid by the female. About 25 species of pipefishes and seahorses occur in the Red Sea.

## 21 Thorny Seahorse

*Hippocampus histrix* Kaup, 1856

Dorsal rays 17 to 19; 11 trunk rings and 33 or 34 tail rings (very small near tip of tail); well-developed, shiny projections on the head and body, including two conspicuous ones on the top of the head; snout long, its length contained about two times in head length; colour variable. Reaches about 15 cm when outstretched. Indo-Pacific. More apt to be found in seagrass beds than coral reefs.

## 22 Bluestripe Pipefish

*Doryrhamphus excisus* Kaup, 1856

Dorsal rays 18 to 20; trunk rings 15 or 16; tail rings 11 or 12; body not very elongate, the depth 12 to 16 in standard length (about 2.5 to 3.0 in head); ridges on body prominent and spiny; snout 2.2 to 2.5 in head, its median dorsal ridge serrate; yellowish to orange with a blue stripe on upper side of body. A small species, it attains only about 6 cm. Indo-Pacific and the eastern Pacific. *D. melanopleura* (Bleeker) is a synonym. Sub-specifically different in the Red Sea where it bears the name *D. excisus abbreviatus* Dawson. The meristic data above are from Red Sea specimens.

33

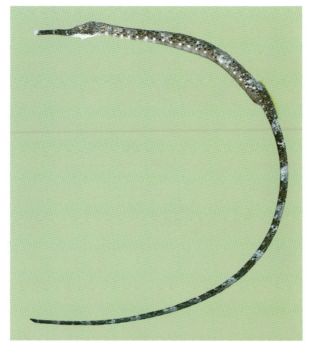

## 23 Double-Ended Pipefish

*Trachyrhamphus bicoarctatus* (Bleeker), 1857

Dorsal rays 24 to 32; trunk rings 21 to 24; tail rings 59 to 64; body relatively smooth and elongate, the greatest depth about 3.7 in head; tail much longer and more slender than trunk; snout long, about 1.7 in head, its dorsal edge smooth; caudal fin rudimentary, often missing; brown, the tail darker than trunk, with small black spots, white dots, and large white saddle-like bars. Reported to 39 cm. East Africa to the western Pacific. Most often found on algal or seagrass bottoms. Most authors have classified this species in the genus *Yozia*, but *Trachyrhamphus* is the older name.

## 24 Gilded Pipefish

*Corythoichthys schultzi* Herald, 1953

Dorsal rays 25 to 31; trunk rings 15 to 17; tail rings 32 to 39; elongate, the depth averaging 4.7 in head; snout long, about 1.7 in head, its upper edge smooth; marked with longitudinal rows of golden spots and broken lines; caudal fin pink with a white border. Largest reported, 15 cm. Red Sea to the Marshall Islands and the Tonga Islands. Snout longer than the two other Red Sea species of the genus: *C. nigripectus* Herald (snout about 2 in head) and *C. flavofasciatus* (Rüppell) (snout about 2.3 in head). Males of the latter species have a deep blue spot around the anus (a pair are shown in the underwater photo with the family discussion on the previous page).

## 25 Multibar Pipefish

*Dunckerocampus multiannulatus* (Regan), 1903

Dorsal rays 20 to 23; trunk rings 16 or 17; tail rings 19 to 21; ridges on body with a recurved spine posteriorly on each ring; elongate, the depth about 7 in head; snout very long, about 1.5 in head; whitish with about 60 or more narrow red or reddish brown bars encircling body; a blackish stripe or series of elongate blackish spots on side of snout; caudal fin red and white. Attains 17.5 cm. Western Indian Ocean. Often seen in pairs. The related *D. dactyliophorus* (Bleeker), which also occurs in the Red Sea, has about 20 broad red bars on the body.

# Frogfishes (Antennariidae)

These odd globular fishes have somewhat compressed bodies, limb-like pectoral fins with an 'elbow' joint, a small round gill opening, a very large, highly oblique mouth, and a greatly modified first dorsal spine, termed the illicium, anteriorly on the top of the head. This consists of a slender stalk tipped with a fleshy or filamentous lure which can be moved enticingly above the mouth to attract the usual prey of fishes to their doom. However, frogfishes do not have to 'angle' in order to feed, and may move slowly to stalk fishes or crustaceans. They are able to engulf prey longer than themselves as their abdomen can expand enormously. They are sedentary and often coloured like their surroundings (hence individuals of a species may vary greatly in colour); their skin, which is loose on the body, may be adorned with warty, fleshy, or filamentous appendages. Because of their camouflage and infrequent movement, they are rarely seen by divers. An underwater photo is shown here of a common species, *Antennarius commersonii* (Shaw). A representative of the 11 Red Sea species is discussed below.

## 26 Freckled Frogfish

*Antennarius coccineus* (Lesson), 1829

Illicium (first dorsal spine) short, about as long as second spine, its tip a small, knob-like mass of fleshy tentacles; third dorsal spine curved posteriorly and joined by a web of skin to the back; dorsal soft rays 12, the last two or three branched; anal rays 7, all branched; pectoral rays usually 10, all unbranched; rear base of anal fin nearly in alignment with caudal fin base; commonly light brown to yellowish, mottled with numerous small brown blotches. Reported to 11.5 cm. Indo-Pacific.

35

# Flashlight Fishes (Anomalopidae)

This unique family of fishes is a member of the order Beryciformes, most of which are deep-water residents. The flashlight fishes have I,5 pelvic rays, a forked tail, a moderately deep compressed body, bluntly rounded head, and very large eyes. Just below each eye is a large, elliptical, luminescent organ filled with bacteria which generate the light. The fishes are able to switch the light on and off by a mechanism varying with the genus. They hide in reefs, generally at depths of 30 metres or more, by day and venture out at night; they are more apt to move into shallower water on moonless nights. They use their light to attract their zooplankton prey as well as to see their prey. The light apparently also allows them to communicate with one another and to confuse predators. Three genera are known, one with two species confined to the New World, the other two Indo-Pacific and monotypic. One species ranges into the Red Sea.

## 27 Flashlight Fish

*Photoblepharon palpebratus* (Boddaert), 1781

A single dorsal fin of two spines and 18 to 20 rays; anal rays II,14 or 15; pectoral rays 16 or 17; light organ below eye covered at will by an eyelid-like structure raised from below; mouth moderately large and oblique; small conical teeth in bands in jaws; caudal fin forked; blackish, the opercular membrane and lateral line pale blue; fin membranes transparent. Attains about 11 cm. Red Sea to Indonesia and the Philippines. Unusual in its occurrence in the northern Red Sea at depths of only a few metres.

# **Squirrelfishes** (Holocentridae)

This family, also of order Beryciformes, consists of very spiny fishes with relatively deep, compressed bodies and large eyes; their colour is usually dominated by red. They have I,7 pelvic rays, IV anal spines, and coarse ctenoid scales. As their large eyes might suggest, they are nocturnal; they feed mainly on crustaceans. During the day most of these fishes hide in caves or crevices in reefs. The family is divisible into two subfamilies; the Holocentrinae (*Adioryx* and *Flammeo*, and in the Atlantic, *Holocentrus*), characterized by a strong spine (may be moderately venomous) on the cheek at the angle of the preopercle; and the Myripristinae (*Myripristis* and allies, popularly called soldierfishes), which lack this spine or have only a weakly developed one. Eight species of holocentrid fishes occur in the Red Sea.

While this book was in press, a paper was published in the *Japanese Journal of Ichthyology* showing that the generic name *Sargocentron* is an earlier valid name for the species classified herein as *Adioryx*.

## 28 Sabre Squirrelfish

*Adioryx spinifer* (Forsskål), 1775

Dorsal rays XI,14 to 16 (usually 15) and anal rays IV,9 or 10 (usually 10); scale rows between lateral line and middle dorsal spines $3\frac{1}{2}$ ($2\frac{1}{2}$ on other Red Sea species); lateral-line scales 40 to 46; dorsal profile of head straight and steep; spine on cheek very large, longer than eye diameter; red, the scales edged posteriorly with silver; spinous dorsal fin solid deep red, the remaining fins with orange-yellow rays. The largest of the squirrelfishes; reaches 45 cm. Indo-Pacific. Feeds mainly on crustaceans, especially crabs, occasionally on small fishes.

## 29 Silverspot Squirrelfish

*Adioryx caudimaculatus* (Rüppell), 1838

Dorsal rays XI,14; anal rays IV,9; pectoral rays 14; lateral-line scales 40 to 43; dorsal profile of head straight; mainly red, this colour deepest at tips of membranes of dorsal spines; in life a silvery white spot anterodorsally on caudal peduncle. Attains 24 cm. Indo-Pacific. A common Red Sea reef species. *Holocentrum andamanense* Day is a synonym.

## 30 Crown Squirrelfish

*Adioryx diadema* (Lacepède), 1801

Dorsal rays XI,13 or 14; anal rays usually IV,9; pectoral rays usually 14; lateral-line scales 46 to 50; dorsal profile of head convex; red with narrow silvery white stripes, the spinous dorsal fin blackish red with a disjunct white band, the triangular membrane tips whitish. To 16 cm. Indo-Pacific. Common and tends to occur in aggregations.

## 31 Redcoat

*Adioryx ruber* (Forsskål), 1775

Dorsal rays XI,12 or 13; anal rays IV,8 or 9 (usually 9); pectoral rays usually 14; lateral-line scales 33 to 37; dorsal profile of head convex, the snout short with a steep profile; upper side of first suborbital bone with a small horizontal recurved spine; body with alternating dusky red and silvery white stripes of about equal width; the third and fourth red stripes joining to one which crosses caudal peduncle to midbase of caudal fin, and the fourth and fifth stripes joining as one which crosses lower part of peduncle. Reaches 33 cm. East Africa to Samoa. A recent immigrant to the Mediterranean Sea via the Suez Canal. Generally found in shallow, dead-reef areas.

## 32 Spotfin Squirrelfish

*Flammeo sammara* (Forsskål), 1775

Dorsal rays XI,11 or 12; anal rays IV,7 or 8; pectoral rays 13 or 14 (usually 14); lateral-line scales 39 to 43; body relatively slender, the depth about 3.3 in standard length; lower jaw projecting; last dorsal spine longer than penultimate spine and closely applied to soft dorsal fin; silvery with a tinge of red, the scales of body with a dark reddish spot, thus forming longitudinal bands; a large reddish black spot anteriorly in dorsal fin. Attains 25 cm. Indo-Pacific.

## 33 Blotcheye Soldierfish

*Myripristis murdjan* (Forsskål), 1775

Dorsal rays X–I,13 to 15; anal rays IV,11 to 13 (rarely 11); pectoral rays 14 to 16 (usually 15); lateral-line scales 27 to 32 (modally 29); a single pair of tooth patches at front of lower jaw just outside mouth; red, the centres of the scales silvery red; black on upper opercular membrane and upper unscaled portion of axil of pectoral fin. Reaches 23 cm. East Africa to the Marshall Islands and Samoa. *M. parvidens* Cuvier is a synonym.

## 34 Yellowtip Soldierfish

*Myripristis xanthacrus* Randall and Guézé, 1981

Dorsal rays X–I,13 to 15; anal rays IV,10 to 13; pectoral rays 14 or 15; lateral-line scales 26 to 29 (modally 27); two pairs of tooth patches at front of lower jaw just outside mouth, one above the other; silvery pink, the edges of the scales red; opercular membrane dark brownish red, continuing as a band to pectoral axil; tips of soft dorsal fin, anal fin, and caudal lobes yellow. Largest specimen, 17 cm. Middle and southern Red Sea and the Gulf of Aden.

# Scorpionfishes (Scorpaenidae)

Scorpionfishes derive their name from the venomous spines possessed by many of the species. Family characteristics include the suborbital stay (an external body reinforcing plate running from the second suborbital bone across the cheek below the eye to the preopercle), other ridges and spines on the head, a large mouth, and small villiform teeth. Often there are fleshy flaps or cirri on the head and body; there may be an elongate flap or tentacle above the eye. There is great variation in the development of these cutaneous structures within a species. These fishes are generally coloured much like the bottom on which they rest; some species exhibit considerable colour variation. The lionfishes (*Dendrochirus*) and turkeyfishes (*Pterois*), sometimes called zebrafishes because of their dark bands, do not alter their colour pattern. The turkeyfishes may swim slowly just off the bottom in contrast to most scorpionfishes which rarely move. Scorpionfishes are lie-and-wait predators, feeding on small fishes and crustaceans that make the mistake of venturing near. The dorsal, anal, and pelvic spines are all venomous. The spines are T-shaped or anchor-shaped in cross section; the glandular tissue producing the venom lies in the longitudinal groove on each side of the spines (or in the case of the stonefishes as a large oblong gland protruding from the side of the spine, the apical end narrowing to a venom duct which runs in the groove to the spine tip). Wounds from the venomous spines vary from bee-sting intensity in some species to unbelievable agony in *Synanceia* and *Pterois*. Immersing the injured limb in water as hot as one can tolerate helps alleviate the pain from spine wounds. Approximately 35 species of scorpionfishes are known from the Red Sea. Only the most common large species are discussed below.

## 35 Bearded Scorpionfish

*Scorpaenopsis barbatus* (Rüppell), 1838

Dorsal rays XII,9; anal rays III,5; pectoral rays usually 18; scale rows from upper end of gill opening to base of caudal fin 50 to 55; an indentation in dorsal profile between snout and eye; a shallow pit middorsally behind eyes and a deeper one below front of eye; back not highly arched beneath front of dorsal fin, the depth of body about 2.9 in standard length; eye about equal to snout length or a little smaller. Attains 22 cm. Red Sea to at least the coast of Somalia. The related *S. oxycephalus* Bleeker (see underwater photo) is larger (to at least 36 cm), more elongate (depth about 3.2 in standard length), has a smaller eye (the diameter about 2 in snout), 19 or 20 pectoral rays, and about 65 scale rows.

## 36 Devil Scorpionfish

*Scorpaenopsis diabolus*
(Cuvier and Valenciennes), 1829

Dorsal rays XII,9; anal rays III,5; pectoral rays 18; an indentation in dorsal profile between snout and eye; a mid-dorsal pit behind eyes, and a deep one below front of eye; back highly arched beneath front of dorsal fin, giving a hump-backed effect; longitudinal scale rows about 45; pelvic fins with a pale outer margin; a bright orange, yellow, and black-spotted pattern inside pectoral fin which is flashed when the fish is disturbed (as warning colouration). Reaches 30 cm. Indo-Pacific.

## 37 Stonefish

*Synanceia verrucosa* Bloch and Schneider, 1801

Dorsal rays usually XIII,6, the fleshy skin covering the spines and hiding a large venom gland on each side of each spine; anal rays III,5 or 6; pectoral rays 18 or 19; no scales, the skin thick and warty; head broad, the eyes oriented upward; mouth vertical with a fringe of cirri at the edge; a deep pit behind each eye and another below front of eye. To 30 cm. Indo-Pacific. Matches its surroundings perfectly and can bury in sand. The most feared venomous fish in the sea; wounds from the spines are terribly painful, and deaths have been reported. Most injuries occur from stepping on the spines. Bleeding of wounds should be encouraged; an antivenin has been produced. The smaller *S. nana* Eschmeyer and Rama Rao has XIV,5 dorsal spines and 14 or 15 pectoral rays.

## 38 Shortfin Lionfish

*Dendrochirus brachypterus* (Cuvier and Valenciennes), 1829

Dorsal rays XIII,9, the spines not connected by membranes except basally; anal rays III,5 or 6; pectoral rays usually 17 and joined by membranes, the fin not extending posterior to dorsal and anal fins; reddish brown with broad irregular dark bars on body and diagonal dark bands on postorbital head; fin rays with black spots in rows, those on paired fins joined by dark bands. Reported to 15 cm, but usually much smaller. East Africa to western Pacific.

# 39 Turkeyfish

*Pterois volitans* (Linnaeus), 1758

Dorsal rays XIII,11, the spines very long (the longest about half standard length), the membranes incised nearly to base; anal rays III,7; pectoral rays 14, extremely long, reaching posterior to caudal fin base, the membranes deeply cleft, those of upper rays broad and plume-like; supraorbital tentacle long, without cross bands; body with black bars alternating with very narrow whitish to light red interspaces; head with similar bands, those on posterior part diagonal and continuing onto chest. Attains about 35 cm. Indo-Pacific. The needle-sharp dorsal, anal, and pelvic spines are highly venomous. Spine wounds are agonizing, and some fatalities have resulted. The turkeyfish and other *Pterois* direct their dorsal spines towards an intruder; if provoked, they can strike forward with these spines.

# 40 Clearfin Turkeyfish

*Pterois radiata* Cuvier and Valenciennes, 1829

Dorsal rays XII,11, the spines very long (the longest half standard length), without membranes except basally; anal rays III,6; pectoral rays usually 16, extremely long (extending beyond base of caudal fin), connected by membranes on only about their basal third; supraorbital tentacle long and without cross bands; body with broad white-edged reddish brown bars, the first and second separated by a triangular bar dorsally and the third and fourth by a similar but red triangle dorsally and another ventrally; side of caudal peduncle with a broad longitudinal reddish band; head with a white-edged dark bar from nape across operculum and a diagonal one from eye across cheek; fin spines and rays red, the pectoral rays becoming white distally; fin membranes clear without spots. Reaches 20 cm. Indo-Pacific.

43

# Groupers & Seabasses (Serranidae)

The Serranidae is a large family in the largest order of fishes, the Perciformes. It is among the least specialized, hence difficult to define briefly. In general, these fishes share the following characteristics: pelvic fins I,5 (number of rays reduced in a few species), located slightly anterior or posterior to pectoral fin base; caudal fin with no more than 17 principal rays (those which extend to posterior margin of fin); mouth large, the maxilla not forming part of the gape, its posterior end fully exposed on the cheek; lower jaw usually projecting anterior to upper; jaws with bands of slender sharp teeth, the medial rows inwardly depressible, and usually a few stout canines at the front; preopercular margin nearly always serrate, and the opercle usually with three flattened spines posteriorly; scales small and ctenoid (tiny spinules on edges) or secondarily cycloid (smooth-edged); postorbital part of head scaled. The groupers and their allies are carnivorous, feeding mainly on fishes and crustaceans. Many are important commercial fishes. Typically they are protogynous hermaphrodites, beginning maturity as females and switching to males later in life. Some, such as the species of *Serranus*, are synchronously hermaphroditic; both ripe ova and sperm develop at the same time in one sex organ; the spawning pairs of fish cross-fertilize. Some of the groupers have different colour phases and all possess the ability

## 41 Peacock Grouper
*Cephalopholis argus* Bloch and Schneider, 1801

Dorsal rays IX,16 or 17 (usually 16); anal rays III,9; pectoral rays 16 or 17 (usually 17); lateral-line scales 46 to 50; lower-limb gill rakers 17 to 19 (other *Cephalopholis* 13 to 16); dark brown with numerous black-edged blue spots on head, body and fins; about five whitish bars may be present on posterior half of body and a whitish triangular area on chest. Reaches 50 cm. Indo-Pacific. Very common throughout most of its range, but not in the Red Sea. The oldest scientific name for this species is *C. guttata* (Bloch); however, application has been made to the International Commission for Zoological Nomenclature to suppress this name in favour of the currently used *C. argus*. About 80 per cent of the diet is fishes and most of the rest crustaceans.

## 42 Halfspotted Grouper
*Cephalopholis hemistiktos* (Rüppell), 1830

to rapidly alter the density of their colour. For example, they become markedly paler when moving from a dark hole in a reef over light-coloured sand. Individuals from deep water tend to have more red colour. Four different subfamilies of serranid fishes occur in the Red Sea: Serraninae (one species of *Serranus*); Epinephelinae (23 species of groupers); Liopropominae (two small species of *Liopropoma*); and Anthiinae (four species of *Anthias* and one of *Plectranthias*). Some authors prefer to classify the anthiines in a separate family. These lovely little fishes, dominated by hues of pink, lavender and yellow, may be sexually dichromatic. More species occur in deep water than shallow.

Dorsal rays IX,14; anal rays III,9; pectoral rays 16 or 17 (usually 17); lateral-line scales 48 to 51; posterior corners of dorsal and anal fins angular; dark brown to red (red in depths of about 30 m or more) with small dark-edged blue spots on head (especially ventrally) and lower half of body; one colour phase exhibits a large light yellowish area posteriorly on back; another has irregular dark brown bars on the body and blotches on the head. A small species; attains only 25 cm. Red Sea to the Arabian Gulf; the most common grouper of the genus in the Red Sea.

45

## 43 Coral Grouper

*Cephalopholis miniata* (Forsskål), 1775

Dorsal rays IX,15; anal rays III,9; pectoral rays 17 or 18; lateral-line scales 47 to 54; lower-limb gill rakers 14 to 15; dorsal spines relatively short, the longest 3.3 to 3.5 in head; posterior corners of dorsal and anal fins rounded; red-orange to reddish brown with numerous blue spots on head, body, and median fins; can assume a colour pattern of diagonal light olivaceous bars; the young have a yellow colour phase. Attains a maximum of nearly 40 cm. Indo-Pacific. Found mainly in well developed coral reefs in clear water. *C. formosanus* Tanaka is a junior synonym.

## 44 Vermilion Grouper

*Cephalopholis oligosticta* Randall and Ben-Tuvia, 1982

Dorsal rays IX,15; anal rays III,9; pectoral rays 16 to 18; lateral-line scales 60 to 71; ventral margin of preopercle serrate (smooth on other Red Sea *Cephalopholis*); dorsal spines not short, 2.9 to 3.15 in head; posterior corners of dorsal and anal fins rounded to slightly angular; orange-red with a few scattered light blue spots on head, body and fins. Largest specimens, 27.5 cm. Known only from the Red Sea; the preferred habitat appears to be relatively deep (25 to 45 m), dead reefs.

## 45 Sixspot Grouper

*Cephalopholis sexmaculata* (Rüppell), 1830

Dorsal rays IX,14 or 15 (usually 15); anal rays III,9; pectoral rays usually 17; lateral-line scales 49 to 56; dorsal spines not short, 2.95 to 3.2 in head; posterior corners of dorsal and anal fins rounded; orange-red with numerous small blue spots on body and head (there may be blue lines radiating forward and backward from the eye) and six squarish blackish spots on the back (four at base of dorsal fin which extend into the fin, and two dorsally on caudal peduncle); faint dark bars may extend ventrally from blackish spots on back, the first four as double bars. Reaches 50 cm. Indo-Pacific. Most often found in caves in reefs, particularly at drop-offs. *C. coatesi* Whitley is a synonym.

## 46 Redmouth Grouper

*Aethaloperca rogaa* (Forsskål), 1775

Dorsal rays IX,17 or 18 (usually 18); anal rays III,9; pectoral rays 17 or 18 (usually 18); body deep, the depth 2.1 to 2.5 in standard length; pelvic fins long, extending posterior to anus, 1.4 to 1.6 in head; caudal fin truncate; dark brown, the mouth largely orange-red; often a whitish bar centred on abdomen; juveniles have a broad white border on the caudal fin. Attains about 60 cm. East Africa to the western Pacific. Usually seen in caves or lurking in their vicinity.

## 47 Blacktip Grouper

*Epinephelus fasciatus* (Forsskål), 1775

Dorsal rays XI,16 or 17 (usually 16); anal rays III,8; pectoral rays 18 or 19 (usually 19); lateral-line scales 50–53; lower-limb gill rakers 15 to 17; dorsal spines relatively long, the longest 2.4 to 2.7 in head; light pinkish grey to pale yellowish red with five dusky to dark orange-red bars on body; tips of membranes of spinous portion of dorsal fin black. Attains about 35 cm. Indo-Pacific. The most common grouper of the genus *Epinephelus* in the Red Sea. Although usually found in relatively shallow water, it has been recorded at depths of 160 m. Among the 11 synonyms are *E. marginalis* Bloch and *E. emoryi* Schultz.

## 48 Smalltooth Grouper

*Epinephelus microdon* (Bleeker), 1856

Dorsal rays XI,14 or 15; anal rays III,8; pectoral rays 16 or 17 (usually 17); lateral-line scales 47 to 52; lower-limb gill rakers 16 to 18; pectoral fins relatively long, 1.65 to 1.95 in head; dorsal profile of head smoothly convex; light brown with numerous small dark brown spots and large irregular dark brown blotches; a saddle-like black spot dorsally on caudal peduncle. Largest specimen examined, 61 cm. Indo-Pacific. Easily approached underwater. Feeds mainly on benthic crustaceans, especially crabs, with fishes a second major item of the diet.

## 49 Brownmarbled Grouper

*Epinephelus fuscoguttatus* (Forsskål), 1775

Dorsal rays XI,14 or 15 (usually 14); anal rays III,8; pectoral rays 18 to 20 (usually 19); lateral-line scales 49 to 58; lower-limb gill rakers 18 to 21; pectoral fins not very long, 1.9 to 2.4 in head; dorsal profile of head of adults a double convexity, the two curves meeting just behind eye; light yellowish brown with large irregular brown blotches, those along base of dorsal fin darkest; a dark brown saddle-like spot dorsally on caudal peduncle. Largest specimen recorded, 88.5 cm. East Africa to the Marshall Islands and the Phoenix Islands. A wary species for a grouper. Limited data

indicate major food items are fishes, crabs and cephalopods. *Serranus horridus* Cuvier and Valenciennes is a synonym.

## 50 Summana Grouper

*Epinephelus summana* (Forsskål), 1775

Dorsal rays XI,14 to 16 (usually 15); anal rays III,8 or 9 (usually 8); pectoral rays 16 to 18; lateral-line scales 49 to 54; lower-limb gill rakers 16 to 17; maxilla just reaching or extending slightly beyond eye; dorsal margin of opercular flap strongly convex; dark brown with large roundish light brown spots, this pattern overlaid with numerous small white spots; a black streak along upper edge of maxillary groove. Juveniles brownish grey with large dark-edged white spots. Largest specimen examined, 52 cm. Red Sea; the closely related *E. ongus* (Bloch) ranges from East Africa to

Micronesia. Generally found on reefs in lagoons or other protected waters; will enter brackish environments.

## 51 Malabar Grouper

*Epinephelus malabaricus* (Bloch and Schneider), 1801

Dorsal rays XI,14 to 16; anal rays III,8; pectoral rays 19 or 20 (usually 19); lateral-line scales 58 to 64; lower-limb gill rakers 15 to 18; teeth on side of lower jaw in two rows; snout relatively long, its length 3.6 to 4.4 in head; light greyish brown to greenish tan with five slightly diagonal dark bars on body which tend to bifurcate ventrally; head and body with numerous small dark spots; adults, in addition, with small indistinct whitish spots. Recorded to 88.5 cm. East Africa to the western Pacific. Has entered the Mediterranean Sea via the Suez Canal. A species of protected reefs and adjacent habitats; readily penetrates turbid water and estuarine areas. *E. salmoides* (Lacepède) is a synonym.

## 52 Greasy Grouper

*Epinephelus tauvina*
(Forsskål), 1775

Dorsal rays XI,14 to 16; anal rays III,8; pectoral rays 18 or 19; lateral-line scales 67 to 74; lower-limb gill rakers 18 to 20; teeth on side of lower jaw in three or four rows; snout not very long, 4.5 to 5.0 in head; greenish grey to pale brown dorsally, shading to whitish ventrally, with numerous round dark spots; a large blackish spot often present at base of last four dorsal spines and extending into lower part of fin; five faint slightly diagonal dusky bars may be visible on body. Reported to 70 cm. A coral reef inhabitant. *E. elongatus* Schultz, *E. salonotus* Smith and Smith, and *E. chewa* Morgans are synonyms. Groupers of immense size, identified as *E. tauvina*, probably represent misidentification of the giant *Promicrops lanceolatus* (Bloch).

## 53 Areolate Grouper

*Epinephelus areolatus* (Forsskål), 1775

Dorsal rays XI,15 to 17 (usually 16); pectoral rays 17 or 18 (more often 17); lower-limb gill rakers 14 to 16; caudal fin slightly emarginate; posterior anal fin rounded to slightly angular, the longest rays 2.3 to 2.6 in head; pectoral fins relatively long, 1.6 to 1.8 in head; whitish with numerous close-set roundish brown to brownish yellow spots. Largest reported, 45 cm. East Africa to the western Pacific. Generally found in somewhat turbid water in grass beds or silty sand bottoms around isolated small rock outcrops or soft coral. *Serranus angularis* Cuvier and Valenciennes is a synonym.

## 54 Brownspotted Grouper

*Epinephelus chlorostigma* (Cuvier and Valenciennes), 1828

Dorsal rays XI,16 to 18 (usually 17); anal rays III,8; pectoral rays 17 or 18 (usually 18); lower-limb gill rakers 15 to 18; caudal fin slightly emarginate; posterior anal fin distinctly angular, the longest rays 1.9 to 2.5 in head; pectoral fins not long, 1.75 to 2.0 in head; whitish with numerous close-set roundish to hexagonal dark brown spots (largest on adults about half pupil diameter). Reaches 75 cm. East Africa to the western Pacific. *E. geoffroyi* Klunzinger is a synonym. Frequently confused with *E. areolatus*.

49

## 55 Sand Grouper

*Epinephelus stoliczkae* (Day), 1875

Dorsal rays XI,16 to 18; anal rays III,8; pectoral rays 17 or 18; lateral-line scales 48 to 51; lower-limb gill rakers 13 to 15; yellowish grey with a dark grey-brown bar below rear of spinous portion of dorsal fin, two more beneath soft portion and one on caudal peduncle; head and body with numerous dark reddish spots except ventrally and posteriorly. To 38 cm. Red Sea to Pakistan. The typical habitat is around small rocks or coral heads on shallow sandy bottoms. Not observed on well developed coral reefs.

## 56 Slender Grouper

*Anyperodon leucogrammicus* (Cuvier and Valenciennes), 1828

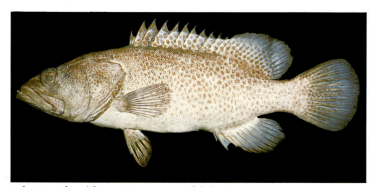

Dorsal rays XI,14 to 16; anal rays III,8 or 9 (usually 9); pectoral rays 15 to 17; lateral-line scales 63 to 71; no palatine teeth (present on other Red Sea groupers); body slender, the depth 3.3 to 3.7 in standard length; greenish grey with numerous small orange-red spots. Reported to attain 50 cm. East Africa to the Marshall Islands and the Phoenix Islands. *Serranus urophthalmus* Bleeker is a synonym based on the juvenile stage which is blue-and-red striped with a blue-edged black spot on the base of its caudal fin. Outside the Red Sea this grouper generally has four longitudinal pale streaks (the pattern on which the scientific name is based) and, modally, one more pectoral ray.

## 57 Lunartail Grouper

*Variola louti* (Forsskål), 1775

Dorsal rays IX,14; anal rays III,8; pectoral rays 16 to 18; lateral-line scales 66 to 77; depth of body 2.8 to 3.2 in standard length; caudal fin lunate; soft portions of dorsal and anal fins very angular; pelvic fins long, 1.2 to 1.6 in head; yellowish brown to orange-red (more red in deeper water) with numerous small irregular pink to blue spots; posterior margins of fins broadly yellow; juveniles with an irregular black stripe from eye to below rear base of dorsal fin and an irregular black spot on upper caudal fin base. Largest collected, 81 cm. Indo-Pacific. Feeds principally on a wide variety of reef fishes.

## 58 Roving Grouper

*Plectropomus maculatus* (Bloch), 1790

Dorsal rays VIII,11; anal rays III,8; pectoral rays 15 to 17 (usually 16); lateral-line scales 88 to 104; a pair of prominent canine teeth anteriorly in jaws and one to three on side of lower jaw in addition to two rows of small teeth; depth of body 3.25 to 3.65 in standard length; suborbital depth 5.8 to 7.8 in head; caudal fin emarginate; brownish orange-red with well-separated, dark-edged blue spots, some of which are usually elongate. Attains at least 90 cm. East Africa to the western Pacific. Feeds mainly on fishes.

## 59 Squaretail Grouper

*Plectropomus truncatus* Fowler and Bean, 1930

Dorsal rays VIII,11; anal rays III,8; pectoral rays 15 or 16 (usually 16); lateral-line scales 88 to 105; one or two pairs of prominent canine teeth anteriorly in jaws and one to three canines on side of lower jaw (in addition to two rows of small teeth); depth of body 3.1 to 3.7 in standard length; suborbital depth 8.0 to 9.9 in head; caudal fin truncate to slightly emarginate; orangish brown with numerous small round black-edged blue spots (spots close-set, often within a spot diameter of adjacent spots); caudal fin with a white posterior margin and blackish submarginal zone. Largest reported, 52 cm. East Africa to Samoa and the Marshall Islands.

## 60 Scalefin Anthias

*Anthias squamipinnis* (Peters), 1855

Dorsal rays X,16 to 18 (usually 17); anal rays III,7; pectoral rays usually 17; lateral-line scales 37 to 41; auxiliary scales (small scales basally on large scales) present; fins heavily scaled; third dorsal spine prolonged in adults, especially so in males; caudal fin deeply emarginate to lunate, the lobes prolonged in males; females (see *right*) orange-yellow with a violet-edged dark orange stripe from eye to pectoral base; males fuchsia, the scales on side of body with a small yellow spot, with the same stripe and a large deep orange spot on upper outer part of pectoral fin. The large males attain 15 cm (including caudal filaments). East Africa to the western Pacific. Huge swarms of these zoo-plankton-feeding fishes occur on shallow

Red Sea reefs, each tied to a prominent rock or coral head. Males (see *opposite*) maintain large harems; removal of a male from such a group results in sex reversal of a dominant female to assume the male role.

## 61 Striped Anthias

*Anthias taeniatus* Klunzinger, 1884

Dorsal rays X,16 or 17 (usually 16); anal rays III,7; pectoral rays 18 or 19 (usually 18); lateral-line scales 44 to 50; no auxiliary scales; caudal fin deeply emarginate; females orange with a broad zone of pink on lower side, becoming white ventrally, with a diagonal pale lavender line from lower snout under eye to pectoral base and orange-red tips on caudal lobes; males develop a narrow pale yellowish to white lateral stripe on body and a broad white ventral stripe commencing on chin. Reaches 13 cm. Red Sea.

# Soapfishes (Grammistidae)

The soapfishes are named for the copious mucus they are able to produce when frightened. This contains a toxic substance, grammistin, which is very bitter and serves to deter predators. In a confined body of water, such as an aquarium, a soapfish under stress can produce enough toxin to kill other residents of the tank. It is not affected by its own toxin, however. The author noted the disappearance of a small goldstriped soapfish in an aquarium one morning; subsequently he determined it was eaten by a larger member of the same species. Morphological family characteristics include a large mouth with projecting lower jaw, small villiform teeth in jaws, the upper end of the opercle connected by skin to the head, and preopercle serrate or with a few spines. Closely related to the groupers, it is sometimes classified as a subfamily of the Serranidae.

## 62 Goldstriped Soapfish

*Grammistes sexlineatus* (Thunberg), 1792

Dorsal rays VII,13 or 14; anal rays II,9; pectoral rays 14 to 16; scales cycloid, small and embedded; depth of body 2.3 to 2.8 in standard length; a small fleshy flap on chin; posterior preopercular margin with two to four broad-based spines; dark brown with light yellow stripes (three in young, increasing to six to eight in adults; stripes break up into series of dashes in older fish). Largest recorded, 27 cm. Indo-Pacific. The skin toxin is produced in multicellular glands in the dermis. An individual fed by the author to a turkeyfish in an aquarium was quickly expelled unharmed and avoided thereafter.

## 63 Yellowface Soapfish

*Diploprion drachi* Estève, 1955

Dorsal rays VIII,15 or 16; anal rays II,12; pectoral rays 15 or 16; scales ctenoid and small; depth of body 2.4 to 2.6 in standard length; no flap on chin; preopercular margin coarsely serrate; pelvic fins long, reaching beyond origin of anal fin; lavender grey, with a large patch of orange-yellow enclosing eye anteriorly on head; spinous portion of dorsal fin mostly blackish, this colour continuing as a broad band along base of soft portion of fin. Recorded to 14 cm. Red Sea and the Gulf of Aden. Has been observed to swim alongside or just behind large nonpredatory fishes to get closer to its prey of small fishes and crustaceans.

# Bigeyes (Priacanthidae)

These fishes are characterized by moderately deep compressed bodies, very large eyes (indicative of their nocturnal habits), highly oblique mouths with projecting lower jaw, small conical teeth in a narrow band in jaws, rough ctenoid scales, a continuous dorsal fin with X spines, and large pelvic fins, the fifth ray broadly joined to abdomen by a membrane. The colour is dominantly red. Some species of *Priacanthus*, at least, are able to rapidly change from solid red, through mottled or barred with silver, to nearly solid silver. These fishes feed mainly on the larger elements of the zooplankton such as larval fishes and crab larvae. Two species can be found in the Red Sea, one of which, the large-finned *Cookeolus boops* (Schneider), occurs in deep water.

## 64 Goggle-Eye

*Priacanthus hamrur* (Forsskål), 1775

Dorsal rays X,14 or 15; the last five spines of nearly equal length; anal rays III,14 or 15; lateral-line scales 71 to 78; depth of body about 2.7 in standard length; preopercular margin serrate, the spine at angle small; caudal fin emarginate; pelvic fins slightly shorter than head length; red with a series of small brownish red blotches along lateral line. To 35 cm. East Africa to the western Pacific. Recently recorded off Tunisia, hence a probable immigrant to the Mediterranean via the Suez Canal. Easily approached underwater. *Cookeolus boops* differs in its deeper body, huge pelvic fins (about 1.5 times longer than head),

slightly rounded caudal fin, progressively longer dorsal spines and elevated soft portion of dorsal fin.

# Hawkfishes (Cirrhitidae)

This family is distinctive in having pectoral fins of 14 rays, the lower five to seven of which are unbranched and usually enlarged; there is a single dorsal fin of X spines which is notched between the spinous and soft portions; anal rays III,6 or 7 (usually 6); one or more cirri projecting from the tips of the dorsal spines, and a fringe of small cirri on the posterior edge of the anterior nostril. Most of these fishes sit on the bottom, often wedging themselves in place with their thickened lower pectoral rays. They are carnivorous, darting out rapidly for small fishes and crustaceans that come within their striking range. Four species of hawkfishes occur in the Red Sea; all are discussed below.

## 65 Stocky Hawkfish

*Cirrhitus pinnulatus* (Bloch and Schneider), 1801

Dorsal rays X,11; lower seven pectoral rays unbranched; lateral-line scales 42 to 44 (39 to 43 outside the Red Sea); four rows of scales above lateral line; scales on cheeks small; body robust; dark brown to dark olive dorsally, whitish ventrally, with whitish blotches in about three rows on body; head and body with small orangish brown spots (more evident on head); fins with dark brown spots. Reaches 28 cm. Indo-Pacific. Lives inshore on reefs or rocky bottoms exposed to surge. Feeds predominantly on crabs but also takes shrimps, other crustaceans, fishes, small sea urchins and brittle stars.

## 66 Blackside Hawkfish

*Paracirrhites forsteri* (Bloch and Schneider), 1801

Dorsal rays X,11; lower seven pectoral rays unbranched; lateral-line scales 45 to 49; five rows of scales above lateral line; large scales on cheek in five or six rows; body yellowish with a broad blackish band on upper side ending in middle of caudal fin; head (and sometimes anterior body) with small dark reddish spots. One colour form is dark brown, shading to orange-yellow on caudal peduncle and fin, with dark spots anteriorly. Largest recorded, 22.5 cm. Indo-Pacific. Feeds mainly on fishes, occasionally on shrimps.

## 67 Pixy Hawkfish

*Cirrhitichthys oxycephalus* (Bleeker), 1855

Dorsal rays X,12; lower six pectoral rays unbranched; lateral-line scales 41 to 45; three rows of scales above lateral line; four rows of large scales on cheek; whitish with three rows of large, oblong, red-edged dark brown spots on body (spots larger dorsally) and smaller red spots among the larger ones; dark brown to red spots in diagonal rows on head. A small species, it attains only 8.5 cm. Indo-Pacific.

## 68 Longnose Hawkfish

*Oxycirrhites typus* Bleeker, 1857

Dorsal rays X,13; lower five or six pectoral rays unbranched; lateral-line scales 51 to 53; four rows of scales above lateral line; snout extremely long, its length about 2 in head; whitish with horizontal and near-vertical red bands forming a cross-hatch pattern. Reaches 13 cm. Indo-Pacific and the eastern Pacific. Generally found deeper than

30 m; usually seen perched on black coral or gorgonians. Feeds principally on small crustaceans, both planktonic and benthic. Lays demersal eggs.

# Dottybacks (Pseudochromidae)

These are small perciform fishes which have a continuous dorsal fin with I to III spines and 21 to 37 rays, an anal fin with II or III spines and 13 to 19 rays; pelvic fins with I spine and 3 to 5 rays (spines in fins sometimes feeble); and the tubed lateral line consisting of two disjunct series or one dorsoanterior series (which may be reduced to a single scale). In a recent study, the families Pseudoplesiopidae and Anisochromidae were merged with the Pseudochromidae. The different species vary greatly in colour pattern, some being very brightly coloured. A few exhibit sexual dichromatism. The dottybacks are closely tied to coral reefs or rocky substrata, rarely venturing far from shelter. They feed mainly on small benthic crustaceans and polychaete worms and zooplankton. The spawning of two Red Sea species of *Pseudochromis* has been observed; a spherical mass of eggs is laid which is guarded by the male. Seven species of *Pseudochromis* and three of *Pseudoplesiops* (*Chlidichthys* is a synonym) occur in the Red Sea.

## 69 Sunrise Dottyback
*Pseudochromis flavivertex* Rüppell, 1835

Dorsal rays III,26 to 28; anal rays III,13 to 15; anterior tubed lateral-line scales 27 to 33; gill rakers 18 to 20; caudal fin truncate; blue, shading to whitish on abdomen, with a yellow stripe commencing on snout, running on top of head and following dorsal contour of body; caudal fin yellow, this colour continuing onto upper and lower edges of peduncle; dorsal fin rays yellow. Largest specimen, 7.2 cm. Red Sea and the Gulf of Aden. Usually found around bases of small rocks or coral heads on sandy bottoms; known depth range 2 to 30 m.

## 70 Orchid Dottyback

*Pseudochromis fridmani* Klausewitz, 1968

Dorsal rays III,24 to 27; anal rays III,13 to 16; anterior tubed lateral-line scales 24 to 29; gill rakers 21 to 24; caudal fin truncate in young, the lower lobe becoming pointed in adults (more so in males); purple with a dark streak from front of snout and chin through eye to upper end of gill opening; a dark blue spot on opercular flap; upper corner of caudal fin clear. Largest, 6.3 cm. Red Sea. Usually found on vertical rock faces or beneath

overhangs, taking refuge in small holes; recorded from depths of 1 to 60 m.

## 71 Forktail Dottyback

*Pseudochromis dixurus* Lubbock, 1975

Dorsal rays III,25 to 28; anal rays III,14; anterior tubed lateral-line scales 32 to 40; gill rakers 22 or 23; caudal fin deeply emarginate; ground colour varying from olive to yellowish brown or whitish, often with two brownish yellow stripes on side of head and body, the uppermost beginning at front of snout, these stripes continuing broadly onto upper and lower lobes of caudal fin, thus enhancing the forked effect of the fin. Maximum size 9 cm. Red Sea. Most

often seen in caves or around silt-covered rocks; observed in depths from 5 to 60 m.

## 72 Pale Dottyback

*Pseudochromis pesi* Lubbock, 1975

Dorsal rays III,26 to 28; anal rays III,14 or 15; anterior tubed lateral-line scales 34 to 38; gill rakers 17 to 19; caudal fin truncate; pale grey to yellowish, the top of the head, dorsal part of body, and dorsal fin base dark grey; a dark blue spot edged in yellow on opercular flap. Reaches 10 cm. Gulf of Aqaba; found around small isolated rocks or corals on sand at depths of 10 to 45 m (rare in less than 20 m).

## 73 Olive Dottyback

*Pseudochromis olivaceus* Rüppell, 1835

Dorsal rays III,26 to 29; anal rays III,15 or 16; anterior tubed lateral-line scales 39 to 53; gill rakers 16 to 18; caudal fin slightly emarginate; dark olive, shading to yellowish or greyish ventrally, with crescentic dark blue marks on many of scales on side of body; a deep blue spot edged posteriorly with gold on opercular flap. Largest, 9.2 cm. Red Sea to the Arabian Gulf. A common shallow-water species not known below 20 m; associated with well developed coral reefs, often hiding among branches of live coral.

59

## 74 Striped Dottyback

*Pseudochromis sankeyi* Lubbock, 1975

Dorsal rays III,25 to 27; anal rays III,14 to 16; anterior tubed lateral-line scales 28 to 34; gill rakers 21 to 23; caudal fin truncate in juveniles, the lower lobe becoming pointed with increasing size; pink to white with three black stripes, the two lowermost converging at the tip of the pointed lower lobe of caudal fin. Largest, 7.4 cm. Southwestern Red Sea and the Gulf of Aden. Generally found in caves or beneath rocky and coralline ledges at depths of 2 to 10 m; often observed in colonies. In spite of very different colouration, this species is a close relative of *P. fridmani*; the two species have not been observed in the same area.

## 75 Bluestriped Dottyback

*Pseudochromis springeri* Lubbock, 1975

Dorsal rays III,28 to 30; anal rays III,16 to 19; anterior tubed lateral-line scales 15 to 28; gill rakers 17 to 18; caudal fin rounded; dark grey to black with two brilliant blue stripes on head and anterior body, the broadest from lips to pectoral base. A small species, the largest specimen 5.5 cm. Red Sea. Closely tied to coral; found in the depth range of 2 to 60 m. Often seen in pairs.

## 76 Golden Dottyback

*Pseudoplesiops auratus* (Lubbock), 1975

Dorsal rays II,22 or 23; anal rays III (first spine visible only by dissection or X-ray), 13 to 15; pelvic rays I,4 (I,5 in *Pseudochromis*); a single tubed lateral-line scale at shoulder; gill rakers 17 to 19; body slender, the depth 4.1 to 4.9 in standard length; caudal fin rounded; orange-yellow with a narrow bright orange stripe, indistinctly edged in dull bluish, from snout through upper edge of eye to below sixteenth dorsal ray; a similar stripe from interorbital to origin of dorsal fin, and an arc of orange on operculum; scaled basal part of caudal fin bright orange-red. Largest, 4.6 cm. A secretive fish which lives in deep recesses of caves; depth range 3 to 30 m. Gulf of Aqaba to the Gulf of Aden. Two other Red Sea species of the genus are *P. rubiceps* (Lubbock) which is deeper bodied, reddish anteriorly (the snout red), shading to olive posteriorly, and the even deeper bodied *P. lubbocki* Edwards and Randall which is light yellowish, becoming pinkish grey on head; it has been collected in 52 to 70 m.

# Longfins (Plesiopidae)

A small family of five genera characterized by dorsal rays XI to XIV,6 to 16; anal rays III,7 to 20; pelvic rays I,4; and a disjunct lateral line; the preopercle has a double border. Most species have long pelvic fins, and the soft portions of the dorsal and anal fins may be prolonged posteriorly. The tropical species are all small and secretive. Three have been recorded from the Red Sea, the two discussed below and *Plesiops coeruleolineatus* Rüppell which is rarely seen.

## 77 Whitespotted Longfin

*Plesiops nigricans* (Rüppell), 1828

Dorsal rays XII,7; spinous membranes of dorsal fin deeply incised; anal rays III,8; anterior lateral line ending beneath rear base of dorsal fin, the tubed scales 19 to 23; pelvic fins long, reaching posterior to third anal spine; caudal fin rounded, not long, its length about 3.7 in standard length; dark brown, the head, body, median and pelvic fins with small white spots (those on body mostly one per scale and vertically elongate, except on thorax and posteriorly on caudal peduncle where round). Attains about 14 cm. Red Sea.

## 78 Comet

*Calloplesiops altivelis* (Steindachner), 1903

Dorsal rays XI,8 to 10; spinous membranes of dorsal fin not incised; anal rays III,9; anterior lateral line ending beneath rear base of dorsal fin, the tubed scales 19 or 20; pelvic fins very long, extending posterior to midbase of anal fin; caudal fin long and pointed, its length about 1.7 in standard length; black with small round bluish white spots on head and body (one per scale) and scaled basal parts of fins; unscaled part of fins with very small blue spots (except pectorals); a black spot, edged in blue above and yellow below at rear base of dorsal fin. Attains at least 16 cm. Indo-Pacific. Usually not seen out of holes in the reef until dusk. When frightened, its pos-

terior end adopts a posture and appearance much like the head of the moray eel *Gymnothorax meleagris*.

61

# Cardinalfishes (Apogonidae)

The cardinalfishes are named for the red colour of many of the species. They have two separate dorsal fins, the first of VI to VIII spines (first spine may be very small), II anal spines, large eyes, a moderately large oblique mouth, and a double-edged preopercle. Most are small, and all are carnivorous. They are nocturnal, feeding principally on zooplankton (as is the individual of *Apogon coccineus* shown in the underwater photo *below left*). By day they tend to hide in caves and crevices in rocky areas or reefs, sometimes in aggregations. Males incubate the eggs in their mouths. Over 35 species of apogonid fishes occur in the Red Sea; their classification is still under study. The 14 species discussed below and *Apogon leptacanthus* Bleeker (see underwater photo *below right*) include those most apt to be seen by divers during the day.

## 79 Largetooth Cardinalfish

*Cheilodipterus macrodon* (Lacepède), 1802

Dorsal rays VI–I,9; anal rays II,8; pectoral rays 13; body elongate; jaws with very long, well-spaced, nearly straight, slender canine teeth, the upper jaw with a band of villiform teeth posterior to canines; iridescent silver with eight bronze brown stripes; base of caudal fin crossed by a broad blackish bar (a large spot instead of bar in juveniles), this pigment continuing onto edges of caudal lobes; outer half of first dorsal fin blackish. Attains 24 cm. Indo-Pacific.

## 80 Lined Cardinalfish

*Cheilodipterus lineatus* (Linnaeus), 1758

Dorsal rays VI–I,9; anal rays II,8; pectoral rays 13; body elongate; jaws with very long, well-spaced, nearly straight, slender canine teeth, the upper jaw with a band of villiform teeth posterior to canines; iridescent silver with about 14 longitudinal dark yellowish brown lines (every other line broader); a broad blackish band across caudal fin base (a large round blackish spot edged in yellow in juveniles and subadults), with a little dark pigment extending onto upper and lower margins of caudal fin; distal part of first dorsal fin dusky. To 18 cm. Western Indian Ocean.

## 81 Fiveline Cardinalfish

*Cheilodipterus quinquelineatus* Cuvier and Valenciennes, 1828

Dorsal rays VI–I,9; anal rays II,8; pectoral rays 12 or 13; body elongate; jaws with villiform teeth in bands, the upper jaw with incurved canine teeth only anteriorly and the lower with re-curved canines only along side; silvery white with five narrow black stripes on side of body and one midventrally; a large round yellow spot at base of caudal fin with a small black spot in centre. Reaches 12 cm. Indo-Pacific. The related *C. bipunctatus* (Lachner) differs in having a black spot dorsally on the caudal peduncle about half the diameter of the black spot in the centre of the yellow area

on the side of the peduncle. Both species may seek refuge among the long black spines of the sea urchin *Diadema*.

## 82 Golden Cardinalfish

*Apogon aureus* (Lacepède), 1802

Dorsal rays VII–I,9; anal rays II,8; pectoral rays usually 14; body deep, the depth about 2.3 in standard length; only the posterior preopercular border ser-rate, caudal fin forked; coppery dorsally, shading to golden on sides and ventrally, with a broad black band across base of caudal fin; a row of small blackish spots along anterior part of lateral line; two bright blue lines through eye, and one on maxilla. Reaches 14 cm. East Africa to

the western Pacific. May be seen hover-ing near coral heads by day.

## 83 Goldstriped Cardinalfish

*Apogon cyanosoma* Bleeker, 1853

Dorsal rays VII–I,9; anal rays II,8; pectoral rays 14; gill rakers 23 or 24; only the posterior border of preopercle serrate; caudal fin slightly forked; bluish silver with six golden yellow stripes, the third short, beginning at upper edge of eye and ending beneath origin of second dorsal fin. Attains 7 cm. East Africa to the western Pacific. May occur in aggregations.

## 84 Iridescent Cardinalfish

*Apogon kallopterus* Bleeker, 1856

Dorsal rays VII–I,9; anal rays II,8; pectoral rays 13 or 14; gill rakers 17 to 19; both borders of preopercle serrate; caudal fin forked; light brown with blue-green and yellow iridescence; a narrow dark brown stripe from snout to eye, continuing broadly (and sometimes dif-fusely) to base of caudal fin where it ends in a dark spot. Maximum size 15 cm. A common Indo-Pacific species. *Apogon snyderi* Jordan and Evermann is a synonym.

## 85 Bridled Cardinalfish

*Apogon fraenatus* Valenciennes, 1832

Dorsal rays VII–I,9; anal rays II,8; pectoral rays 14 or 15; gill rakers 17 or 18; both borders of preopercle serrate; caudal fin forked; pale coppery to whitish with a lateral black stripe edged in iridescent light blue from snout through eye, narrowing as it ends posteriorly on caudal peduncle; a round black spot nearly as large as pupil centred on caudal base; front of first dorsal fin blackish. Largest recorded 12.5 cm. Indo-Pacific.

## 86 Eyeshadow Cardinalfish

*Apogon exostigma* (Jordan and Starks), 1906

Dorsal rays VII–I,9; anal rays II,8; pectoral rays 13; gill rakers 18 or 19; both borders of preopercle serrate; caudal fin forked; silvery white with some iridescence; a narrow black stripe, edged in pale iridescent blue-green, from front of snout through eye nearly to caudal base, more attenuate posteriorly; a black spot smaller than pupil at caudal base just above end of lateral stripe; front of first dorsal fin and upper and lower margins of caudal fin blackish. Attains 10 cm. Indo-Pacific. Most common around isolated coral heads on sand in protected waters.

## 87 Twobelt Cardinalfish

*Apogon taeniatus* Cuvier and Valenciennes, 1828

Dorsal rays VII–I,9; anal rays II,8; pectoral rays 14; gill rakers 18 to 20; only the posterior preopercular border serrate; caudal fin slightly emarginate centrally, the lobes rounded; light grey with dark stripes following scale rows, a dark bar beneath each dorsal fin, an ocellated dark bluish spot (sometimes faint) above pectoral fin and a diagonal dark streak on cheek; a dark spot may be present anterior to middle of caudal base. Reported to 12.5 cm. East Africa to the western Pacific. A shallow-water species generally found in silty reef environments or mangrove areas.

## 88 Multistripe Cardinalfish

*Apogon multitaeniatus* Cuvier and Valenciennes, 1828

Dorsal rays VII–I,9; anal rays II,8; pectoral rays 15; lateral-line scales 35 (other *Apogon* and *Cheilodipterus* herein with 23 to 25); gill rakers 19 to 21; only the posterior preopercular margin serrate; caudal fin forked with rounded lobes; red with brownish red stripes following scale rows on body; a black spot covering most of first dorsal fin. Reaches 18 cm. Western Indian Ocean. Not often seen by day in spite of its large size.

## 89 Ringtail Cardinalfish

*Apogon annularis* Rüppell, 1829

Dorsal rays VII–I,9; anal rays II,8; pectoral rays 12; gill rakers 26 to 28; only the posterior border of preopercle serrate; caudal fin slightly forked; pinkish mauve dorsally, shading to silvery or coppery on sides and ventrally, with iridescence; a broad black ring, bordered by pale bands encircling posterior part of caudal peduncle; a diagonal blackish streak on cheek. Attains 7 cm. Red Sea.

## 90 Doublebar Cardinalfish

*Apogon bifasciatus* Rüppell, 1838

Dorsal rays VII–I,9; anal rays II,8; pectoral rays 15; gill rakers 18; only the posterior border of preopercle serrate; caudal fin slightly emarginate with rounded lobes; reddish to silvery grey with iridescence; a black bar narrower than eye on body beneath each dorsal fin; a small black spot posteriorly on lateral line just in front of caudal fin base. Attains 14 cm. East Africa to southern Japan. Generally found in silty reef habitats.

## 91 Orangelined Cardinalfish

*Archamia fucata* (Cantor), 1850

Dorsal rays VI–I,9; anal rays II,15 to 17; pectoral rays 13 to 15; gill rakers 20 to 24; only the posterior border of preopercle serrate (broadly over the corner); caudal fin slightly forked; iridescent silvery to coppery with about 25 vertical orange lines on body which curve forward as they pass ventrally; a blackish spot as large or larger than pupil at midbase of caudal fin. Reaches 8 cm. East Africa to Samoa and the Marshall Islands. Usually seen in aggregations in the shelter of reefs or rocky substrata. The related Red Sea species *A. lineolata* (Cuvier and Valenciennes) is similar,

differing in having 13 to 15 anal rays and about half the number of orange vertical lines on the body (the orange of these lines partially obscured by blackish pigment).

## 92 Variegated Cardinalfish

*Fowleria variegata* (Valenciennes), 1832

Dorsal rays VII–I,9; anal rays II,8; pectoral rays 14; lateral line incomplete, the tubed scales ending beneath front of second dorsal fin; both preopercular borders smooth; no palatine teeth (other apogonids herein all with palatine teeth); mottled brown and whitish with about eight or nine faint brown bars on side of body; a large black spot rimmed narrowly in silver, then dark brown, on opercle. Reaches about 8 cm. East Africa

to Samoa. One of four species of the genus recorded from the Red Sea.

# Jacks (Carangidae)

The jacks are strong-swimming, open-water, carnivorous fishes which are usually silvery in colour. They vary in shape from fusiform, such as seen in the species of *Decapterus*, to high-bodied like *Alectis*. The caudal fin is strongly forked or lunate; the caudal peduncle is slender and usually reinforced with a series of external overlapping bony plates called scutes. The lateral line is complete and arched anteriorly, the straight posterior portion consisting of scutes in those fishes possessing them. The scales are small and cycloid (sometimes embedded). The eye is usually protected and streamlined by an adipose eyelid. The opercle lacks spines, and the preopercle is without serrae. There are two dorsal fins (or one so deeply notched as to seem like two), though the first may become embedded with age on a few species. The first two anal spines are separated from the rest of the anal fin; these are usually stout, but in large individuals of a few species they also may become obsolete.

The pectoral fins are narrow and often falcate. Many of the species are highly esteemed food fishes. Over 30 species of carangid fishes are known from the Red Sea. None is a reef fish in the sense that it resides in reefs, but some range over reefs to prey upon the fishes there. The four most apt to be observed entering the Red Sea reef environment are discussed below, and two other common species, *Caranx ignobilis* (Forsskål) *below*, and *Scomberomorus lysan* (Forsskål) *above*, are shown in underwater photos.

## 93 Orangespotted Jack

*Carangoides bajad* (Forsskål), 1775

Dorsal rays VIII–1,24 to 26; anal rays II–I,21 to 24; scutes 19 to 30; gill rakers 27 to 32; teeth small, in villiform bands in jaws; chest completely scaled except for a narrow midventral region anteriorly; brassy, shading to silver on sides, with numerous yellow-orange spots; no dark opercular spot. This jack is able to change its colour to almost entirely orange-yellow. Reaches 53 cm. East Africa to Indonesia and the Philippines. *C. auroguttatus* (Cuvier and Valenciennes) is a synonym.

# 94 Yellowspotted Jack

*Carangoides fulvoguttatus* (Forsskål), 1775

Dorsal rays VIII–I,25 to 30; anal rays II–I,22 to 26; scutes 15 to 25; gill rakers 22 to 28; teeth in villiform bands in jaws; naked area ventrally on chest highest anteriorly, reaching nearly half distance or to pectoral base, and extending well posterior to origin of pelvic fins; iridescent blue-green on back, shading to silvery on the sides, with yellow spots contained within six faint broad dusky bars on body; opercular membrane dusky from level of upper edge of pectoral base to upper end of gill opening. Attains 90 cm. East Africa to the western Pacific, including eastern Australia.

# 95 Bluefin Trevally

*Caranx melampygus* Cuvier and Valenciennes, 1833

Dorsal rays VIII–I,21 to 24; anal rays II–I,17 to 20; scutes 31 to 40; gill rakers 25 to 29; body deep, the depth about 3.4 in total length; teeth in jaws conical, biserial, the outer row larger; chest completely scaled; brassy dorsally with scattered small black and blue spots, silvery ventrally, the entire head and body suffused with blue; median and pelvic fins blue; pectoral fins mainly yellow. Largest collected by author, 80 cm, 6.8 kg; recorded to 100 cm. Indo-Pacific and the tropical eastern Pacific.

# 96 Bigeye Trevally

*Caranx sexfasciatus* Quoy and Gaimard, 1825

Dorsal rays VIII–I,19 to 22; anal rays II–I,15 to 17; gill rakers 22 to 25; scutes 27 to 35; body somewhat elongate, the depth about 4 in total length; eye large; conical teeth in upper jaw in two rows, the outer row largest; teeth in lower jaw in one row with a villiform band of small teeth behind; chest completely scaled; iridescent blue-green to lavender dorsally, shading to silvery white ventrally; scutes blackish; a small blackish spot near upper end of gill opening; median fins dusky, the pointed lobes of the second dorsal fin tipped with white. The scientific name is derived from the six dusky bars of juveniles. Attains 85 cm. Indo-Pacific and tropical eastern Pacific (where it is generally known as *C. marginatus* Gill). Juveniles may be found in estuaries. The giant trevally, *Caranx ignobilis* (Forsskål) (see underwater photo *opposite*), is not uncommon in the Red Sea; it is distinctive in its deep body, steep forehead, and scaleless chest (except for a small mid-ventral patch of scales in front of pelvic fins); its maximum verified size, 165 cm, 52.6 kg.

# Snappers (Lutjanidae)

The snappers are one of the most important commercial families of fishes of tropical and subtropical seas. In addition to the general characteristics of the order Perciformes, they are distinctive in having dorsal rays X to XII,9 to 17, the fin continuous (with or without a notch between spinous and soft portions); anal rays III,7 to 11; mouth fairly large; jaws equal or with the lower slightly project-

near the shelter of reefs. Snappers feed heavily on crustaceans, though some species are primarily piscivorous. The family is represented in the Red Sea by the deep-water *Aphareus rutilans* Cuvier and Valenciennes, *Macolor niger* (Forsskål), *Paracaesio sordidus* Abe and Shinohara (see underwater photo from the Gulf of Aqaba), three species of *Pristipomoides*, and about 15 of *Lutjanus*.

ing, the maxilla slipping under edge of preorbital when mouth closed; teeth in jaws fixed, varying from small and conical to large and caniform (none incisiform or molariform); vomer and palatines usually with small teeth; no spines on opercle; preopercular margin usually finely serrate; scales ctenoid; dorsal spines heteracanthous (successive spines alternating slightly in position left to right); caudal fin truncate, emarginate, or forked, the principal rays 17. These fishes are all carnivorous, usually bottom-dwelling, and many are nocturnal. During the day several species of *Lutjanus* may form large aggregations

## 97 Blackspot Snapper

*Lutjanus ehrenbergi* (Peters), 1869

Dorsal rays X,13; longitudinal rows of scales on back horizontal; preopercular notch not shallow; preorbital narrow, its depth 8.0 to 10.0 in head (4.0 to 7.6 for other *Lutjanus* herein); patch of teeth on vomer triangular with a median posterior projection; caudal fin very slightly emarginate; grey-brown on back, silvery on sides, with four yellow stripes and a large blackish spot on lateral line below anterior soft portion of dorsal fin. To 30 cm. East Africa to the western Pacific.

## 98 Dory Snapper

*Lutjanus fulviflamma* (Forsskål), 1775

Dorsal rays X,12 or 13 (usually 13); longitudinal rows of scales on back oblique; preopercular notch shallow; patch of teeth on vomer triangular with a prominent pointed median posterior projection; caudal fin slightly emarginate; greenish to grey on back, silvery white on sides, with about six yellow stripes and a blackish spot (usually oblong and often broadly pale bordered) on lateral line below anterior soft portion of dorsal fin. Reaches 30 cm. East Africa to Samoa.

## 99 Onespot Snapper

*Lutjanus monostigma* (Cuvier and Valenciennes), 1828

Dorsal rays X,13; longitudinal rows of scales on back oblique, preopercular notch shallow; caudal fin slightly forked; canine teeth in jaws large; patch of teeth on vomer in a V shape; pale yellowish to pink with an oval blackish spot on lateral line beneath anterior soft portion of dorsal fin (spot may be absent in large adults); fins yellow. Reaches 60 cm. Indo-Pacific. Feeds mainly on fishes.

## 100 Bluestripe Snapper

*Lutjanus kasmira* (Forsskål), 1775

Dorsal rays X,14 or 15 (usually 15); longitudinal rows of scales on back oblique; scales on top of head extending anteriorly to a point over centre of eye (scales on head of other *Lutjanus* herein do not extend anterior to rear margin of eye); preopercular notch deep; patch of teeth on vomer in a V shape; caudal fin slightly forked; yellow with four dark-edged blue stripes on upper half of body, whitish to pale pink below; fins yellow; a diffuse blackish spot sometimes present below anterior soft portion of dorsal fin. Largest specimen, 34 cm. Indo-Pacific. Not common in less than 20 m; the author caught one on hook and line in the Red Sea from 265 m.

## 101 Blueline Snapper

*Lutjanus coeruleolineatus* (Rüppell), 1838

Dorsal rays X,12 or 13 (usually 12); longitudinal rows of scales on back oblique; preopercular notch shallow; patch of teeth on vomer in a V shape; caudal fin slightly emarginate; olivaceous yellow dorsally, pale yellow ventrally, with seven or eight narrow blue stripes and a large blackish spot (may be rimmed in whitish in life) on lateral line beneath anterior soft portion of dorsal fin; fins yellow. Attains about 35 cm. Red Sea to the Gulf of Oman.

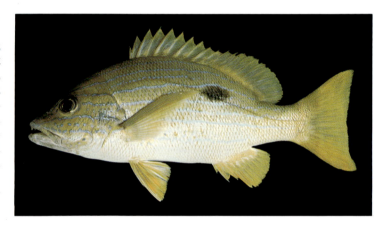

## 102 Humpback Snapper

*Lutjanus gibbus* (Forsskål), 1775

Dorsal rays X,13 or 14; longitudinal rows of scales on back oblique; dorsal profile of head of adults a sinuous curve with the snout slightly concave and the forehead and nape convex; preopercular notch very deep; patch of teeth on vomer in a V shape; caudal fin deeply forked, the lobes rounded; grey to red (those from deeper water more red), the median fins blackish with bluish white margins; juveniles with a very large round black spot at caudal fin base. Reaches 60 cm. Indo-Pacific. May be seen in dense, more-or-less stationary aggregations at edges of reefs during the day. Feeds primarily on crustaceans (especially crabs) and other invertebrates, occasionally on small fishes.

## 103 River Snapper

*Lutjanus argentimaculatus* (Forsskål), 1775

Dorsal rays X,13 or 14; longitudinal scale rows on back horizontal (parallel with lateral line); preopercular notch shallow; patch of teeth on vomer in a V shape; caudal fin truncate; bronze to silvery red; one oblique pale blue line may be present on snout, ending beneath eye. Attains about 80 cm. Capable of living in freshwater. East Africa to the western Pacific. Recently recorded in the Mediterranean Sea; its occurrence there is probably due to passage through the Suez Canal.

## 104 Twinspot Snapper

*Lutjanus bohar* (Forsskål), 1775

Dorsal rays X,13 or 14; longitudinal scale rows on back oblique; preopercular notch shallow; anterior canine teeth large; patch of teeth on vomer in a broad V shape; nostrils of adults set in a deep groove; caudal fin moderately forked; dark reddish brown on back, shading to reddish tan ventrally, with a faint linear pattern from dark edges on the scales; median and pelvic fins blackish orange-red; about upper third of pectoral fins blackish red, the lower two-thirds light reddish; young with two whitish spots on back (one beneath seventh to eighth dorsal spines and one below rear base of dorsal fin, the latter more conspicuous) and a black submarginal band in each caudal lobe. To 100 cm. Indo-Pacific. The preferred habitat is exposed deep

outer reefs. About three-quarters of the diet of adults consists of fishes. The young have been reported to mimic certain damselfishes of the genus *Chromis*, such as *C. ternatensis* (Bleeker), and thereby get closer to their prey.

## 105 Black-and-White Snapper

*Macolor niger* (Forsskål), 1775

Dorsal rays X,13; anal rays III,11 (III,8 on the species of *Lutjanus* discussed above); gill rakers very long, blade-like and numerous (as many as 75 on lower limb of first gill arch); dorsal profile of head smoothly convex; preopercle deeply notched; mouth oblique; vomerine teeth in a V-shaped patch; caudal fin emarginate; fins of adults with ragged edges; body blackish, each scale with a vertically elongate pale blue-green spot; head pale bluish with numerous, close-set, blackish spots, some joined; fins blackish. The young are strongly marked in black and white (see underwater photo in family account). Reported to 61.5 cm. East Africa to Samoa and the Marshall Islands. Adults are often seen in aggregations, as may be seen in the underwater photo on page 69.

# Fusiliers (Caesionidae)

The fusiliers have often been classified as a subfamily in the Lutjanidae; however, they are now given full family status. These fishes have fusiform bodies, the depth 2.4 to 5.5 in standard length; the mouth is small, terminal and oblique, the upper jaw very protrusible; the long ascending process of the premaxilla is a separate ossification; the upper edge of the side of the premaxilla has one or two bony processes which slide medial to the maxilla; the teeth are small and conical (absent in *Dipterygonotus*), none as canines; there is a single dorsal fin with IX to XV slender spines and 9 to 21 soft rays; anal fin with III spines and 9 to 13 rays; last dorsal and anal rays slightly longer than penultimate rays; caudal fin deeply forked; scales small, ctenoid; a supratemporal band of scales separated from scales of rest of nape by a narrow naked band. The caesionids are diurnal, midwater, zooplankton-feeding fishes that are usually encountered in schools. They are generally found over or in the vicinity of coral reefs, though they do not seek refuge in reefs by day; they depend on their swift swimming and elusive movement to escape predators. They come readily to cleaning stations on reefs and retire to the shelter of reefs at night to sleep. There are four genera: *Caesio*, *Pterocaesio*, *Gymnocaesio*, and *Dipterygonotus*, the last-mentioned not known from the Indian Ocean and Red Sea. *Gymnocaesio* is distinguished from *Caesio* and *Pterocaesio* because it lacks scales on the dorsal and anal fins (these fins densely scaled in *Caesio* and *Pterocaesio*).

## 106 Lunar Fusilier

*Caesio lunaris* Cuvier and Valenciennes, 1830

Dorsal rays X,14; anal rays III,11; pectoral rays 19 to 21; lateral-line scales 48 to 52; depth of body 2.7 to 2.8 in standard length; two rows of teeth in upper jaw (those in outer row largest), with a narrow medial band of very small villiform teeth; blue dorsally, shading to white ventrally; tips of caudal lobes black; axil of pectoral fins black, and a small black spot at upper pectoral base. Reaches about 30 cm. East Africa to the western Pacific.

## 107 Suez Fusilier

*Caesio suevicus* Klunzinger, 1884

Dorsal rays X,15; anal rays III,12; pectoral rays 19 to 21 (usually 20); lateral-line scales 53 to 55; depth of body 3.25 to 3.55 in standard length; dentition as in *C. lunaris*; blue dorsally, shading to white or light red ventrally, with a yellow band on back beginning beneath spinous portion of dorsal fin and extending to upper base of caudal fin; caudal lobes tipped with black, each with a submarginal band of white; a triangular black spot at upper pectoral base; pectoral axil black. To about 25 cm. Red Sea.

## 108 Striated Fusilier

*Caesio striatus* Rüppell, 1830

Dorsal rays X,15; anal rays III,12; pectoral rays 18 or 19; lateral-line scales 62 to 67; depth of body 3.9 to 4.4 in standard length; one row of teeth in upper jaw (with a few tiny medial teeth anteriorly in jaw); green to blue-green dorsally with four blackish stripes, the fourth midlateral, narrow, and sometimes faint; ventral half of body silvery white or light red; caudal fin with a black band submarginally in each lobe; upper base and axil of pectoral fin black. Reaches about 18 cm. Western Indian Ocean.

## 109 Goldband Fusilier

*Pterocaesio chrysozona* (Cuvier and Valenciennes), 1830

Dorsal rays X,15; anal rays III,12; pectoral rays 19 to 20; lateral-line scales 65 to 71; depth of body 3.7 to 4.3 in standard length; dorsal edge of side of premaxilla with two bony processes (one in *Caesio*); a single row of teeth in upper jaw; grey-blue on back, the scale edges brown, white on ventral half, the two regions separated by a yellow band about as wide as pupil at level of upper edge of eye which narrows as it passes to base of caudal fin; tips of caudal lobes dark reddish brown; no black spot on pectoral base or axil. Reaches about 18 cm. East Africa to the western Pacific.

# Grunts (Haemulidae)

These fishes, sometimes given the family names Pomadasyidae, Gaterinidae, or Plectorhynchidae, have most of the characteristics listed for the family Lutjanidae. They differ from the snappers principally in that the mouth is smaller and lower on the head, the upper jaw often projecting slightly; the lips are usually thick, particularly in the genus *Plectorhynchus* (species of this genus are called sweetlips in Australia); the teeth in the jaws are conical and small, none developed as canines; there are no teeth on the palate; dorsal rays IX to XIV,13 to 26; anal rays III,6 to 12, the second spine generally longest and stoutest. Grunts are named for the sounds they make by grinding their pharyngeal teeth; the sound is amplified by the gas bladder. They are primarily nocturnal; those on Indo-Pacific reefs during the day (principally species of *Plectorhynchus*) are merely utilizing the reefs for shelter until nightfall when they disperse for feeding. They feed on a wide variety of benthic invertebrates. Some species of *Plectorhynchus* undergo dramatic changes in colour pattern with growth. Other species of this genus not commonly seen in the Red Sea include *P. flavomaculatus* (Cuvier and Valenciennes), *P. nigrus* (Cuvier and Valenciennes) (see underwater photo), and *P. sordidus* (Klunzinger).

## 110 Blackspotted Grunt
*Plectorhynchus gaterinus* (Forsskål), 1775

Dorsal rays XIII,19 or 20; gill rakers 8+18 or 19; third to fifth dorsal spines longest; caudal fin rounded in young, truncate in adults; pelvic fins slightly longer than pectorals; head grey; body whitish with numerous black spots smaller than pupil except ventrally; lips pale salmon; inside of mouth orange-red; median fins light yellow with black spots; paired fins light yellow. Young with three pairs of black stripes on head and body; these break up into spots at a length of about 12 cm. Reaches approximately 45 cm. Western Indian Ocean.

## 111 Painted Grunt
*Plectorhynchus pictus* (Thunberg), 1792

Dorsal rays IX or X (usually X), 22 to 25; gill rakers 7 or 8 + 14 or 15; second dorsal spine longest; second anal spine longer than third; caudal peduncle long and slender; caudal fin rounded in juveniles, truncate in adults; adults light purplish grey with a small bronze spot on each scale and a few scattered large blackish blotches; juveniles with two broad black stripes, the fins yellow and black striped; larger ones lose the yellow, the stripes narrow, and spots begin to form; at 20 cm the stripes are gone but rows of spots may indicate their earlier location. Reported to 90 cm. East Africa to the western Pacific. Most common in and about silty reefs.

## 112 Minstrel
*Plectorhynchus schotaf* (Forsskål), 1775

Dorsal rays XII,18 to 21; gill rakers 10 to 12 + 16 or 17; third to fifth dorsal spines longest; pectoral and pelvic fins about equal in length; caudal fin truncate in juveniles, slightly emarginate in adults; grey, the distal edges of median fins blackish; opercular membrane and sometimes hind edge of preopercle orange-red; edges and inside of mouth orange-red. Reported to 80 cm. Western Indian Ocean.

# Emperors (Lethrinidae)

This important family consists of moderate to large-sized perciform fishes related to the grunts and snappers on one side and the porgies on the other. They have a terminal mouth with fairly thick lips, stout canine teeth anteriorly in the jaws and either conical or molariform teeth at the side of the jaws; there are no teeth on the palate. The preopercle is scaleless. The dorsal fin is continuous, without a notch, with X spines and 9 or 10 soft rays; the anal fin has III spines and 8 to 10 rays; the caudal fin is emarginate to forked. Like the grunts, these fishes feed mainly at night. Those with molariform teeth tend to eat molluscs, sea urchins and other hard-shelled invertebrates which they crush with these teeth. The family consists of five genera: the large genus *Lethrinus*, *Gymnocranius*, and the monotypic *Monotaxis*, *Gnathodentex*, and *Wattsia*. The first three mentioned are represented in the Red Sea, *Lethrinus* by ten species and *Gymnocranius* by one [*G. robinsoni* Gilchrist and Thompson, which replaces *G. rivulatus* (Rüppell), invalid as a homonym]. The usual meristic data are not helpful in distinguishing the species of *Lethrinus*; all listed below have 9 dorsal soft rays, 8 anal soft rays, 13 pectoral rays, and lateral-line scales within the range of 45 to 48. Some species are capable of rapidly adopting a dark mottled or reticular colour pattern and just as rapidly turning it off.

## 113 Blackspot Emperor

*Lethrinus harak* (Forsskål), 1775

Six rows of scales between lateral line and middle dorsal spines; inner base of pectoral fins covered with small scales; depth of body 2.8 to 3.0 in standard length; snout not long, 1.8 to 2.0 in head; jaws ending beneath anterior nostrils; teeth on side of jaws include molars; olive dorsally, shading to silvery white below, with a large elliptical black spot on side of body just below lateral line, this spot broadly edged in dull yellow. Attains 60 cm. East Africa to the western Pacific. A common inshore species usually seen over substrata dominated by

sand. Feeds principally on benthic invertebrates. Among the least wary of the species of *Lethrinus*.

## 114 Yellowlip Emperor

*Lethrinus xanthochilus* Klunzinger, 1870

Five rows of scales between lateral line and middle dorsal spines; inner base of pectoral fins without scales; body elongate, the depth 3.1 to 3.3 in standard length; interorbital flat; snout 1.6 to 1.9 in head; jaws ending beneath anterior nostril; no molariform teeth in jaws; yellowish grey with indistinct scattered small dark spots; lips yellow, particularly the upper; a red spot at upper base of pectoral fin. To 60 cm. East Africa to the Gilbert and Marshall Islands. Feeds on a

wide variety of marine animals, including fishes, crabs and sea urchins. A wary species.

## 115 Longnose Emperor

*Lethrinus elongatus* Cuvier and Valenciennes, 1830

Five or six (usually six) rows of scales between lateral line and middle dorsal spines; inner base of pectoral fins without scales; body moderately elongate, the depth 3.1 to 3.2 in standard length; head very long, 2.4 to 2.7 in standard length (2.7 to 3.3 for other *Lethrinus* herein); snout long, 1.6 to 1.8 in head; jaws ending in front of anterior nostril; no molariform teeth in jaws; grey, whitish ventrally, often with two or three oblique dark streaks on snout passing from eye toward mouth. Reaches 100 cm. Indo-Pacific. Feeds mainly on fishes. This species has long been misidentified as *L. miniatus* (Bloch and Schneider); the name *miniatus*, however, must replace *chrysostomus* Richardson, a species of the southwest Pacific. *L. elongatus* described by Valenciennes from the Red Sea is therefore the oldest available name for the present species. *L. microdon* Cuvier and Valenciennes is similar, but has a shorter head and red fins.

## 116 Variegated Emperor

*Lethrinus variegatus* Cuvier and Valenciennes, 1830

Five rows of scales between lateral line and middle dorsal spines; inner base of pectoral fins without scales; body slender, the depth 3.1 to 3.7 in standard length; snout 2.2 to 2.4 in head; jaws ending beneath posterior nostril; no molariform teeth in jaws; brownish yellow with a broad dark bar passing ventrally from eye, a broad diagonal dark band from eye to corner of mouth, and one across interorbital space. A small species, rarely exceeding 20 cm. East Africa to the western Pacific.

## 117 Redspot Emperor

*Lethrinus lentjan* (Lacepède), 1802

Six rows of scales between lateral line and middle dorsal spines; inner base of pectoral fins with a few small scales or none at all; depth of body 2.6 to 2.9 in standard length; snout 1.9 to 2.1 in head; jaws ending beneath nostrils; adults with molariform teeth on side of jaws; greenish on back, some scales with white centres, shading to whitish ventrally, with a vertically elongate red spot on opercular flap at level of lower edge of eye, and often another on pectoral base. Attains about 40 cm. East Africa to the western Pacific.

## 118 Yellowstripe Emperor

*Lethrinus ramak* (Forsskål), 1775

Six rows of scales between lateral line and middle dorsal spines; inner base of pectoral fins with numerous small scales; depth of body 2.7 to 3.0 in standard length; snout 1.8 to 2.0 in head; jaws ending beneath anterior nostril; teeth on side of jaws may be nodular, but none molariform; head purplish grey, the body whitish (scale edges dusky), with an orange-yellow stripe on lower side at level of pectoral base (sometimes two faint orange-yellow stripes above and one below this stripe); upper basal edge of pectoral fins blue. Reaches 40 cm. East Africa to Micronesia.

## 119 Redfin Emperor

*Lethrinus mahsenoides* Cuvier and Valenciennes, 1830

Six rows of scales between lateral line and middle dorsal spines; inner base of pectoral fins with numerous small scales; body deep, the depth 2.4 to 2.7 in standard length; snout short, 1.9 to 2.2 in head; jaws ending beneath posterior nostril; teeth on side of jaws include large molars; head yellowish brown; body pale greenish yellow, the scale edges dark, sometimes with a faint pattern of irregular broken dusky bars; opercular membrane usually red; fins red, the colour more on rays than membranes. Reaches 30 cm. East Africa to the western Pacific. *L. borbonicus* Cuvier and Valenciennes is a synonym.

## 120 Mahsena

*Lethrinus mahsena* (Forsskål), 1775

Five rows of scales between lateral line and middle dorsal spines; inner base of pectoral fins with numerous small scales; body deep, the depth 2.3 to 2.6 in standard length; snout short, 1.7 to 2.0 in head; jaws ending beneath posterior nostrils; adults with molariform teeth on side of jaws; head purplish grey, the body greenish dorsally, shading to whitish below, usually with nine or ten dusky yellowish bars, the second bifurcating below lateral line (beneath middle of pectoral fin); a red bar at base of pectoral fins, often with a streak of red in upper part of these fins and sometimes another in lower; pelvic fins with a trace of red at base. Attains 50 cm. East Africa to the western Pacific. Sea urchins are a favourite food item; some fish exhibit

small dark purple spots on front of snout, a result of being stuck by the spines of *Diadema*.

## 121 Spangled Emperor

*Lethrinus nebulosus* (Forsskål), 1775

Six rows of scales betwen lateral line and middle dorsal spines; inner base of pectoral fins with numerous small scales; depth of body 2.6 to 2.8 in standard length; snout 1.8 to 2.2 in head; jaws ending beneath anterior nostrils; teeth on side of jaws include small molars; olivaceous to yellowish, each scale with an iridescent light blue spot (more evident on back); usually two or three blue streaks radiating anteroventrally from eye. Attains about 80 cm. East Africa to the western Pacific. An important commercial fish in some areas.

## 122 Bigeye Emperor

*Monotaxis grandoculis* (Forsskål), 1775

Dorsal soft rays 10; anal soft rays 9; five rows of scales between lateral line and middle dorsal spines; depth of body 2.2 to 2.9 in standard length (increasing with age); eye large, 2.7 to 3.4 in head; snout short, its dorsal profile very steep; jaws ending beneath anterior half of eye; large molariform teeth on side of jaws; greenish dorsally, silvery on sides and ventrally, the edges of the scales dark; can rapidly assume a pattern of four broad blackish bars on body; juveniles with four permanent black bars and a more pointed snout. Largest collected by author, 56 cm. Indo-Pacific. Feeds heavily on molluscs, but crabs, sea urchins and hermit crabs are also important items of the diet. A wary fish.

# Porgies (Sparidae)

The porgies, sometimes called the sea breams, share many general characteristics with the Lethrinidae. Most have moderately deep, compressed bodies; the mouth is small, low on the head, horizontal, and not extending posterior to the centre of the eye; the premaxilla, which is only slightly protractile, overlaps the maxilla; the teeth at the front of the jaws are prominent, conical or incisiform, those at side of jaws molariform; the palate is toothless. Most species have scales on the preopercle. The dorsal fin is continuous with X to XIII spines and 10 to 15 soft rays; the anal fin has III spines (the second longest and strongest) and 8 to 12 rays; the pectoral fins are long and pointed; the caudal fin is emarginate or forked. Most of these fishes are carnivorous, feeding principally on molluscs or crustaceans which they crush with their molariform teeth, but some, such as certain species of *Diplodus*, are omnivorous, feeding in part on benthic plants.

Twelve species of sparid fishes are reported from the Red Sea. The three which are most apt to be observed in the reef environment are discussed below.

## 123 Yellowfin Bream

*Rhabdosargus sarba* (Forsskål), 1775

Dorsal rays XI,13 or 14; anal rays III,11; lateral-line scales 56 to 59; body deep, the depth about 2.0 to 2.2 in standard length; somewhat pointed incisiform teeth anteriorly in jaws and molariform teeth in four rows in upper jaw and three in lower, the most posterior tooth largest; silver with brassy yellow stripes following scale rows; anal, caudal, and paired fins yellow. Reaches 40 cm. Indian Ocean. Records from Indonesia and the western Pacific should be checked. Often occurs in brackish environments. Usually encountered in small schools, as seen in the underwater photo above.

## 124 Doublebar Bream

*Acanthopagrus bifasciatus* (Forsskål), 1775

Dorsal rays XI,12 to 14; anal rays III,10 or 11; lateral-line scales 48 to 51; depth of body 1.8 to 2.1 in standard length; compressed conical teeth at front of jaws and molariform teeth in four rows in upper jaw and three in lower; silvery in colour with two black bars on head (the anterior one through eye), the anal and pelvic fins black, the remaining fins yellow. Reaches 50 cm. Western Indian Ocean. In the Arabian Gulf this species has blackish longitudinal lines on the body following the scale rows.

## 125 Arabian Pinfish

*Diplodus noct* (Cuvier and Valenciennes), 1830

Dorsal rays X to XIII (modally XII), 12 to 15; anal rays III,12 to 14; lateral-line scales 60 to 69; depth of body 23 to 26 in standard length; four pairs of strong incisiform teeth anteriorly in jaws and three rows of molariform teeth (largest posteriorly); silvery in colour with a round black spot slightly smaller than eye anteriorly on side of caudal peduncle; juveniles with narrow blackish bars on upper half of body. Attains about 25 cm. Red Sea. A shallow-water species found along exposed rocky shores.

# Threadfin Breams & Spinecheeks (Nemipteridae)

This family consists of the genera *Nemipterus*, *Pentapodus*, *Scolopsis*, and *Parascolopsis*. In some classifications *Scolopsis* and *Parascolopsis* have been placed in a separate family, Scolopsidae. *Pentapodus* has also been grouped in a separate family, the Pentapodidae (sometimes with lethrinids). These are fishes of small to moderate size which have a small terminal mouth, the maxilla not extending posterior to centre of eye (and usually not reaching front edge of eye); bands of small conical teeth in the jaws, with or without canine teeth anteriorly; no teeth on the vomer or palatines. The scales are large and ctenoid. The dorsal fin is continuous, without a notch between spinous and soft portions, with X spines and 8 to 11 soft rays; the anal fin has III spines and 6 to 8 rays; the pectoral rays number 15 to 18 (rarely 15); the caudal fin is emarginate to forked, the upper

lobe of some species of *Nemipterus* and *Pentapodus* with a long filament. The species of *Scolopsis* are easily distinguished by having a strong backward-directed spine just under the eye. *Parascolopsis* also has a suborbital spine, but is much smaller. Nine nemipterid fishes have been recorded from the Red Sea; most occur in deeper than scuba diving depths. The only one commonly seen in the vicinity of shallow reefs is discussed below.

## 126 Dotted Spinecheek

*Scolopsis ghanam* (Forsskål), 1775

Dorsal rays X,9; anal rays III,7; pectoral rays 16; a large posterior-directed spine on suborbital with several lesser spines below it; depth of body 3.1 to 3.3 in standard length; eye large, about 3 in head of adults; small conical teeth in bands in jaws; posterior preopercular margin and protruding rounded corner serrate; greenish grey, shading to whitish on side and ventrally; a white-edged dark line following lateral line; a white line from interorbital to rear base of dorsal fin; white lines extending posteriorly from upper and lower edges of eye; scales on side of body with a round blackish dot (ventrally and posteriorly

the spots are golden). Attains 20 cm. Indian Ocean, with one record from Indonesia. Common inshore; usually seen over sand flats or sand pockets of reefs.

# Sea Chubs (Kyphosidae)

The sea chubs, sometimes called rudder-fishes, are moderately deep-bodied, compressed fishes with a small head and a small terminal mouth; the teeth are incisiform, and the maxilla slips partially under the preorbital bone when the mouth is closed. The scales are small and ctenoid, covering most of the head and soft portions of the median fins. The dorsal fin is continuous, and the caudal fin is emarginate to forked; the paired fins are relatively short, the origin of the pelvics posterior to the pectoral base. These fishes are omnivorous, but feed mainly on benthic algae, their digestive tract is very long as would be expected from their heavy feeding on plants. They sometimes occur in small aggregations. The family is divisible into two sub-families, the Kyphosinae and the Girellinae (often regarded as a separate family). The latter group is mainly subtropical or temperate in distribution; none occurs in the western Indian Ocean or the Red Sea. Of the Kyphosinae, only

*Kyphosus* is found in the Indo-Pacific (except for waifs of the eastern Pacific *Sector* to eastern Oceania). The Kyphosinae have X or XI (usually XI) dorsal spines.

## 127 Brassy Chub

*Kyphosus vaigiensis* (Quoy and Gaimard), 1825

Dorsal rays XI,14 (rarely 13); anal rays III,13; depth of body 2.3 to 2.5 in standard length; dorsal profile of snout forming an angle of about 60° to the horizontal; soft portion of dorsal fin not higher than longest dorsal spine; silvery grey with bronze stripes following scale rows; opercular membrane dark brown; two diagonal bronze bands on head, the lowermost passing from upper lip to corner of preopercle. Attains 60 cm. Indo-Pacific. The similar *K. bigibbus* (Lacepède) has 12 dorsal soft rays.

## 128 Snubnose Chub

*Kyphosus cinerascens* (Forsskål), 1775

Dorsal rays XI,12; anal rays III,11; depth of body 2.25 to 2.5 in standard length; dorsal profile of snout forming an angle of about 70° to the horizontal; soft portion of dorsal fin distinctly longer than spinous (longest spine of adults contained 1.3 to 1.7 times in longest soft ray); silvery grey, the edges of the scales brown, giving a linear effect; opercular membrane dark brown; caudal, pelvic, and soft portions of dorsal and anal fins dark brown. Attains 45 cm. Indo-Pacific.

# Spadefishes (Ephippidae)

These most distinctive fishes have deep, nearly circular, compressed bodies. The mouth is small and terminal (or nearly so); the teeth in the jaws are brush-like (those of *Platax* with tricuspid tips); no teeth on roof of mouth (except a few on vomer reported as sometimes present on *Platax teira*); posterior nostril elongate; gill membranes broadly joined to isthmus; branchiostegal rays 6; dorsal fin continuous with V to IX spines and 19 to 40 rays; anal fin with III spines and 17 to 28 rays; scales small, ctenoid, the soft portions of the median fins densely scaled, at least basally. The colour pattern is often silvery with dark bars. Of the seven genera, only *Platax* (sometimes given the common name batfishes) is associated with coral reefs.

## 129 Circular Spadefish

*Platax orbicularis* (Forsskål), 1775

Dorsal rays V,34 to 38, with no notch between spinous and soft portions; anal rays III,26 to 28; body of juveniles very deep, the depth greater than standard length; on large adults the depth about 1.4 in standard length; dorsal and anal fins of juveniles enormously elevated, gradually shortening with growth; pelvic fins of juveniles also very elongate, becoming shorter in adults; caudal fin of juveniles rounded, of adults slightly double emarginate; teeth tricuspid, the middle cusp largest; adults silvery grey with a broad dark brown bar anteriorly on body and one on head passing through eye; juveniles brownish yellow. Attains 40 cm. Indo-Pacific. The young sometimes lay on their side and mimic drifting leaves. *P. teira* (Forsskål) (see underwater photo above) also occurs in the Red Sea, though less commonly than *orbicularis*; it has dorsal rays V,30 to 33; anal rays III,23 or 24; and the three cusps on its teeth are about equal in size.

# **Monos** (Monodactylidae)

A small family of two genera characterized by a high compressed body and angular head; a small, very oblique mouth, the lower jaw slightly protruding; brush-like teeth in jaws; villiform teeth on vomer and palatines; vestigial pelvic fins; a continuous unnotched dorsal fin of VII or VIII spines and 26 to 36 soft rays; anal fin of III spines and 27 to 37 soft rays, soft portions of dorsal and anal fins very elevated anteriorly; caudal fin emarginate; scales small, weakly ctenoid, about 50 to 60 in lateral line; dorsal and anal fins completely scaled. These are silvery fishes often seen in schools. They are more apt to be found in estuarine habitats than full salinity marine environments and are able to live in freshwater.

## 130 Mono

*Monodactylus argenteus* (Linnaeus), 1758

Dorsal rays VII or VIII,28 to 30; anal rays III,28 to 30; pelvic fins I,2 or 3, extremely small; depth of body 1.3 to 1.6 in standard length; head 2.9 to 3.0 in standard length; brush-like teeth in bands in jaws, the tips tricuspid; silvery, the young with a dark bar through eye and sometimes a second bar from nape through pectoral base; median fins yellowish, silvery at base, the dorsal and anal with a large blackish area at the ends of the elevated lobes. Attains 23 cm. East Africa to Samoa. An active schooling fish occasionally seen over silty reefs. *M. falciformis* Lacepède has a more ovoid body (the depth 1.5 to 2.0 in standard length); its pelvic fins are a little larger and have 5 soft rays.

# Sweepers (Pempherididae)

The sweepers are a small family of only two genera, *Pempheris* and the luminescent *Parapriacanthus*. They have moderately deep compressed bodies, with a strongly tapering tail and narrow caudal peduncle, very large eyes, no adipose eyelid, a highly oblique mouth with a projecting lower jaw, the maxilla broad posteriorly, exposed on the cheek and not reaching beyond pupil of eye; the teeth are small, incurved, in bands in jaws; there are small teeth in a V-shaped patch on vomer and on palatines. There is a single short unnotched dorsal fin of IV to VII spines and 7 to 12 soft rays, the fin entirely anterior to middle of body; the anal fin has a long base and consists of III spines and 17 to 45 soft rays; the caudal fin is emarginate or forked. The lateral line is arched anteriorly, the tubes short and broad; it reaches to the end of the middle caudal rays on *Pempheris* but not on *Parapriacanthus*, the Red Sea species of which is *P. guentheri* (Klunzinger) (see underwater photo). The sweepers are usually found in large aggregations in caves or deep crevices in reefs by day. Limited data indicate they are nocturnal and feed on zooplankton. The classification of the family is in need of revision.

## 131 Vanikoro Sweeper

*Pempheris vanicolensis*
Cuvier and Valenciennes, 1831

Dorsal rays VI,9; anal rays III,39 to 43; lateral-line scales 55 to 60; depth of body 2.2 to 2.4 in standard length; maxilla reaching to below centre of eye; coppery with a large blackish spot at apical end of dorsal fin. Attains 18 cm. East Africa to Samoa.

# Left-Eye Flounders (Bothidae)

The left-eye flounders are one of seven families of flatfishes that comprise the order Pleuronectiformes. These fishes are unique because they have both eyes on one side of the head. The most primitive family, the Psettodidae [*Psettodes erumei* (Bloch and Schneider) is a Red Sea representative, but it is not found in the vicinity of reefs], has spines in the dorsal and pelvic fins, but all the other families lack spines. The dorsal and anal fins are very long, the dorsal commencing on the head. The flatfishes all begin life as larvae with an eye on each side of the head, but as development nears completion, one eye gradually migrates over the top of the head to the other side, and soon thereafter the post-larvae settle out of the plankton to the bottom with the blind side down. The Bothidae have their eyes on the left side. The pelvic fin on the blind side is short-based, and its first ray is posterior to the first ray of the pelvic fin on the ocular side. The lateral line is usually highly arched at the front. Like most flatfishes, the bothids can change their colour to match the substratum on which they are residing. They can also partially bury themselves in the sediment and thus camouflage themselves further. All are carnivorous; they feed mainly on small fishes and crustaceans that fail to detect these hidden lie-and-wait predators. Nine bothid fishes are recorded from the Red Sea. The species which is most often encountered in shallow water is discussed below.

## 132 Panther Flounder

*Bothus pantherinus* (Rüppell), 1830

Dorsal rays 85 to 95; anal rays 64 to 72; pelvic rays 6; depth of body 1.75 to 1.9 in standard length; eye 3.5 to 5.0 in head; interorbital width nearly equal to eye diameter in male, narrower in female; mature males with a small tentacle on the posterior part of each eye, some short spines in front of the lower eye, and greatly prolonged upper pectoral rays; ocular side light brown with a large blackish spot on lateral line in middle of body and a fainter one on lateral line beneath pectoral fin, small pale spots of variable size (often with a dark spot in centre), and usually with dark-edged yellowish spots; blind side not pigmented. Reaches 23 cm. Indo-Pacific. Found on sandy or silty sand bottoms, sometimes near reefs.

# Soles (Soleidae)

The Soleidae is another flatfish family of the order Pleuronectiformes. It differs from the Bothidae in having no free preopercular margin, no ribs, the lower jaw not projecting, and the eyes on the right side (hence the illustrations of the Moses sole herein are of the right side in contrast to other fishes in this book for which, by ichthyological tradition, the left side is figured). The soles share all the above characteristics with the tongue-fishes (Cynoglossidae) except the side on which the eyes are found; in the Cynoglossidae they are on the left side. The cynoglossids differ further in having a pointed caudal fin which is continuous with the dorsal and anal fins; the caudal fin of soleids is rounded and distinct from the dorsal and anal fins.

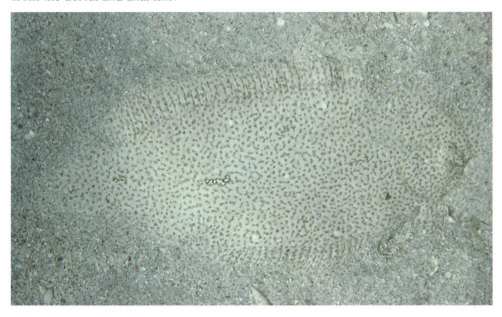

## 133 Moses Sole

*Pardachirus marmoratus* (Lacepède), 1802

Dorsal rays 63 to 72; anal rays 48 to 55; no pectoral fins; pelvic rays 5; lateral-line nearly straight, the pored scales 83 to 102; scales cycloid; depth of body 2.3 to 2.5 in standard length; a fringe of cirri from front of head to pelvic fins; light brown with numerous dark brown dots, dark-edged pale spots (mostly larger than eye), and still larger brown spots irregularly edged in dark brown (a few of these spots on lateral line containing bright orange-yellow flecks). Reaches 26 cm. East Africa to Sri Lanka. Secretes a highly toxic milky fluid from poison glands, one at the base of all dorsal and anal rays except the first and last. The skin is extremely bitter, which serves to repel predators. A shallow-water species, it is usually completely buried in sand

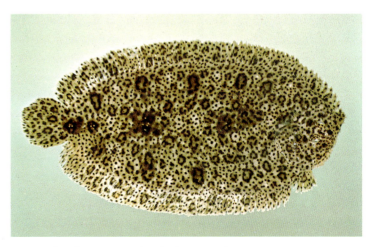

except for its eyes and tubular anterior nostril.

# Goatfishes (Mullidae)

The most distinctive feature of the goatfishes is a pair of long barbels on the chin. Only the beryciform family Polymixiidae has a similar pair of barbels, but these fishes are found in deep water, and none is recorded from the Red Sea. Other mullid characteristics are two well separated dorsal fins, the first of VI to VIII spines (the initial spine sometimes very small), and the second fin of 9 or 10 (usually 9) soft rays; the anal fin has one small spine and 6 or 7 soft rays; the caudal fin is forked. The body is elongate and slightly compressed. The scales are relatively large and finely ctenoid. The mouth is small, ventral in position, the upper jaw slightly projecting; the teeth are relatively small and conical. The five genera are differentiated mainly on dentition. Three genera occur in the Red Sea, *Upeneus, Parupeneus,* and *Mulloides* (*Mulloidichthys* of most authors): *Upeneus,* which has teeth on the vomer and palatines, is represented by four species in the sea, but they are found on open stretches of sand or mud (mainly in deep water) and not apt to be seen around coral reefs. *Parupeneus* and *Mulloides* lack teeth on the roof of the mouth. *Parupeneus* has one row of conical teeth in the jaws. The species of *Mulloides* have bands of villiform teeth. All of these fishes are carnivorous; they often feed on invertebrates, particularly worms and crustaceans, that live in the sediment. They use their barbels, which possess chemosensory organs, to probe into the bottom in search of food organisms; once food is found they root into the bottom with their snouts. When the barbels are not used in the search for food (or in the case of males when wiggling them during courtship), they are held back between the lower part of the gill covers.

## 134 Longbarbel Goatfish

*Parupeneus macronema* (Lacepède), 1801

Pectoral rays 15 or 16; lateral-line scales 27 or 28; gill rakers 35 to 39; depth of body 3.35 to 3.65 in standard length; snout 1.65 to 1.75 in head; barbels long, 1.0 to 1.2 in head; tan, sometimes lavender or magenta ventrally, with a blackish stripe from eye along upper side to front of caudal peduncle, followed by a blackish spot larger than eye more posteriorly on caudal peduncle, the spot and stripe separated by a whitish area that continues dorsal to posterior part of stripe; base of second dorsal fin broadly blackish, this pigment continuing to distal end of last ray. Largest specimen collected by author 29.5 cm, from

Bahrain. East Africa to Indonesia and the Philippines. Records from Tahiti and Hawaii are erroneous.

## 135 Forsskål's Goatfish

*Parupeneus forsskali* (Fourmanoir and Guézé), 1976

Pectoral rays 15 or 16; lateral-line scales 27 or 28; gill rakers 26 to 32; depth of body 3.6 to 3.7 in standard length; snout 1.6 to 1.7 in head; barbels not long, 1.55 to 1.7 in head; greenish grey on back, white below, becoming yellow dorsally on caudal peduncle and all of caudal fin; a black stripe from front of snout, through eye, ending beneath rear of second dorsal fin; a black spot about as large as eye on upper side of caudal peduncle; no black on second dorsal fin. Attains 28 cm. A common species, endemic to the Red Sea and the Gulf of Aden.

## 136 Yellowsaddle Goatfish

*Parupeneus cyclostomus* (Lacepède), 1801

Pectoral rays 16 or 17; lateral-line scales 27 to 29; gill rakers 29 to 32; depth of body 3.4 to 3.9 in standard length; snout 1.65 to 2.0 in head; barbels long, extending to or beyond posterior end of head; yellowish, the scales dorsally on body broadly blue; a yellow saddle dorsally on caudal peduncle; irregular blue lines extending anteriorly and posteriorly from eye; second dorsal and anal fins with alternating stripes of yellow and blue; another colour phase which does not attain large size is entirely yellow, the caudal peduncular saddle a brighter yellow. Reaches 50 cm. Indo-Pacific. Unusual for a goatfish in its heavy feeding on fishes (about 70 per cent of stomach contents); has been observed to use its barbels to frighten prey from small crevices in the reef. *Mullus chryserydros* Lacepède and *Upeneus luteus* Cuvier and Valenciennes are synonyms.

## 137 Rosy Goatfish

*Parupeneus rubescens* (Lacepède), 1801

Pectoral rays 15 to 17; lateral-line scales 27 or 28; gill rakers 29 to 31; depth of body 3.0 to 3.3 in standard length; snout 1.9 to 2.2 in head; barbels 1.3 to 1.5 in head; brown on back, usually shading to red on ventral half of body, with a whitish saddle-like spot anteriorly on caudal peduncle, followed by one of about equal size in black; a dark band bordered above and below with whitish extending posteriorly from eye to about middle of body; another pale streak across cheek to pectoral base. Attains about 30 cm. East Africa to the western Pacific. *Mullus dispilurus* Playfair and

Günther and *M. pleurotaenia* Playfair and Günther are synonyms.

## 138 Cinnabar Goatfish

*Parupeneus cinnabarinus* (Cuvier and Valenciennes), 1829

Pectoral rays usually 16; lateral-line scales 27 or 28; gill rakers 26 to 29; depth of body 3.15 to 3.4 in standard length; snout 1.8 to 2.0 in head; barbels 1.25 to 1.4 in head; yellowish on back, the scales with a pale blue spot, shading to silvery white on sides and ventrally; a small brown spot just below lateral line beneath sixth to seventh dorsal spines; snout mainly pink; irregular blue lines often present passing anteriorly and posteriorly from eye; deeper water individuals suffused with light red. Largest collected by author, 29 cm, from Lord Howe Island. East Africa to the Marshall Islands. Usually seen over silty sand bottoms or seagrass beds. *Upeneus pleurospilos* Bleeker is a synonym.

## 139 Yellowstripe Goatfish

*Mulloides flavolineatus* (Lacepède), 1801

Pectoral rays 16 or 17; lateral-line scales 33 to 38; gill rakers 25 to 30; depth of body 3.6 to 4.7 in standard length; snout 1.7 to 2.6 in head; barbels 1.4 to 1.8 in head; silvery white with a yellow stripe on body at level of eye; a blackish spot often present in yellow stripe beneath first dorsal fin; fins whitish. Attains 40 cm. Indo-Pacific. Appears to feed mainly at night on a wide variety of invertebrates, such as small crustaceans, polychaete worms and molluscs, and occasionally on small fishes. *Mulloides samoensis* Günther is a synonym.

## 140 Yellowfin Goatfish

*Mulloides vanicolensis* (Cuvier and Valenciennes), 1831

Pectoral rays 16 or 17; lateral-line scales 35 to 38; gill rakers 32 to 36; depth of body 3.3 to 3.9 in standard length; snout 2.1 to 2.7 in head; barbels 1.2 to 1.6 in head; whitish to pink with yellow stripe, edged in pale blue, passing from eye to upper caudal fin base; median and pelvic fins yellow. Reaches 38 cm. Indo-Pacific. Often seen in aggregations. Very closely related to *M. martinicus* (Cuvier and Valenciennes) of the Atlantic.

# Sand Tilefishes (Malacanthidae)

The sand tilefishes (or blanquillos) have elongate bodies (the depth 3.4 to 8.3 in standard length); a long unnotched dorsal fin of I to X spines and 13 to 60 soft rays; anal fin of I or II spines and 12 to 56 rays; opercle with a single spine; jaws with both canine and villiform teeth; no teeth on the roof of the mouth; and small scales, those on body ctenoid. They are closely related to, and sometimes classified in, the family Branchiostegidae. The latter are deeper bodied fishes with a fleshy median ridge in front of the dorsal fin. The malacanthids live on sandy or rubble bottoms; they seek refuge in burrows (or in the case of one species of *Hoplolatilus*, in a rubble mound of its own construction). They are often encountered in pairs. Three

species are recorded from the Red Sea, *H. oreni* (Clark and Ben-Tuvia) (known from only a single specimen from the southern Red Sea) and the following two species of *Malacanthus*.

## 141 Quakerfish

*Malacanthus brevirostris* Guichenot, 1848

Dorsal rays I to IV, 52 to 60; anal rays I,46 to 55; pectoral rays 15 to 17 (usually 16); lateral-line scales 146 to 181; body elongate, the depth 6.3 to 8.3 in standard length; snout short, 2.7 to 3.45 in head; grey on the back, white below, the grey extending onto sides as a series of slightly diagonal bars; caudal fin with two prominent black bands, the upper horizontal, the lower slightly diagonal. Reaches at least 32 cm. Indo-Pacific and the eastern Pacific. Usually seen in pairs which are believed to be male and female; they construct a burrow in sand, often under a rock; they may pile coral rubble near the entrance to the burrow. *M. hoedtii* Bleeker is a synonym.

## 142 Striped Blanquillo

*Malacanthus latovittatus* (Lacepède), 1801

Dorsal rays III or IV,43 to 47; anal rays I,37 to 40; pectoral rays 16 or 17 (usually 17); lateral-line scales 116 to 132; depth of body 5.0 to 6.7 in standard length; snout relatively long, 2.1 to 2.7 in head; blue on back, bluish white below, with a broad black stripe on side which extends into caudal fin where it forms a large irregular C-shaped mark in lower part of fin; head blue; juveniles white with a broader black stripe which continues across head to mouth. Largest recorded, 43.5 cm. Indo-Pacific. Also builds a burrow, but less inclined than the preceding to seek shelter in it; a wary fish.

# Sandperches (Mugiloididae)

The Mugiloididae (Parapercidae of some authors) consists of three genera, only one of which, *Parapercis*, occurs in the Indo-Pacific region. The fishes of this family have a moderately elongate, slightly compressed body, a terminal protractile mouth, a long dorsal fin with IV to VII spines and 20 to 24 soft rays, an anal fin of 15 to 21 soft rays, a truncate to emarginate caudal fin (some with only the upper lobe prolonged) with 15 or 17 principal rays, well-separated pelvic fins which lie below or in advance of pectoral fins, a complete lateral line, and small ctenoid scales. The species of *Parapercis* are carnivorous and benthic on sedimentary bottoms; they prop themselves above the substratum on their pelvic fins.

Three species are recorded from the Red Sea, but only the one discussed below is found in the reef environment.

## 143 Spotted Sandperch

*Parapercis hexophtalma* (Cuvier and Valenciennes), 1829

Dorsal rays V,21 or 22 (usually 21), the membrane connecting last spine to first ray at level of spine tip; anal rays 18 or 19 (usually 19); pectoral rays 17 or 18; eight canine teeth in outer row of lower jaw; palatine teeth absent; brown on back with small dark brown spots, white on sides and ventrally, with a brown line from axil of pectoral fin to lower caudal base separating a midlateral band of white from the brown of the back, this band divided into sections containing a brown spot or pair or trio of spots by vertical brown lines; a horizontal row of small yellow-edged black spots ventrally on body; median fins with small black spots, the caudal with a very large central black spot; head of females with small dark brown spots, of males with diagonal dark brown lines. Attains 23 cm. East Africa to the western Pacific. Lives on sand and rubble bottoms in and about shallow reefs. *P. polyophtalma* (Cuvier and Valenciennes) is a synonym based on the female phase.

# Remoras (Echeneididae)

The remoras are unique in possessing a sucking disc on the top of the head which consists of a series of transverse laminae. With this disc they attach themselves to sharks and rays, bony fishes, sea turtles and even aquatic mammals. Some are host specific, such as *Remorina albescens* (Temminck and Schlegel) which lives in the mouth and gill chamber of manta rays, whereas others may hitch a ride on a variety of aquatic animals. These fishes have no spinous dorsal fin, but a study of development indicates that the sucking disc is derived from this fin. Of the eight species of the family, three are known from the Red Sea. Only the one discussed below is apt to be seen in coral reefs.

## 144 Sharksucker

*Echeneis naucrates* Linnaeus, 1758

Dorsal rays 33 to 45; anal rays 31 to 41; pectoral rays 20 to 26; disc laminae 21 to 27; body elongate, the depth 8 to 13 in standard length (larger individuals, in general, deeper bodied); a midlateral pale-edged black stripe which is attenuated at either end. Attains 100 cm. Indo-Pacific and the Atlantic. Attaches to a wide variety of hosts; often encountered free living.

# Mojarras (Gerreidae)

These are silvery fishes with moderately deep compressed bodies and a distinctive concave ventral profile to the head; the mouth is very protractile, extending downward when protruded; maxilla broad posteriorly and exposed on the cheek; the teeth in the jaws are brush-like (small, slender, numerous, and close-set) and none exists on the roof of the mouth; there is a single dorsal fin, elevated anteriorly, of IX spines and 10 rays; anal fin with II or III spines and 6 to 8 rays; the dorsal and anal fins fold into a scaly sheath at their base; the caudal fin is deeply forked; the scales are large and finely ctenoid. These fishes are found on sand or mud bottoms, often in brackish environments. The species below, however, is often seen over sandy bottoms within or around reefs. *Gerres argyreus* (Bloch and Schneider) (see underwater photo) is occasionally observed near reefs too.

## 145 Slenderspine Mojarra

*Gerres oyena* (Forsskål), 1775

Dorsal spines slender, the second not greatly prolonged (about 1.6 in head); anal rays III,7; pectoral rays 15 or 16; lateral-line scales 39 to 42; depth of body 2.4 to 2.8 in standard length; silvery with a series of faint paired pink spots in rows on side of body; no black on dorsal fin. Largest collected by author, 32 cm. East Africa to the western Pacific. Feeds by taking in mouthfuls of sand, sorting the small animals therein, and expelling the sand from the gill openings.

# Mullets (Mugilidae)

The mullets are shallow-water, schooling fishes of moderate size which are silvery except for the back which is dark-coloured. The body is nearly cylindrical anteriorly, becoming more compressed toward the tail; the head is depressed, the snout generally short and broadly rounded; the mouth is small, usually shaped like a broad inverted V when viewed from the front; the teeth are minute or absent. Many species have an adipose eyelid partially covering the eye anteriorly and posteriorly. Mugilid fishes have two short-based, well-separated dorsal fins, the first of IV spines; the anterior three dorsal spines are close together at the base, while the fourth is more distant; the caudal fin varies from truncate to emarginate or forked; the pelvic fins, of I,5 rays, lie well behind the pectorals. The scales are moderately large and usually cycloid; there is no well defined lateral line. Most species have a thick-walled, gizzard-like stomach and a very long intestine. Typically they feed on fine algal and detrital material from

the surface of bottom sediments, and they may be seen expelling the inorganic sediment from their gill openings. Mullets are most often found in brackish water (some live as adults in purely freshwater), but the two species discussed below are marine inhabitants that occasionally range in small schools over shallow reefs.

## 146 Fringelip Mullet

*Crenimugil crenilabis* (Forsskål), 1775

Second dorsal rays I,8; anal rays III,9; pectoral rays 17 or 18; scale rows from upper end of gill opening to caudal base 37 to 40; depth of body 3.5 to 3.9 in standard length; preorbital bone not notched; edge of lower lip with a forward-directed fringe of dorsoventrally flattened, fleshy papillae; caudal fin moderately forked; silvery, the back blackish; a small black spot at upper base of pectoral fin; edges of caudal fin dusky. Reported to 50 cm. Indo-Pacific. Often occurs in small schools as seen in the above underwater photo.

## 147 Thicklip Mullet

*Oedalechilus labiosus* (Cuvier and Valenciennes), 1836

Second dorsal rays I,7 or 8; anal rays III,9; pectoral rays 17; scale rows from upper end of gill opening to caudal base 34 to 36; depth of body about 3.3 in standard length; preorbital bone with a deep V-shaped notch ending beneath posterior nostril; mouth horizontal, the lower lip with a median V-shaped notch, the edge smooth; caudal fin emarginate; silvery, the back dark greenish; a small black spot at upper base of pectoral fin; median fins yellowish. To 23 cm. East Africa to the Marshall Islands.

# Barracudas (Sphyraenidae)

The barracudas are very elongate fishes whose bodies are cylindrical anteriorly; they have pointed heads, a large mouth with projecting lower jaw, and a formidable array of long sharp-edged teeth on the jaws and palatines; developed gill rakers (higher than base) are few or absent. Like the mullets to which they are related, the barracudas have two widely separated, short-based dorsal fins; the first has V dorsal spines and the second I,9 rays; the caudal fin is forked; the pelvic fins are clearly posterior to the base of the pectorals. The scales are small and cycloid, and there is a distinct lateral line. Barracudas are carnivorous; they may be either diurnal or nocturnal. Some species occur primarily in schools, others are solitary. Although barracudas have attacked man, this danger has been exaggerated. In clear water without anything that might serve as an attractant, such as a wounded fish struggling on a spear or a metal object that flashes in the sun, there should be no reason to fear a barracuda.

## 148 Great Barracuda

*Sphyraena barracuda* (Walbaum), 1792

Anal rays II,7 or 8; lateral-line scales 69 to 84; depth of body 5.5 to 8.2 in standard length; dark green on back, silvery on sides, with faint dark oblique bars on upper side and usually with scattered blackish blotches on lower side; second dorsal, anal, and caudal fins blackish, the distal ends whitish. Although reported to 300 cm, no length over 200 cm has been authenticated. Indo-Pacific and the Atlantic. Juveniles usually in estuaries or mangrove areas. Diurnal and usually solitary; feeds mainly on fishes. Attacks on humans have nearly all occurred in murky water

where a limb might be mistaken for prey or by provocation, as by spearing. *S. picuda* Bloch and Schneider, 1801 is a synonym.

## 149 Pickhandle Barracuda

*Sphyraena jello* Cuvier and Valenciennes, 1829

Anal rays II,8; lateral-line scales 123 to 133; depth of body 7.9 to 8.9 in standard length; tip of lower jaw blunt; maxilla usually reaching to or slightly posterior to a vertical at front edge of eye; dusky green dorsally, silvery on sides and ventrally, with about 20 wavy dark bars that extend a short distance below lateral line; caudal fin yellowish. Reaches at least 150 cm. East Africa to the western Pacific. Diurnal; usually seen in schools.

## 150 Chevron Barracuda

*Sphyraena putnamiae* Jordan and Seale, 1905

Anal rays II,8; lateral-line scales 129 to 131; depth of body 7.3 to 8.5 in standard length; lower jaw with a fleshy pointed tip; maxilla approaching but not reaching a vertical at front edge of eye; dark green on back, silvery on sides and below, with about 20 angled dark bars that reach about two-thirds distance to ventral edge of body; caudal fin dusky, the margins black. Attains about 90 cm. East Africa to the western Pacific. Primarily nocturnal; a schooling species. Described as *S. bleekeri* in 1959 by Williams; however, this name is pre-occupied, so a new name is needed. Most specimens have been confused in the past with *S. jello.*

## 151 Blackfin Barracuda

*Sphyraena qenie* Klunzinger, 1870

Anal rays II,8; lateral-line scales 113 to 123; depth of body 6.2 to 7.9 in standard length; tip of lower jaw blunt; maxilla reaching to or beyond a vertical at front edge of eye; dark blue on back, silvery on sides and below, with about 20 dark bars, broader than interspaces, which usually reach two-thirds or more of distance to ventral edge of body (bars angled slightly anteriorly, the angle below lateral line); median fins blackish except last one or two rays of anal which are whitish; upper two-thirds of inside of pectoral fins blackish. Attains at least 160 cm. Indo-Pacific. Appears to be mainly nocturnal; may be solitary or occur in schools.

## 152 Yellowtail Barracuda

*Sphyraena flavicauda* Rüppell, 1838

Anal rays I,9 or 10; lateral-line scales 72 to 82; developed gill rakers (distinctly higher than base) 2 (none in above species of *Sphyraena*); depth of body 6.8 to 8.3 in standard length; corner of preopercle with a pronounced membranous flap (not present on above species); opercle with a single membranous spine (above species with two spines, though the upper one may be poorly developed); tip of lower jaw blunt; maxilla not approaching a vertical at front edge of eye; origin of first dorsal fin behind tip of pectoral fin; height of first dorsal fin greater than postorbital length of head; iridescent yellow-green on back, silvery on sides and ventrally, the lateral line dark yellowish brown; two faint dark stripes in life, the lowermost passing through base of pectoral fin; fins yellowish, particularly the caudal. Attains about 45 cm. East Africa to the western Pacific. The closely related *S. obtusata* Cuvier and Valenciennes differs in that the origin of the first dorsal fin lies in front of the tip of the pectoral fin; also the height of this fin is equal to or greater than the postorbital length of the head.

# Damselfishes (Pomacentridae)

The Pomacentridae is a large family of small, often colourful, shallow-water fishes, most of which are associated with coral reefs or rocky substrata. They have rather deep compressed bodies, small mouths with teeth which are conical or incisiform, and they lack teeth on the roof of the mouth. Only a single nostril is present on each side of snout, or the posterior nostril is very small. There is a single continuous dorsal fin of VIII to XV spines and 10 to 21 soft rays, the base of the spinous portion longer than the soft; the anal fin has II spines and 10 to 16 rays; the caudal fin varies from slightly emarginate to forked or lunate. The scales are moderately large and ctenoid; the head is largely scaled, as are the basal parts of median fins; the lateral line is interrupted, the anterior part ending beneath the dorsal fin. Most damselfishes are territorial and very pugnacious. They lay elliptical demersal eggs which are guarded by the male parent. The species of *Dascyllus*, *Chromis*, *Neopomacentrus*, *Pristotis*, and *Teixeirichthys* are mainly zooplankton feeders and usually occur in aggregations, while the species of other Red Sea genera are omnivorous; some such as *Amphiprion* tend to feed more on animal material than algae, whereas others are principally herbivorous. *Teixeirichthys jordani* (Rutter) (see underwater photo of the blue fish) is usually found in small aggregations over seagrass or open sandy

areas. The young of many *Pomacentrus* and *Chrysiptera* are very brightly coloured, particularly in shades of blue, yellow and orange (see underwater photo,.*above*, of juvenile *Pomacentrus trilineatus*); the adults tend to be a sombre dark brown.

## 153 Twobar Anemonefish

*Amphiprion bicinctus* Rüppell, 1830

Dorsal rays X,15 to 17; anal fin rays II,13 or 14; poectoral fin rays 17 to 21 (usually 19); tubed lateral-line scales 37 to 40; suborbital bones scaleless, their lower edges strongly serrate; preopercular margin serrate; teeth conical, in one row; caudal fin slightly emarginate; orange, sometimes brown anterodorsally, with two dark-edged bluish white bars, the first from nape across head behind eye and the second below front of soft portion of dorsal fin. Attains about 12 cm. Red Sea and the Gulf of Aden. Lives in close association with stoichactid sea anemones; since it is not stung by the anemone, it hides among the tentacles when frightened.

## 154 Domino

*Dascyllus trimaculatus* (Rüppell), 1829

Dorsal rays XII,14 to 16 (usually 15); anal rays II,14 (rarely 15); pectoral rays 19 to 21; tubed lateral-line scales 18 or 19; suborbital bones scaled, their lower margins finely serrate; preopercular margin finely serrate; teeth conical; black, the centres of the scales lighter, with a whitish spot above lateral-line scales 10 to 13; juveniles with a larger white spot and another on forehead. Reaches 14 cm. Indo-Pacific. Feeds mainly on zooplankton. The young are associated with anemones or branching corals.

## 155 Blackbordered Dascyllus

*Dascyllus marginatus* (Rüppell), 1829

Dorsal rays XII,14 or 15; anal rays II,13 or 14 (usually 13); pectoral rays 17 to 19; tubed lateral-line scales 15 to 19 (usually 17 or 18); suborbital bones scaled and finely serrate; preopercular margin finely serrate; teeth conical; head and chest brown; body pale yellowish (sometimes blackish anteriorly); with a vertical light blue line; spinous portion of dorsal fin with a broad black margin which narrows as it continues onto anterior soft portion; anal fin black anteriorly; caudal fin with light grey rays, the membranes and upper and lower borders light blue; pelvic fins largely black; pectoral fins with a large black spot at base. Attains about 6 cm. Red Sea to the Gulf of Oman.

## 156 Banded Dascyllus

*Dascyllus aruanus* (Linnaeus), 1758

Dorsal rays XII,11 to 13 (usually 12); anal rays II,11 to 13 (usually 12); pectoral rays 17 to 19; tubed lateral-line scales 15 to 19 (usually 17 or 18); suborbital bones scaled and finely serrate; preopercular margin finely serrate; teeth conical; white with three broad black bands, the first diagonal from nape and upper head through eye to chin. Attains 7.5 cm. Indo-Pacific. An abundant species which lives in small colonies in branching corals, generally on isolated coral heads in shallow protected waters. Feeds principally on zooplankton in the water column above the coral, but takes shelter among the branches with the approach of danger.

## 157 Duskytail Chromis

*Chromis pelloura* Randall and Allen, 1982

Dorsal rays XIV,13 or 14; anal rays II,12 or 13; pectoral rays 18 or 19; tubed lateral-line scales 15 to 17; upper and lower edges of caudal fin base with two small spines; suborbital bones scaled, their lower edges smooth; preopercular margin smooth; teeth conical; bluish white, the top of the head blackish; a broad black bar across base of caudal fin, the posterior edge of which parallels hind edge of the forked caudal fin; rest of fin lightly dusky; axil and upper edge of base of pectoral fins black. Largest specimen 13 cm. Known only from the Gulf of Aqaba at depths greater than 30 m. Closely related to *C. axillaris* (Bennett) of the Indian Ocean, differing in its smaller eye (2.7 to 2.9 in head).

## 158 Yellow-Edge Chromis

*Chromis pembae* Smith, 1960

Dorsal rays XIII,11 or 12 (usually 12); anal rays II,11; pectoral rays 17 to 19; upper and lower edges of caudal fin base with three small spines; tubed lateral-line scales 15 or 16; suborbital bones scaled, their lower edges smooth; margin of preopercle smooth; teeth conical; caudal fin deeply forked; brown, the caudal fin and edge of spinous portion of dorsal fin yellow. Reaches 13 cm. Red Sea south at least to Tanzania. Common on steep rocky substrata at depths of 25 to 50 m.

### 159 Weber's Chromis

*Chromis weberi* Fowler and Bean, 1928

Dorsal rays XIII,10 or 11 (usually 11); anal rays II,10 or 11 (usually 11); pectoral rays 17 to 20 (usually 18 or 19); upper and lower edges of caudal fin base with three small spines; tubed lateral-line scales 17 to 19; suborbital bones scaled, their lower margins smooth (though largely hidden by scales); pre-opercular margin smooth; teeth conical; caudal fin deeply forked; brown, the edges of the scales darker, the centres sometimes bluish or olive; preopercular edge and upper edge of opercular membrane blackish; a broad blackish band at upper and lower margins of caudal fin, the lobe tips black. Attains 13.5 cm. Indo-Pacific.

## 160 Ternate Chromis

*Chromis ternatensis* (Bleeker), 1856

Dorsal rays XII,10 to 12; anal rays II,11 or 12 (usually 11); pectoral rays 17 to 19; upper and lower edges of caudal fin base with three small spines; tubed lateral-line scales 14 to 17 (usually 15 or 16); suborbital bones scaled, their lower margins smooth (though hidden by scales); margin of preopercle smooth; teeth conical; caudal fin deeply forked; olivaceous, shading to whitish ventrally, the centres of the scales often iridescent blue or green; a suffusion of yellow over upper head and nape in life; upper and lower edges of caudal fin broadly black; base of pectoral fins yellow. Reaches 11 cm. East Africa to Micronesia. A shallow-water species closely associated with branching corals. Feeds on zooplankton; descends to the shelter of the coral when danger approaches.

## 161 Half-and-Half Chromis

*Chromis dimidiata* (Klunzinger), 1871

Dorsal rays XII,11 or 12 (usually 12); anal rays II,12; pectoral rays 15 to 17; upper and lower edges of caudal fin base with two small spines; tubed lateral-line scales 14 to 16; suborbital bones scaled, their lower edges smooth; preopercular margin smooth; teeth conical; caudal fin forked, the lobe tips with two filamentous rays; head and anterior half of body dark brown, becoming abruptly white posteriorly; a black spot at base of pectoral fins. Reaches 9 cm. Indian Ocean. A common shallow-water species.

## 162 Triplespot Chromis

*Chromis trialpha* Allen and Randall, 1980

Dorsal rays XII,10 or 11; anal rays II,10 or 11; pectoral rays 16 to 18; upper and lower edges of caudal fin base with two small spines; tubed lateral-line scales 15 or 16; suborbital bones scaled, their lower edges smooth; preopercular margin smooth; teeth conical; caudal fin forked, the lobe tips filamentous; brown on back shading to light blue ventrally, the edges of the scales dark brown; dorsal and anal fins very dark brown except posteriorly where clear with flecks of brown; a white spot at rear base of dorsal and anal fins and another at midbase of caudal fin; upper and lower edges of caudal fin broadly black. To 6 cm. Red Sea. Closely related to *C. elerae* Fowler and Bean from outside the

Red Sea which lacks the black bands and the white basal spot in the caudal fin.

## 163 Bluegreen Chromis

*Chromis caerulea* (Cuvier and Valenciennes), 1830

Dorsal rays XII,9 or 10 (usually 10); anal rays II,10 or 11 (usually 10); pectoral rays 17 to 19; upper and lower edges of caudal fin base with three small spines; tubed lateral-line scales 15 or 16; suborbital bones scaled, their lower margins smooth (but scaled over); preopercular margin smooth; teeth conical; caudal fin forked; blue-green, shading to whitish ventrally; a faint dusky spot at upper base of pectoral fin; a blue line from front of snout to eye. Males in courtship exhibit a black (except posteriorly where yellow) dorsal fin. Reaches 9.5 cm. Indo-Pacific. Abundant on protected shallow reefs, taking refuge in branching corals (often the genus *Acropora*).

## 164 Bluedotted Damselfish

*Pristotis cyanostigma* Rüppell, 1838

Dorsal rays XIII,11 or 12 (usually 12); anal rays II,12 or 13 (usually 13); pectoral rays 17 or 18; tubed lateral-line scales 15 to 17; preorbital bone notched; suborbital bones not scaled, the lower edges smooth to weakly serrate; preopercular margin finely serrate; teeth in one row, incisiform, the ends bluntly rounded except larger anterior teeth which may be somewhat pointed; caudal fin forked; blue-green, shading to whitish ventrally, with a blue spot on each scale; a wash of yellow on head and back. Attains 10 cm. Red Sea and the Gulf of Aden, in protected waters. Feeds on zooplankton and retreats to coral for shelter.

## 165 Sulphur Damselfish

*Pomacentrus sulfureus* Klunzinger, 1871

Dorsal rays XIII or XIV,13 to 15; anal rays II,14 or 15; pectoral rays 17 to 19; tubed lateral-line scales 15 to 18 (usually 17); suborbital bones not scaled, the first suborbital with a flat, posteriorly directed spine, the second suborbital with a few serrae; margin of preopercle serrate; teeth incisiform, close-set, in two rows (the second row buttressing the first); caudal fin slightly forked; yellow with a large black spot at base and axil of pectoral fins; juveniles with a black spot near base of soft portion of dorsal fin. Reaches 10 cm. Western Indian Ocean.

## 166 Sombre Damselfish

*Pomacentrus aquilus* Allen and Randall, 1980

Dorsal rays XIV,13 to 15; anal rays II,14 or 15; pectoral rays 17 to 19; tubed lateral-line scales 17 to 19; suborbital bones with a few or no scales, the first with a flat posteriorly directed spine; remaining suborbitals serrate; margin of preopercle serrate; teeth incisiform with rounded tips, close-set, in two rows, the second row smaller, reinforcing the first; caudal fin forked; mature adults dark brown with a black spot at upper base of pectoral fin; juveniles yellow, becoming brown on nape and dorsally on head; four bright blue stripes on head; a small blue spot on scales on side of body; a blue-edged black spot larger than eye at juncture of spinous and soft portions of dorsal fin. Largest specimen, 10.7 cm. Western Indian Ocean.

## 167 Reticulated Damselfish

*Pomacentrus trichourus* Playfair and Günther, 1867

Dorsal rays XIV,14 to 16; anal rays II,15 to 17; pectoral rays 16 or 17 (usually 17); tubed lateral-line scales 17 or 18; preorbital and suborbital bones without scales and serrate, the first with a large posteriorly directed spine; preopercular margin serrate; teeth incisiform, close-set, in two rows, the inner row buttressing the outer; caudal fin slightly forked; adults dark brown, the scale centres paler, resulting in an overall reticulated effect; posterior part of caudal peduncle darker than rest of body (or there may be a large black spot); a small black spot on opercle near upper end of gill opening; a black spot covering base of pectoral fin; base of caudal fin abruptly white, shading to transparent distally; margin of dorsal fin black (except posteriorly); juveniles

are blue on the nape and dorsally on the head. Reaches 11 cm. Red Sea to Mozambique.

## 168 Whitetail Damselfish

*Pomacentrus albicaudatus* Baschieri-Salvadori, 1957

Dorsal rays XIII,14 or 15; anal rays II,15; pectoral rays 15 or 16 (usually 15); tubed lateral-line scales 15 or 16; suborbital bones without scales, their lower edges smooth or with a few serrae; preopercular margin serrate; teeth incisiform, close-set, in two rows, the inner row buttressing the outer; caudal fin slightly forked; head and chest brown; body dark brown, the centres of the scales yellowish on sides, the abdomen largely yellow-orange; one to three blue dots on scales of head and body except posteriorly; caudal fin abruptly white. Attains 6.5 cm. Central and southern Red Sea.

## 169 Threeline Damselfish

*Pomacentrus trilineatus* Cuvier and Valenciennes, 1830

Dorsal rays XIII,14 or 15 (usually 15); anal rays II,14 to 16; pectoral rays 17 or 18 (usually 17); tubed lateral-line scales 16 to 19 (usually 18); suborbital bones scaleless and serrate; margin of preopercle serrate; teeth incisiform, close-set, in two rows, the inner row reinforcing the outer; caudal fin forked; yellowish brown, the edges of the scales darker brown, shading to dull yellow on caudal peduncle, chest, and lower abdomen; one to three blue dots on scales of body between pectoral tips and caudal peduncle; a blue-edged black spot dorsally on caudal peduncle; diagonal blue lines on side of snout and dorsally on head (better developed in juveniles; may be broken lines in adults); juveniles yellow with iridescent blue lines and small spots and a large blue-edged black

spot at juncture of spinous and soft portions of dorsal fin. Attains 11 cm. Western Indian Ocean. Has been misidentified as *P. tripunctatus* Cuvier and Valenciennes, a western Pacific species.

## 170 Slender Damselfish

*Pomacentrus leptus* Allen and Randall, 1980

Dorsal rays XIII,13 or 14; anal rays II,13 or 14; pectoral rays 16 or 17; tubed lateral-line scales 15 to 17; suborbital bones scaleless, their lower edges smooth or with a few serrae; margin of preopercle finely serrate; teeth incisiform, close-set, in two rows, the inner row buttressing the outer; body relatively elongate, the depth 2.3 to 2.7 in standard length (1.9 to 2.1 for other Red Sea *Pomacentrus*); caudal fin slightly forked; brown, suffused with orange-yellow (and in life sometimes with blue-violet); scales on side of body with two or three blue dots (sometimes faded); a small deep blue to black spot on opercle near upper end of gill opening; a small black spot at

upper base of pectoral fin; caudal fin abruptly white to pale yellowish; distal third of posterior soft portion of dorsal fin yellow. Largest specimen, 6.8 cm. Red Sea.

103

## 171 Black Damselfish

*Stegastes nigricans* (Lacepède), 1802

Dorsal rays XII,15 or 16; anal rays II,12 or 13; pectoral rays 18 to 20; tubed lateral-line scales 18 or 19; suborbital bones scaled, their lower edges serrate; preopercular margin serrate; teeth incisiform, close-set, in a single row; caudal fin forked with rounded lobes; dark brown, almost black; suborbital may be blue, and centres of some scales of operculum may be blue; a vertical blue line sometimes present on scales of middle of body; a black spot about size of pupil at upper base of pectoral fin; males guarding eggs may exhibit a very broad whitish bar in middle of body and a pale blue stripe from mouth to above pectoral base; juveniles are whitish, shading to yellow posteriorly, the dorsal part of head and anterior body and front of dorsal fin blackish; fins otherwise yellow to yellowish; a small black spot at rear base of dorsal fin. Attains 13 cm. Indo-Pacific. A very common shallow-water species usually found in thickets of staghorn coral (*Acropora*); feeds mainly on the algae growing on the dead basal branches of the coral. Very aggressive; will bite intruders, including man. *S. lividus* (Bloch and Schneider) is reported from the Red Sea but evidently rare (see underwater photo at the top of page 97, taken by the author off Djibouti); it has a deep preorbital, a large ocellated black spot at rear base of dorsal fin, and 15 to 19 lower-limb gill rakers (*S. nigricans* with 12 to 14).

## 172 Regal Damselfish

*Neopomacentrus cyanomos* (Bleeker), 1856

Dorsal rays XIII,11; anal rays II,10 or 11; pectoral rays 17 or 18; tubed lateral-line scales 17 to 19; suborbital bones scaled, their lower margin hidden by scales; lower part of posterior margin of preopercle weakly serrate; teeth incisiform, close-set, in two rows anteriorly, those of second row serving as buttresses, each behind a space between front teeth; caudal fin lunate; middle soft dorsal and anal rays prolonged; dark brown, the scales of nape and ventrally on body with iridescent blue centres; a black spot about as large as eye at upper end of gill opening; posterior part of median fins abruptly pale yellowish to yellow. Attains 9.5 cm. East Africa to the western Pacific.

Generally found in vicinity of hard substrata in silty environments such as dead reefs or harbours. *Chromis*-like in habits.

# 173 Miry's Damselfish

*Neopomacentrus miryae* Dor and Allen, 1977

Dorsal rays XIII,11 to 13; anal rays II,11; pectoral rays 18 or 19; tubed lateral-line scales 17 or 18; suborbital bones scaled, their lower margins covered by scales; preopercular margin smooth; teeth incisiform, close-set, in one row; caudal fin deeply forked; head and body olive with a dusky patch on each scale; upper half of caudal peduncle and outer edges of caudal fin yellow-orange; a prominent white spot slightly smaller than pupil on caudal peduncle just behind last dorsal ray; a small black spot on upper pectoral base. Reaches 11 cm. Northern and central Red Sea, more common in the north. Forms aggregations which feed on zooplankton well above the coral reefs.

# 174 Yellowtail Damselfish

*Neopomacentrus xanthurus* Allen and Randall, 1980

Dorsal rays XIII,10 to 12; anal rays II,10 or 11; pectoral rays 16 or 17; tubed lateral-line scales 15 to 17; suborbital bones with scales, their lower margins smooth; preopercular margin smooth; teeth incisiform, close-set, in two rows, the second buttressing the first; caudal fin lunate; middle soft dorsal and anal rays prolonged; bluish grey, shading to yellow posteriorly on caudal peduncle and on caudal fin; posterior half of soft portion of dorsal fin abruptly yellow; a black spot at upper base of pectoral fins. Largest specimen, 8 cm. Red Sea and the Gulf of Aden.

# 175 Jewel Damselfish

*Plectroglyphidodon lacrymatus* (Quoy and Gaimard), 1825

Dorsal rays XII,16 to 18; anal rays II,13 or 14; pectoral rays 18 to 20; tubed lateral-line scales 18 or 19; suborbital bones scaled, their lower margins smooth; preopercular margin smooth; teeth incisiform, elongate, close-set, and in one row; caudal fin forked; brown, shading to yellowish posteriorly on caudal peduncle and fin, with small bright blue spots on head and body. Reaches 11 cm. Indo-Pacific. Feeds mainly on benthic algae, occasionally on small invertebrate animals.

## 176 Whitebar Damselfish

*Plectroglyphidodon leucozona* (Bleeker), 1859

Dorsal rays XII,15 or 16 (usually 15); anal rays II,12 or 13 (usually 12); pectoral rays 19 or 20; tubed lateral-line scales 19 or 20; suborbital bones scaled, their margins smooth; preopercular margin smooth; teeth incisiform, slender, close-set, and in one row; caudal fin forked; brown, the edges of scales darker than centres, with a large tan area on anterior two-thirds of body below lateral line or with a whitish bar about as broad as eye centred on base of eighth dorsal spine; some blue marks on scales behind and beneath eye; a black spot on upper base of pectoral fin; median fins yellow posteriorly; juveniles with a large yellow-edged black spot basally in rear spinous portion of dorsal fin and a small black spot dorsally on caudal peduncle. Reaches 12 cm. Indo-Pacific; Red Sea fish are differentiated from the species elsewhere by having yellow posteriorly on the median fins and more upper-limb gill rakers; the Red Sea form is *P. l. cingulus* Klunzinger. Prefers reef flats and inshore rocky substrata exposed to wave action; feeds predominantly on benthic algae.

## 177 Royal Damselfish

*Paraglyphidodon melas* (Cuvier and Valenciennes), 1832

Dorsal rays XIII,14 or 15 (usually 14); anal rays II,13 to 15; pectoral rays 17 to 19; tubed lateral-line scales 16 to 18; suborbital bones scaled, their lower edges smooth; margin of preopercle smooth; teeth slender, incisiform, with rounded tips, close-set, and in two rows, the second buttressing the first; caudal fin slightly forked; adults bluish black; juveniles greyish white, the dorsal part of head and body and anterior dorsal fin above a demarcation from front of snout through middle of eye to tip of longest dorsal ray yellow; upper and lower edges of caudal fin yellow; a broad black band followed by blue anteriorly in soft portion of anal and pelvic fins. Attains 18 cm. East Africa to the western Pacific. The author has observed this species feeding on soft coral. *Glyphisodon melanopus* Bleeker is a synonym based on the juvenile stage.

## 178 Footballer

*Chrysiptera annulata* (Peters), 1855

Dorsal rays XIII,12 or 13; anal rays II,12 or 13; pectoral rays 17 or 18 (usually 17); tubed lateral-line scales 17 or 18 (usually 17); suborbital bones without scales, their lower edges smooth; preopercular margin irregularly and finely serrate; teeth incisiform with rounded tips, close-set, and in two rows, the inner row serving as a buttress for the outer; caudal fin slightly forked with rounded lobes; yellowish white with five black bars, the first on head through eye and the last at caudal fin base; pelvic fins black. Reaches 9 cm. Western Indian Ocean. A shallow-water fish of sheltered waters, often seen in seagrass or man- grove areas or isolated coral heads or rocks within these habitats.

## 179 Onespot Damselfish

*Chrysiptera unimaculata* (Cuvier and Valenciennes), 1830

Dorsal rays XIII,13 or 14 (usually 13); anal rays II,12 or 13 (usually 12); pectoral rays 18 or 19 (usually 18); tubed lateral-line scales 17 to 19; suborbital bones scaleless, their lower edges smooth; margin of preopercle smooth; teeth incisiform with rounded tips, close-set, and in two rows, the second buttres-sing the first; caudal fin slightly forked with rounded lobes; yellowish brown, shading to yellowish ventrally, with a blue-edged black spot larger than pupil at rear base of dorsal fin; a blue line from eye to mouth; juveniles are yellow with a blue band from snout through upper edge of eye along base of dorsal fin to join a blue-edged black spot larger than eye basally on last three or four dorsal spines and first soft ray; blue dots on scales of head and body. Reaches 8 cm. East Africa to the western Pacific. Occurs on shallow reef flats; feeds mainly on benthic algae.

## 180 Whitebelly Damselfish

*Amblyglyphidodon leucogaster* (Bleeker), 1847

Dorsal rays XIII,12 or 13; anal rays II,12 to 14; pectoral rays 16 to 18; tubed lateral-line scales 14 to 17; suborbital bones scaled, their lower edges smooth; preopercular margin smooth; teeth incisiform, in one row; body deep, the depth 1.6 to 1.7 in standard length; caudal fin moderately forked; pelvic fins long, the filamentous tips reaching posterior to spinous portion of anal fin; light blue-green dorsally, the scale edges slightly dusky, shading to white ventrally; edges of preopercle and subopercle and opercular membrane blackish; a small black spot at upper pectoral base; upper and lower edges of caudal fin black. Reaches 14 cm. East Africa to Micronesia and Samoa. More study is needed to ascertain if alleged colour forms are all this species.

## 181 Yellowflank Damselfish

*Amblyglyphidodon flavilatus* Allen and Randall, 1980

Dorsal rays XIII,11 to 13; anal rays II,11 to 14; pectoral rays 15 or 16 (rarely 16); tubed lateral-line scales 15 to 17; suborbital bones with scales, their lower edges smooth; preopercular margin smooth; teeth incisiform, the edges bilobed, in two rows at front of jaws, the teeth of second row small; body deep, the depth 1.6 to 1.7 in standard length; caudal fin moderately forked; pelvic fins long, the tips filamentous, reaching well beyond origin of anal fin; greyish green dorsally, shading to whitish ventrally and to yellow on posterior half of body (the yellow most evident dorsally); all fins pale; a small black spot at upper base of pectoral fins. Largest specimen, 9.5 cm. Red Sea and the Gulf of Aden.

## 182 Sergeant Major

*Abudefduf saxatilis* (Linnaeus), 1758

Dorsal rays XIII,12 to 14; anal rays II,11 to 13; pectoral rays 17 to 20 (usually 18 or 19); tubed lateral-line scales 20 to 22; suborbital bones scaled, their margins and that of preopercle smooth; teeth incisiform, close-set, the tips flat to slightly notched; caudal fin forked; blue-green dorsally, shading to white ventrally, with five broad black bars (narrower than pale interspaces), the first from origin of dorsal fin to upper pectoral base, and the last on caudal peduncle. Reaches 18 cm. Circumtropical. Slight differences from the Atlantic to the Indo-Pacific have led some authors to regard the Indo-Pacific form as a distinct species, *A. vaigiensis* (Quoy and Gaimard); however, this might best

serve as a subspecific name. This shallow-water species is usually found in colonies. It appears to feed mainly on zooplankton, but will ingest a great variety of benthic organisms.

## 183 Scissortail Sergeant

*Abudefduf sexfasciatus* (Lacepède), 1801

Dorsal rays XIII,12 to 14; anal rays II,12 or 13; pectoral rays 18 to 20; tubed lateral-line scales 20 to 22; suborbital bones scaled, their lower edges smooth; preopercular margin smooth; teeth incisiform with truncate or slightly notched tips, close-set, and in one row; caudal fin forked; blue-green dorsally, shading to white ventrally, with five broad black bars (broader dorsally than pale interspaces), the first from nape to above pectoral base and the last at caudal fin base; last dark bar joined in its upper part to a submarginal black band in upper lobe of caudal fin; a separate black submarginal band in lower lobe

of fin. Reaches 19.5 cm. Indo-Pacific. *Glyphisodon coelestinus* Cuvier and Valenciennes is a synonym.

## 184 Blackspot Sergeant

*Abudefduf sordidus* (Forsskål), 1775

Dorsal rays XIII,15 or 16 (usually 15); anal rays II,14 or 15; pectoral rays 18 to 20; tubed lateral-line scales 20 to 23; posterior suborbital bones scaled, their edges and that of preopercle smooth; teeth incisiform with tips truncate to slightly notched, close-set, and in one row; caudal fin forked; body whitish to light yellowish grey with six dark brown bars broader than pale interspaces; a black spot about as large as eye on caudal peduncle at upper end of sixth dark bar (hence just behind rear base of dorsal fin); small blackish spots on scales above and posterior to eye; a small black spot at upper base of pectoral fin. Reaches 22 cm. Indo-Pacific. Generally found along exposed rocky shores; the diet consists primarily of benthic algae.

# Wrasses (Labridae)

The wrasses are the most diverse family of Indo-Pacific fishes in terms of form and size. They vary in size from the tiny *Minilabrus striatus* Randall and Dor (see underwater photos) to the enormous humphead wrasse, *Cheilinus undulatus* Rüppell. They are also one of the most speciose families of fishes, second in the number of species within the Indo-Pacific only to the gobies (Gobiidae). They usually have a terminal mouth which varies from small to moderate in size; the maxilla is not exposed on the cheek; the teeth at the front of the jaws are usually well developed canines that are often projecting; there are no teeth on the roof of the mouth, but the pharyngeal dentition is strong, consisting of conical, nodular or molariform teeth on the paired upper pharyngeal plates and the single T- to Y-shaped lower pharyngeal bone; the lips are generally thick. There is a single continuous dorsal fin, not obviously notched between spinous and soft portions, the tropical species with from VIII to XIV spines which vary from flexible to sharp-tipped; the anal fin has III spines (rarely II). The scales are cycloid; the lateral line may be continuous or interrupted; when continuous, it usually has a part below the soft portion of the dorsal fin which angles sharply downward to a straight peduncular part. Most wrasses are brightly coloured, often with complex patterns. Juveniles are frequently of different colour than adults, and the adults are usually sexually dichromatic. Some males and females are so different in colour that they have been described as different species. Sex reversal has been demonstrated for a number of labrids; these fishes commence their adult life as females and later may alter their sex to male. Usually this terminal male pattern is gaudier than the initial colour phase. For some species there are both mature males and females in the initial phase; these tend to spawn in aggregations, whereas terminal males reproduce with single females. Wrasses are carnivorous; some, like the species of *Cirrhilabrus* and *Paracheilinus*, rise above the bottom to feed on zooplankton (see underwater photo of *C. blatteus* Springer and Randall in Introduction). Others, such as *Labroides dimidiatus* and the young of *Larabicus quadrilineatus*, *Thalassoma lunare*, and *T. klunzingeri*, are cleaners, i.e. they feed on crustacean ectoparasites of other fishes (and mucus as well). The majority of labrids, however, are benthic feeders; they prey mainly on invertebrates with hard parts such as shelled molluscs, sea urchins, and crustaceans; they crush these animals with their pharyngeal teeth. The wrasses are diurnal; they are among the first fishes to retire to an inactive state on the bottom with the approach of darkness and among the last to resume activity the following morning. Most of the smaller species bury themselves in the sand at night. Wrasses normally swim with their pectoral fins; only when greater speed is needed are their tails brought into action. Sixty species of labrid fishes are known from the Red Sea. Those most apt to be

encountered on coral reefs are discussed below. Among those not often seen because of their secretive habits are *Pteragogus cryptus* Randall (see underwater photo *above*) and *Wetmorella nigropinnata* (Seale).

## 185 Axilspot Hogfish

*Bodianus axillaris* (Bennett), 1831

Dorsal rays XII,9 or 10; anal rays III,11 or 12; pectoral rays 15 to 17; lateral-line complete, a smooth curve, the pored scales 30 or 31; scales on top of head extending anterior to front edge of eye; a sheath of scales at base of dorsal and anal fins; snout pointed; caudal fin varying from slightly rounded to very slightly double emarginate; juveniles black, the front of snout and chin white; three large white spots along back, three ventrally on body, and two at caudal base; the initial phase in the Indian Ocean has essentially the same pattern but the ground colour is brown (in the Pacific the black, white-spotted pattern appears to be restricted to juveniles); terminal males are brown or reddish brown, shading to whitish posterior to a diagonal running from middle of abdomen to soft portion of dorsal fin and to orange-yellow on caudal peduncle; a round black spot at pectoral base which is larger than eye and edged in yellow posteriorly; a black spot about as large as eye on soft portions of dorsal and anal fins; soft rays of median fins yellow. Reaches 20 cm. East Africa to Samoa and the Mariana Islands. Juveniles are usually found in caves; they have been observed picking at the bodies and fins of other fishes. *Lepidaplois albomaculatus* Smith is a synonym based on the initial phase.

## 186 Diana's Hogfish

*Bodianus diana* (Lacepède), 1801

Dorsal rays XII,9 or 10; anal rays III,10 to 12; pectoral rays 16; lateral-line complete, a smooth curve, the pored scales 30 or 31; scales on top of head not extending anterior to front edge of eye; a sheath of scales at base of dorsal and anal fins; snout pointed; posterior edge of preopercle finely serrate; caudal fin slightly rounded in juveniles, slightly double emarginate in adults; juveniles reddish with rows of white spots on body, two large ocellated black spots in dorsal and anal fins and one in pelvic fins; a large white-edged black spot at pectoral base and a small one at midbase of caudal fin; adults have a reddish brown head, yellowish body, the scales with a brown posterior edge (except dorsoposteriorly where scales have a round black spot); three small yellow spots on back; median fins with red rays, the anal with two black spots and the caudal with a small one at midbase; a large black spot on pelvics. Reported to 25 cm, but rarely exceeds 18 cm. East Africa to the western Pacific. *Lepidaplois aldabrensis* Smith is a synonym based on the juvenile form.

## 187 Lyretail Hogfish

*Bodianus anthioides* (Bennett), 1830

Dorsal rays XII,9 or 10 (usually 10); anal rays III,11 or 12 (usually 12); pectoral rays 15 to 17; lateral-line complete, a smooth curve, the pored scales 29 or 30; scales dorsally on head extending anterior to nostrils; a scaly sheath at base of dorsal and anal fins; snout bluntly rounded; posterior edge of preopercle coarsely serrate; caudal fin deeply emarginate; reddish brown on head, chest, and abdomen; nape and dorsoanterior part of body yellowish brown to a curved irregular black band extending from distal edge at front of soft portion of dorsal fin to beneath pectoral fin; body posterior to this band whitish with scattered small brown spots; upper and lower edges of caudal peduncle black, these bands continuing onto upper and lower edges of caudal fin; a large black spot at front of dorsal fin; juveniles are coloured similarly but have a white snout and chin, the rest of head and anterior body orange-yellow, the posterior body more white; the caudal fin is very large. Reaches 21 cm. Indo-Pacific.

## 188 Mental Wrasse

*Cheilinus mentalis* Rüppell, 1828

Dorsal rays IX,10; anal rays III,8; pectoral rays 12; lateral line interrupted, the anterior pored scales 15 or 16; body slender, the depth 2.8 to 3.5 in standard length; snout pointed, the lower jaw protruding; preopercular margin smooth; caudal fin slightly rounded (in small individuals) to double emarginate; brown or reddish brown, usually with a dark stripe from mouth through eye nearly to caudal base, the edges of this stripe darker than centre (individual fish may rapidly lose the stripe or cause it to reappear); a large whitish spot may be present at caudal base at end of stripe; a dark spot may be evident in shoulder region; large males have narrow red bands radiating from the eye. Attains at least 20 cm. Western Indian Ocean; common in the Red Sea.

111

### 189 Bandcheek Wrasse

*Cheilinus digrammus* (Lacepède), 1801

Dorsal rays IX,10; anal rays III,8; pectoral rays 12; lateral line interrupted, the anterior pored scales 15 or 16; body slender, the depth 2.8 to 3.3 in standard length; lower jaw projecting; preopercular margin smooth; caudal fin slightly rounded (lobe tips may be slightly prolonged on large males); seven to nine diagonal maroon lines on cheek nearly at right angle to diagonal orange-red lines passing anteriorly and posteriorly from eye; head and most of caudal fin of adults green; ability to assume a broad striped pattern. Attains 30 cm. East Africa to Micronesia and Samoa.

### 190 Humphead Wrasse

*Cheilinus undulatus* Rüppell, 1835

Dorsal rays IX,10; anal rays III,8; pectoral rays 12; lateral line interrupted, the anterior pored scales 15 or 16; depth of body 2.2 to 2.7 in standard length (body relatively deeper on larger individuals); adults develop a prominent hump on forehead; mouth terminal or lower jaw slightly projecting; preopercular margin smooth; caudal fin rounded; body green to olive with a vertical dark line on scales; head of adults blue-green to blue with highly irregular undulating yellow lines; two black lines extending posteriorly from eye (juveniles with two more extending diagonally from upper edge of eye and two extending diagonally downward on snout from front of eye); posterior edge of caudal fin pale. Reaches immense size; largest reliably recorded, 2290 cm, 190.5 kg, from Queensland. Indo-Pacific. Feeds on a wide variety of molluscs, fishes, sea urchins, crustaceans, and other invertebrates. In spite of its size, it is a wary fish.

### 191 Broomtail Wrasse

*Cheilinus lunulatus* (Forsskål), 1775

Dorsal rays IX,10; anal rays III,8; pectoral rays 12; lateral line interrupted, the anterior pored scales 15 or 16 (usually 16); depth of body 2.4 to 2.7 in standard length; lower jaw slightly protruding; preopercular margin smooth; caudal fin rounded, the rays of adults prolonged and free of membranes (particularly in large males); greenish, with dark double bars on body and a midlateral row of blackish spots (lost in males); scales of body with a vertical orange-red line; head with scattered orange-red dots, the opercular flap dark with a curved bright orange-yellow mark and a spot of the same colour below it; large males may exhibit a dark blue-green body except for a broad bar of light greenish yellow passing beneath outer part of pectoral fin, a green head and a dark purplish blue caudal fin. Reaches 50 cm. Red Sea to the Gulf of Oman.

## 192 Redbreasted Wrasse

*Cheilinus fasciatus* (Bloch), 1791

Dorsal rays IX,10; anal rays III,8; pectoral rays 12; lateral line interrupted, the anterior pored scales 14 to 16; depth of body 2.3 to 2.6 in standard length; mouth terminal, the lower jaw slightly projecting in large individuals; preopercular margin smooth; caudal fin rounded, becoming emarginate in adults (some central rays may be prolonged and free of membranes); brown, the scales with vertical dark line, with narrow whitish bars on body which extend basally into dorsal and anal fins; chest, front of abdomen and anterior side of body to

level of lateral line red-orange; head brownish grey with some bluish black markings posteriorly (also one at pectoral base, and some may be present on chest). Attains 36 cm. East Africa to Micronesia and Samoa.

## 193 Abudjubbe

*Cheilinus abudjubbe* Rüppell, 1835

Dorsal rays IX,10; anal rays III,8 pectoral rays 12; lateral line interrupted, the pored anterior scales 16; depth of body 2.3 to 2.6 in standard length; mouth terminal; preopercular margin smooth; caudal fin rounded, the rays of large males projecting posteriorly free of membranes (some rays longer than others); posterior part of dorsal and anal fins very angular in adults; greenish with orange-red dots anteriorly on body and a vertical orange-red line on each scale posteriorly; orange-red lines radiating from eye; large males, in addition, with pale greenish dots in middle of body and pale greenish lines posteriorly; median fins with blue-green rays and light orange-red membranes (becoming yel-

lowish posteriorly on caudal fin) fins finely spotted overall with pale green; pectoral fins with yellowish rays and clear membranes; pelvic fins with blue-green rays dotted with pale greenish, the membranes orange-red. Reaches about 40 cm. Red Sea. Related to *C. trilobatus* Lacepède from elsewhere in the Indo-Pacific.

## 194 Slingjaw Wrasse

*Epibulus insidiator* (Pallas), 1770

Dorsal rays IX,10; anal rays III,8 or 9; pectoral rays 12; lateral line interrupted, the pored anterior scales 14 or 15; body deep, the depth 2.0 to 2.3 in standard length; jaws extremely protractile; preopercular margin smooth; caudal fin emarginate; posterior part of dorsal and anal fins very prolonged, particularly the anal; pelvic fins long, reaching posterior to origin of anal fin on mature adults; females brown or yellow; males with dark green edges on scales of body, a diffuse yellow bar on side behind pectoral fin, a red and orange area dorso-anteriorly on body, and a light grey head with dark lines radiating from eye (the longest and broadest from eye to upper end of gill opening); small juveniles brown with three complete narrow white bars on body, one on caudal fin base, and five narrow white bands radiating from

eye. Attains 35 cm. Indo-Pacific. Feeds by very rapid extension of the jaws; the diet consists mainly of small fishes, crabs, and shrimps.

## 195 Rockmover Wrasse

*Novaculichthys taeniourus* (Lacepède), 1801

Dorsal rays IX,12, the origin of fin over preopercular margin, the first two spines flexible (very prolonged on juveniles); anal rays III,12; pectoral rays 13; lateral line interrupted, the anterior pored scales 19 or 20 (usually 20); head scaleless except for two scales on upper part of opercle and a near-vertical row of small scales behind eye; depth of body 2.8 to 3.0 in standard length; preopercular margin smooth; caudal fin rounded; dark brownish grey with a vertically elongate pale spot on each scale; a red patch often present on abdomen; four pale-edged dark bands extending posteriorly and ventrally from eye; a curved black bar beneath proximal part of pectoral fin; a black spot on first two membranes of dorsal fin; a broad white bar on basal part of caudal fin; juveniles mottled green, brown, or reddish with dark-edged, white blotches on body and head, and clear areas in fins. Attains 27 cm. Indo-Pacific. Feeds on a variety of mol-luscs, brittle stars, echinoids, polychaete worms, and crustaceans. Often turns over rocks with its jaws to get to the invertebrate animals beneath. The young mimic drifting clumps of algae. *Julis bifer* Lay and Bennett is a synonym based on the juvenile stage. *N. macrolepidotus* (Bloch) is usually found in seagrass beds; it has a more slender body (depth 3.6 to 3.9 in standard length) and is often green like the seagrass.

## 196 Sixstripe Wrasse

*Pseudocheilinus hexataenia* (Bleeker), 1857

Dorsal rays IX,11; anal rays III,9; pectoral rays 16; lateral line interrupted, the anterior pored scales 16 to 18; head scaled except interorbital, snout, and ventrally; a sheath of scales at base of dorsal and anal fins; eye with an apparent double pupil from a division of the cornea; preopercular margin smooth; caudal fin slightly rounded; upper two-thirds of body with alternating stripes of purplish blue and orange-yellow; caudal fin green; a small black spot on upper part of caudal peduncle near caudal fin base. Reaches 6.5 cm. Indo-Pacific. A secretive species not often seen in the open.

## 197 Disappearing Wrasse

*Pseudocheilinus evanidus* Jordan and Evermann, 1903

Dorsal rays IX,11; anal rays III,9; pectoral rays 14; lateral line interrupted, the anterior pored scales 14 to 16; head scaled except interorbital, snout, and ventrally; a sheath of scales at base of dorsal and anal fins; eye with an apparent double pupil; preopercular margin smooth; caudal fin rounded; red with numerous fine longitudinal whitish lines on body; a bluish white streak extending posteriorly from corner of mouth; edge of preopercle often purple and a near-vertical purple streak usually present on opercle. Reaches nearly 8 cm. Indo-Pacific. Also a secretive species.

## 198 Social Wrasse

*Cirrhilabrus rubriventralis* Springer and Randall, 1974

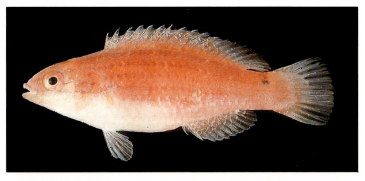

Dorsal rays XI,10; anal rays III,10; pectoral rays 14 or 15 (usually 14); lateral line interrupted, the anterior pored scales 15 to 17; eye with a double pupil; three pairs of canine teeth anteriorly in upper jaw, the two posterior pairs recurved; posterior margin of preopercle finely serrate; first two dorsal spines of males very elongate; a fleshy cirrus near tip of each dorsal and anal spine; caudal fin rounded, the lobe tips slightly prolonged in males; pelvic fins of males very long; females orange-red with longitudinal blue lines and a small black spot dorso-posteriorly on caudal peduncle; males red, mottled with light pink and blue, becoming whitish ventrally; a horizontal violet line passing posteriorly from corner of mouth; pelvic fins bright red; caudal fin mainly blue. Attains 7.5 cm. Known from the northern half of the Red Sea. Occurs from 3 to 43 m; usually seen over bottoms of coral rubble. Feeds on zooplankton. Males maintain harems. Another Red Sea species of the genus, *C. blatteus* Springer and Randall, occurs in deeper water; it is larger and has a pointed caudal fin.

## 199 Eightline Wrasse

*Paracheilinus octotaenia* Fourmanoir, 1955

Dorsal rays IX,11; anal rays III,9; pectoral rays 14; lateral line interrupted, the anterior pored scales 14 to 16; a double pupil; three pairs of canine teeth anteriorly in upper jaw, the two posterior pairs recurved; posterior margin of pre-opercle finely serrate; no elongate rays in dorsal fin; caudal fin rounded; orange-red with longitudinal blue lines on body (four or five in females, eight in males). Attains 9 cm. Red Sea. Occurs in aggre- gations. Feeds on zooplankton. Males maintain harems.

## 200 Cleaner Wrasse

*Labroides dimidiatus* (Cuvier and Valenciennes), 1839

Dorsal rays IX,10 or 11; anal rays III,10; pectoral rays 13; lateral line complete, bent downward below posterior part of dorsal fin, the pored scales 52 to 54; preopercular margin smooth; lower lip divided into two prominent forward-projecting lobes; caudal fin truncate; light blue with a black stripe from front of snout through eye, along upper side of body, and ending at hind edge of caudal fin, this stripe broadening as it passes posteriorly; juveniles more black, the blue deeper and restricted to a narrow dorsal stripe. Largest specimen examined, 11 cm. Indo-Pacific. Feeds on crustacean ectoparasites and mucus of other fishes; even enters the mouth and gill chambers of some fishes. Maintains stations on the reef to which the host fishes come for its services.

## 201 Fourline Wrasse

*Larabicus quadrilineatus* (Rüppell), 1835

Dorsal rays IX,11; anal rays III,10; pectoral rays 13; lateral-line scales 26 or 27; preopercular margin smooth; lips thick, forming a short tube when mouth closed; lower lip not bi-lobed; caudal fin rounded in juveniles, truncate in adults (may be slightly emarginate on large males); juveniles and females dark purplish grey with two bright blue stripes; males lose the blue stripes but develop a curved blue band on head below eye. Largest specimen, 11.5 cm. Red Sea and the Gulf of Aden. The young are cleaners; adults appear to feed primarily on coral polyps.

## 202 Bluelined Wrasse

*Stethojulis albovittata* (Bonnaterre), 1788

Dorsal rays IX,11; anal rays III,11; pectoral rays 14 or 15 (usually 14); lateral line complete, bent downward beneath rear of dorsal fin, the pored scales 26 or 27; head scaleless; scales on chest not smaller than those of rest of body; gill rakers 25 to 30; preopercular margin smooth; no canine teeth anteriorly in jaws, but one at corner of mouth; remaining teeth incisiform; caudal fin small, slightly rounded; initial-phase fish brown to greenish dorsally, whitish ventrally, with a faint pink stripe on lower side; a bright orange-red spot above pectoral base and a yellow streak across cheek under eye; one or two small pale-edged black spots midlaterally on posterior part of caudal peduncle; may exhibit two narrow whitish stripes, the lowermost a continuation of the yellow streak on head; terminal males with four narrow blue bands on head, the uppermost continuing along base of dorsal fin and the two lower ones extending full length of body. Reaches 12 cm. Western Indian Ocean. An active fish, like others of the genus, it is always on the move.

## 203 Cutribbon Wrasse

*Stethojulis interrupta* (Bleeker), 1851

Dorsal rays IX,11; anal rays III,11; pectoral rays 12 or 13 (usually 13); lateral line complete, bent downward beneath rear of dorsal fin, the pored scales 26 or 27; head scaleless; scales on chest not smaller than those of rest of body; gill rakers 20 to 23; preopercular margin smooth; no canine teeth anteriorly in jaws, but one at corner of mouth; remaining teeth incisiform; caudal fin small, slightly rounded; initial-phase fish with upper half of body brown, greenish, or yellowish with tiny pale blue dots, the lower half white with rows of black dots, the two regions often separated by a narrow blackish stripe; terminal males with three blue lines on head, the most dorsal continuing along base of dorsal fin; a short midlateral blue line anteriorly on body, ending at lower base of pectoral fin and reappearing on posterior half of

body. To 13 cm. East Africa to the western Pacific. *Julis kalosoma* Bleeker is a synonym based on the initial phase.

## 204 Checkerboard Wrasse

*Halichoeres hortulanus* (Lacepède), 1801

Dorsal rays IX,11; anal rays III,11; pectoral rays 14; lateral-line scales 26, the anterior scales with one pore; a patch of small scales dorsally on opercle and a near vertical band of small scales in two or three rows just behind eye; scales on chest smaller than those of rest of body (true of other *Halichoeres, Macropharyngodon* and *Thalassoma*); two pairs of projecting canine teeth anteriorly in upper jaw; a tooth at corner of mouth (also present in other *Halichoeres*); preopercular margin smooth (true of remaining wrasses of this book); caudal fin slightly rounded; body of females with a longitudinal series of black-edged white blotches following scale rows; a yellow

spot on back at base of fourth and fifth dorsal spines, followed by a large blackish blotch; head and nape with pink bands; caudal fin yellow; males similar, but ground colour green; juveniles white with large black areas on body and a yellow-edged black spot in dorsal fin. Reaches 27 cm. Indo-Pacific. *Labrus centiquadrus* Lacepède is a synonym.

## 205 Zigzag Wrasse

*Halichoeres scapularis* (Bennett), 1831

Dorsal rays IX,11; anal rays III,11; pectoral rays 14; lateral-line scales 26, the anterior scales with one pore; a patch of small scales dorsally on opercle, but no small scales behind eye; two pairs of projecting canine teeth anteriorly in upper jaw; caudal fin slightly rounded; whitish (pale greenish in terminal males), with a dark stripe from eye along upper side (following anterior part of lateral line) to upper caudal base (stripe zigzag on body); pink bands on upper half of head. Reaches 20 cm (but does not attain this size in the Red Sea). East Africa to

the western Pacific. Usually found in protected waters of lagoons or bays, associated more with sand, rubble, or seagrass bottoms near reefs than the reefs themselves.

117

## 206 Nebulous Wrasse

*Halichoeres nebulosus* (Cuvier and Valenciennes), 1839

Dorsal rays IX,11; anal rays III,11; pectoral rays 13 to 15 (nearly always 14); lateral-line scales 27, the anterior scales with one to three pores; no scales on operculum; two pairs of large canine teeth anteriorly in upper jaw, the second pair smaller than the first and recurved; caudal fin slightly rounded; initial phase mottled brown and white with large dusky blotches dorsally on body, a large pink area on abdomen, a small black spot behind eye, a less distinct one on opercular flap, a yellow-rimmed black spot in middle of dorsal fin and a smaller one at front of fin; males green with irregular pink bands on head and large blackish blotches dorsally, two of which extend ventrally in middle of body; pink area on abdomen reduced or lost, as are the black spots except the one on opercular flap. Largest specimen, 11.5 cm. East Africa to

the western Pacific where it ranges from southern Japan to southern New South Wales. A shallow-water reef species. *Julis reichei* Bleeker is a synonym. *Halichoeres margaritaceus* (Cuvier and Valenciennes) is a closely related species which does not occur in the western Indian Ocean.

## 207 Dusky Wrasse

*Halichoeres marginatus* Rüppell, 1835

Dorsal rays IX,13 or 14 (usually 13); anal rays III,12 or 13 (usually 12); pectoral rays 14 or 15 (usually 14); lateral-line scales 27 or 28 (usually 27), the anterior scales with two to four pores; no scales on operculum; canine teeth anteriorly in jaws not markedly longer than adjacent posterior teeth and not recurved; caudal fin rounded; initial phase dark brown with faint lighter stripes following scale rows, two yellow-edged deep blue spots in dorsal fin, the smaller one anterior, and a whitish caudal fin (larger individuals develop a broad blackish crescent in fin); terminal males yellowish brown with a dark bluish spot on each scale, narrow diagonal dark blue bands on head, and complexly coloured fins; juveniles with alternating narrow pale yellowish and broad dark brown stripes. Attains 17 cm. Indo-Pacific. *Julis notopsis* (Cuvier and Valenciennes) is a synonym based on the initial phase (which may be either female or male).

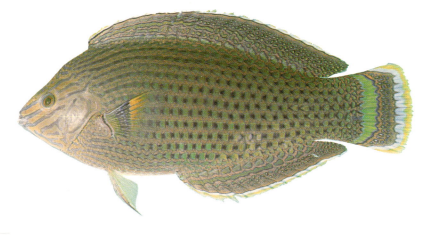

## 208 Vermiculate Wrasse

*Macropharyngodon bipartitus* Smith, 1957

Dorsal rays IX,11; anal rays III,11; pectoral rays 12; lateral-line scales 27, the anterior scales with two or three pores; head scaleless; no median predorsal scales; two pairs of canine teeth anteriorly in upper jaw, the first pair projecting, the second recurved; pharyngeal dentition dominated by a few very large molars; free margin of preopercle short, especially the lower edge; caudal fin rounded; initial phase orange on body with white spots becoming black over abdomen and chest with very irregular light blue spots; head yellow with blue-edged black spots posteriorly; terminal males dusky to blackish red with irregular greenish yellow spots. Reaches 13 cm. Western Indian Ocean. The Red Sea population has a slightly lower gill-raker count, and the terminal male is somewhat different in colour; it has been named *M. b. marisrubri* by the author. *M. varialvus* Smith is a synonym based on the initial phase.

## 209 Spottail Coris

*Coris caudimacula* (Quoy and Gaimard), 1834

Dorsal rays IX,12, the first two spines of adults flexible, longer, and closer together than remaining spines; anal rays III,12; pectoral rays 13; lateral-line scales 50 to 52; head scaleless except side of nape; two pairs of prominent canine teeth anteriorly in upper jaw; a small canine at corner of mouth; caudal fin rounded; upper two-thirds of body striped, the lowermost of salmon pink breaking up posteriorly into irregular vertically elongate spots; upper half of body usually with an overlying pattern of broad dark and narrow pale bars; a large diffuse blackish spot usually present at caudal fin base; a black spot on opercular flap edged posteriorly in yellow; distal part of first two membranes of dorsal fin blackish. Reaches 20 cm. East Africa to Indonesia.

## 210 African Coris

*Coris gaimard* (Quoy and Gaimard), 1824

Dorsal rays IX,12, the first two spines flexible, notably longer than third spine (except in juveniles), and close together; anal rays III,12; pectoral rays 13; lateral-line scales 70 to 79; head scaleless; front pair of canine teeth in jaws nearly twice as large as second pair; a tooth at corner of mouth; caudal fin slightly rounded; adults reddish brown with green bands on head and small green spots (one per scale, blue in small individuals) on body and caudal fin; males with a pale green bar on body above origin of anal fin; juveniles red with three black-edged white spots dorsally on body and two similar but smaller spots on head. Reaches 38 cm. Indo-Pacific. In the eastern Indian Ocean and Pacific this species has a yellow caudal fin and scattered small blue spots. Smith named the western Indian Ocean form *C. g. africana.* Feeds mainly on molluscs, crabs, and hermit crabs. *Julis greenovii* Bennett is a synonym based on the juvenile stage.

## 211 Clown Coris

*Coris aygula* (Lacepède), 1801

Dorsal rays IX,12, the first two spines flexible, elongate in adult males, and close together; anal rays III,12; pectoral rays 14; lateral-line scales 60 to 65; head scaleless; males develop a prominent hump on forehead; anterior pair of canine teeth in jaws clearly the longest; a tooth (or pair of teeth) at corner of mouth; caudal fin slightly rounded, the rays prolonged and free of membranes in males; initial phase light greenish anteriorly with dark reddish spots, a pale bar across body above anus; body posterior to bar greenish, the edges of the scales dark; males dark blue-green, often with a broad pale bar above origin of anal fin; juveniles whitish with small dark spots anteriorly and two large semi-circular orange-red spots on back with a large ocellated black spot above each in dorsal fin. Attains at least 60 cm. Indo-Pacific. Feeds chiefly on shelled molluscs, hermit crabs, sea urchins, and crabs. This and the preceding *Coris* will turn over rocks in search of prey. *C. angulata* Lacepède is a synonym.

## 212 Dapple Coris

*Coris variegata* (Rüppell), 1835

Dorsal rays IX,11; anal rays III,11; pectoral rays 13 to 15 (usually 14); lateral-line scales 51 to 54; head scaleless except dorsally behind eye; a pair of canine teeth anteriorly in jaws and one or two canines at corner of mouth; caudal fin slightly rounded; whitish to pale greenish with six dark bars on back (may be faint) much broader than white interspaces and scattered light red to blackish spots (one per scale) on body which may form irregular longitudinal lines; a small dark spot behind eye; a small blackish spot anteriorly in dorsal fin (small individuals have a large yellow-edged black spot anteriorly in soft portion of dorsal

fin); a narrow black bar at base of pectoral fins. Reaches 20 cm. East Africa to the Marshall Islands.

## 213 Ring Wrasse

*Hologymnosus annulatus* (Lacepède), 1801

Dorsal rays IX,12; anal rays III,12; pectoral rays 13; lateral-line scales 100 to 118; head scaleless; body elongate, the depth 3.3 to 5.1 in standard length (larger individuals, in general, deeper bodied); head moderately long and pointed, 3.0 to 3.3 in standard length; two pairs of protruding canine teeth anteriorly in jaws, none at corner of mouth; caudal fin slightly rounded in juveniles, emarginate in adults; initial phase brown to dark olive with 18 to 19 dark brown bars on body and a large white crescentic area posteriorly in caudal fin; terminal males green to blue-green with about 20 narrow orange-brown to light purple bars on body and a broader whitish or pale yellow bar above origin of anal fin; head yellowish brown, suffused with green, with irregular bright green to blue-green bands radiating from eye; caudal fin with lobes broadly yellowish brown to purple, the large centroposterior region green to blue-green; juveniles yellow with a red line dorsally

on head and body and a very broad dark brown stripe on lower side. Reaches 40 cm. Indo-Pacific. Feeds mainly on fishes. *Labrus semidiscus* Lacepède is a synonym.

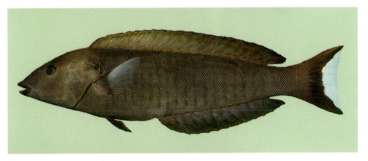

121

## 214 Barred Wrasse

*Hemigymnus fasciatus* (Bloch), 1792

Dorsal rays IX,11; anal rays III,11; pectoral rays 14; lateral-line scales 27; a few rows of small scales on cheek behind and below eye; lips very thick; a pair of protruding canine teeth anteriorly in jaws; teeth on side of jaws small and compressed, the upper jaw with some small nodular teeth medially; gill membranes broadly attached to isthmus (thus restricting gill opening to side); caudal fin truncate to slightly rounded; whitish with five black bars much broader than interspaces; blue-edged pink bands on head; median fins dark brown to black. Reported to 75 cm but probably does not exceed 50 cm. Observed feeding by ingesting mouthfuls of sand, sorting the material for a few moments to extract the animal material, and ejecting the inorganic sediment from its mouth or gill openings. Stomach contents reveal a wide variety of small invertebrates such as crustaceans, polychaete worms, brittle stars, and foraminifera; also feeds directly on larger shelled invertebrates such as sea urchins and molluscs.

## 215 Thicklip Wrasse

*Hemigymnus melapterus* (Bloch), 1791

Dorsal rays IX,11; anal rays III,11; pectoral rays 14; lateral-line scales 27; a few rows of small scales on cheek behind and below eye; lips very thick; dentition and gill membranes as in above species; caudal fin truncate to slightly rounded; head and anterior body light grey, the upper half of head with irregular, blue-edged pink bands; most of body dark purplish, the edges of the scales black, with a curved vertical pale blue line or spot on each scale; median fins dark purplish with fine blue markings; juveniles with a white bar from front of dorsal fin to abdomen; head and body before this bluish grey; body posterior up to white bar is black, becoming yellow on posterior caudal peduncle and fin. Reaches 50 cm. Indo-Pacific.

## 216 Bluespotted Wrasse

*Anampses caeruleopunctatus* Rüppell, 1829

Dorsal rays IX,12; anal rays III,12; pectoral rays 13; lateral-line scales 27; head scaleless; no median predorsal scales; depth of body 2.3 to 3.0 in standard length; a pair of forward-projecting incisiform teeth at front of jaws, the uppers with upcurved pointed tips, the lowers nearly conical and down-curved; remaining teeth very small, none at corner of mouth; caudal fin slightly rounded to truncate; females reddish brown with a dark-edged blue spot on each scale and dark-edged blue bands on head; males greenish with a vertical blue line on each scale, a broad green bar in pectoral region of body, a blue band across interorbital, narrow irregular blue bands on head, and blue bands on fins. Largest specimen, 42 cm. Indo-Pacific. Generally found inshore on rocky bottom exposed to surge. *Anampses diadematus* Rüppell is a synonym based on the male form.

122

## 217 Yellowbreasted Wrasse
*Anampses twistii* Bleeker, 1856

Dorsal rays IX,12; anal rays III,12; pectoral rays 13; lateral-line scales 26; head scaleless; depth of body 3.0 to 3.3 in standard length; dentition as above; caudal fin rounded; brown with dark-edged blue dots, shading to yellow on lower half of head and on chest (the yellow sometimes continuing broadly onto abdomen); a black spot on opercular flap; a large blue-edged black spot posteriorly in dorsal and anal fins; caudal fin light red with pale blue spots and a whitish posterior border. To 18 cm. Indo-Pacific.

## 218 Yellowtail Wrasse
*Anampses meleagrides* Cuvier and Valenciennes, 1839

Dorsal rays IX,12; anal rays III,12; pectoral rays 13; lateral-line scales 26; head scaleless; no median predorsal scales; body moderately elongate, the depth 3.1 to 3.4 in standard length; dentition typical of the genus; caudal fin rounded in juveniles, truncate to emarginate in adults; females dark brown with round white spots, those on body one per scale; caudal fin bright yellow; males dark orangish brown with a vertical blue line on each scale of body (except caudal peduncle where the scales have a round blue spot); dorsal and anal fins dull orange with blue stripes; caudal orange with blue spots and a white crescent edged at the front with blue posteriorly in fin. Reaches 21 cm. Indo-Pacific. *A. amboinensis* Bleeker is a synonym based on the male form.

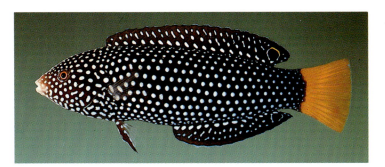

## 219 Lined Wrasse
*Anampses lineatus* Randall, 1972

Dorsal rays IX,12; anal rays III,12; pectoral rays 13; lateral-line scales 26; head scaleless; no median predorsal scales; depth of body 3.15 to 3.4 in standard length; dentition typical of the genus; caudal fin rounded; orangish brown with dark-edged, light blue-green lines (some broken into series of dashes) following longitudinal scale rows; head and chest with pale blue-green spots and irregular lines; a black spot on opercular flap; caudal fin white with a very large black area covering most of outer half of fin (leaving only a narrow whitish posterior border). Reaches 12 cm. Indian Ocean. Rare in less than 20 m. Originally described as a subspecies of the Pacific *A. melanurus* Bleeker.

## 220 Klunzinger's Wrasse

*Thalassoma klunzingeri* Fowler and Steinitz, 1956

Dorsal rays VIII,13; anal rays III,11; pectoral rays 16 (rarely 15); lateral-line scales 26, most with the external tubes branched (true of other *Thalassoma*); small scales dorsally on opercle; free preopercular margin short, especially the lower edge (true of other *Thalassoma*); one pair of large canines anteriorly in jaws; no tooth at corner of mouth of this and other *Thalassoma*; caudal fin truncate to very slightly rounded in young, emarginate in adults; green with a midlateral red stripe connected by numerous narrow bars of lavender pink to a stripe of the same colour along back; head with alternating broad red and narrow green curved bands; a submarginal red band in each lobe of caudal fin; a small dark blue spot at upper base of pectoral fins; males with outer upper part of pectoral fins dusky. Reaches 20 cm. Red Sea; one of the most abundant of reef fishes. Usually identified as *T. rueppellii* Klunzinger, but this name is preoccupied. Closely related to *T. quinquevittatum* (Lay and Bennett) from outside the Red Sea.

## 221 Moon Wrasse

*Thalassoma lunare* (Linnaeus), 1758

Dorsal rays IX,13; anal rays III,11; pectoral rays 15; lateral-line scales 26; a patch of small scales dorsally on opercle; body elongate for the genus, the depth 3.4 to 3.8 in standard length; a pair of prominent canine teeth anteriorly in jaws, the remaining conical teeth gradually smaller; caudal fin varying from truncate in juveniles to lunate with filamentous lobes in large males; adults green to blue with a vertical red line on scales of body; head with irregular curved red bands; a broad red band in pectoral fin and one in each lobe of caudal fin; a large hemispherical yellow area posteriorly in caudal fin; juveniles with a large blackish spot at base of caudal fin and another in middle of dorsal fin. Reaches 25 cm. Indo-Pacific. Relatively more common than other *Thalassoma* in silty dead reef areas.

## 222 Surge Wrasse

*Thalassoma purpureum* (Forsskål), 1775

Dorsal rays IX,13; anal rays III,11; pectoral rays 16 (rarely 15 or 17); lateral-line scales 26; two short rows of small scales dorsally on opercle; a pair of large canines anteriorly in jaws; caudal fin slightly rounded, becoming double emarginate in large adults; initial phase green with a midlateral red stripe on body and another on lower side; scales on upper two-thirds of body with a narrow vertical red bar (groups of these scales in rows with the bar brownish red); head with numerous small red to brownish red spots and short irregular markings; a small blackish spot anterior in dorsal fin and another at upper pectoral base; terminal males blue to blue-green with three pink stripes on body and irregular pink bands on head (a prominent diagonal one from eye across cheek, branching as it approaches pectoral base). Reaches 43 cm. Indo-Pacific. The usual habitat is rocky shore exposed to surge; although the largest species of the genus, it readily penetrates the shallowest water. Feeds on crabs, fishes, sea urchins, molluscs, and polychaete worms. *Julis umbrystygma* Rüppell is a synonym based on the initial phase. The closely related *T. fuscum* (Lacepède) apparently does not occur in the Red Sea.

## 223 Red Sea Bird Wrasse

*Gomphosus caeruleus* Lacepède, 1801

Dorsal rays VIII,13; anal rays III,11; pectoral rays 15; lateral-line scales 26; base of dorsal fin scaled; body moderately elongate, the depth 3.7 to 4.0 in standard length; snout extremely long and slender (except small juveniles), its length more than half length of head; teeth conical, those at front of jaws incurved, the most anterior pair as moderate canines; caudal fin varying from slightly rounded in juveniles to lunate with filamentous lobes in large males; initial phase with upper half of head and body blackish, the lower half whitish, shading to yellow posteriorly where scales may have a central blackish spot; dorsal fin dark with some yellow distally on first two membranes; anal and caudal fins yellow; a black spot at upper base of pectoral fins; terminal males are deep blue-green, the outer part of soft por-tions of dorsal and anal fins and a large hemispherical area posteriorly in caudal fin yellowish green; pectoral fins blackish with whitish outer edge. Reaches 26 cm. Indian Ocean. Coloured differently in the Red Sea where it has been named *G. c. klunzingeri* by Klausewitz.

## 224 Cigar Wrasse

*Cheilio inermis* (Forsskål), 1775

Dorsal rays IX,12 or 13; anal rays III,11 or 12; pectoral rays 12 or 13; lateral-line scales 45 to 47; head scaleless except for a few scales behind eye on preopercle and opercle; body very elongate, the depth 5.5 to 7.8 in standard length; snout long, its length 2.2 to 2.4 in head; teeth conical, those at front of jaws recurved, the anterior pair of upper jaw as moderate canines; caudal fin rounded or rhomboid; dorsal half of body green, brown or brownish yellow, the lower half whitish, often with a narrow blackish midlateral stripe or row of spots separat-ing the two colour zones; large males may lack the blackish stripe and develop a pink spot or spots on upper side above pectoral fin. Attains 50 cm. Indo-Pacific. Found more in beds of seagrass or on algal-covered flats than coral reefs. Feeds chiefly on molluscs, hermit crabs, crabs, sea urchins, and shrimps.

## 225 Chiseltooth Wrasse

*Pseudodax moluccanus* (Cuvier and Valenciennes), 1839

Dorsal rays XI,12; anal rays III,14; pectoral rays 15; lateral-line scales 31; head scaled except interorbital, snout, and chin; base of dorsal and anal fins scaled; body moderately deep, the depth 2.5 to 2.7 in standard length, and compressed; jaws with a pair of large spatulate incisiform teeth anteriorly, the lower jaw with a second adjacent smaller pair; teeth on sides of jaws coalesced into a bony ridge; pharyngeal teeth more like those of parrotfishes than wrasses; caudal fin rounded; adults grey with a reddish brown spot on each scale of body; a wash of orange or orange-red on nape; upper lip yellow with a blue streak above it which extends almost to corner of pre-opercle; caudal fin blackish with a broad pale yellowish bar across base and a narrow blue posterior margin; dorsal and anal fins orange-yellow with a blue margin; juveniles with two bright blue stripes, one commencing on snout and passing dorsally on body and the other from lips along ventral part of body. Attains 25 cm. Indo-Pacific.

# Parrotfishes (Scaridae)

The parrotfishes are well named for their bright colours and the fusion of their teeth to form beak-like dental plates. Their pharyngeal dentition is also unique; each of the interlocking upper pharyngeal bones has one to three rows of molariform teeth; these teeth form a convex surface that bears against the concave surface of the lower pharyngeal bone which is also studded with rows of molariform teeth. This pharyngeal mill, as it is often called, is used to grind the algal food with the coral rock or sediment that is usually ingested with the algae. These fishes have oblong, somewhat compressed bodies, and the head is usually bluntly rounded anteriorly. All have an unnotched dorsal fin with IX,10 dorsal rays, the spines usually slender and flexible, and III,9 anal rays; the scales are large and cycloid, with 22 to 24 in the lateral line which angles downward beneath the rear part of the dorsal fin to a straight midlateral peduncular part; the fins have no scales except for a basal row that may be present on the median fins; there is no true stomach, and the intestine is very long. The dental plates have a median suture; the adults of many species have one to three canine teeth posteriorly on the side of the dental plates. When these fishes graze algae on limestone rock, they often scrape into the rock and leave characteristic grooves showing the median suture. The rock is ground into sand with the algae. Like other herbivores, parrotfishes feed much of the time during the day. They are more important in sand production than any other group of marine animals. At night they sleep on the bottom, usually beneath ledges or in small caves; some species secrete a veil-like mass of mucus around themselves during the night. Like the Labridae from which they have evolved, scarid fishes often exhibit differences in colour from juveniles to adults and during sex reversal. The first adult colour form, termed the initial phase, is usually drab, generally grey, brown, or reddish brown. For some scarids this phase is only female. Males of such species (called terminal males) result from sex change. With the development of testes these fishes adopt a new colour pattern which is often dominated by green. The initial phase of most parrotfishes may be either male or female (the males are then called primary males). Terminal males of these species appear to result mainly from sex reversal, but primary males can also alter their colour to the terminal phase. Spawning

of parrotfishes takes two forms: aggregations of like-coloured females and males (with the numbers of males much greater) and by pairs of different colour. In both cases, the release of eggs and sperm takes place at the peak of a sudden upward rush. Parrotfishes swim with their pectoral fins except when rapid movement is needed, as during the spawning rush or to avoid predation; then the tail is brought into play. The Scaridae is divisible into two subfamilies, the more primitive Sparisomatinae and the Scarinae. The former, which is characterized by a single row of scales on the cheek below the eye and a lower pharyngeal bone which is much wider than long, is represented by two species in the Red Sea, *Calotomus viridescens* (Rüppell) and *Leptoscarus vaigiensis* (Quoy and Gaimard), a resident of seagrass beds. There are 13 species of Scarinae in the Red Sea.

## 226 Dotted Parrotfish

*Calotomus viridescens* (Rüppell), 1835

Pectoral rays 12 or 13 (usually 13); median predorsal scales 4; one row of scales on cheek; teeth not fully fused to form dental plates (overlapping pointed incisiform teeth clearly distinct); one or two recurved canine teeth posteriorly on side of upper jaw; caudal fin rounded in juveniles, slightly double emarginate in large individuals; initial phase mottled grey-brown with numerous very small black spots on operculum and pectoral region of body; a blackish spot on first membrane of dorsal fin; dark pigment around anus; terminal males mottled greenish grey with black dots as seen in initial-phase fish and an orange-red spot on scales of lower half of body; head dull blue-green anteriorly and ventrally with red bands radiating from eye and orange-red spots on lower part; median fins greenish to blue-green with orange-red markings, the dorsal with a blackish spot anteriorly; anus black. Attains 27 cm. Red Sea. May be seen in seagrass beds as well as on coral reefs and rocky sea bottom.

## 227 Longnose Parrotfish

*Hipposcarus harid* (Forsskål), 1775

Pectoral rays 15; median predorsal scales 4; cheek scales small, in an isolated subtriangular patch of three or four rows; head rather pointed for a scarid, the snout long, 1.8 to 2.35 in head; caudal fin lunate, the lobes of large males very long; initial phase light tan, the dorsal and anal fins pale yellowish with light blue margins; caudal fin pale yellowish, the rays light blue; terminal males green, the scales edged in light orange except chest and abdomen; head orange with submarginal blue bands on lips; fins largely orange-yellow, the large central posterior area of caudal fin blue, streaked with orange-yellow. Reported to 75 cm. Indian Ocean. The related *H. longiceps* (Cuvier and Valenciennes) occurs in the Pacific. A species of protected waters often seen over sandy substrata near reefs.

## 228 Bicolour Parrotfish

*Cetoscarus bicolor* (Rüppell), 1829

Pectoral rays 14 or 15 (usually 14); median predorsal scales 5 to 7 (usually 6); three rows of scales on cheek, the lower row with 3 to 7 scales; each upper pharyngeal bone with three longitudinal rows of molariform teeth, the outer row rudimentary (the species of *Scarus* and *Hipposcarus* with two rows; when there are two, the outer row is rudimentary); outer surface of dental plates granular; no canine teeth on dental plates; dorsal profile of head not steep and without a hump; snout long, 1.8 to 2.2 in head; caudal fin of adults emarginate (deeply emarginate in terminal males); initial phase reddish, yellow on the back, the scales of side edged and spotted with black; terminal males green, the edges of scales orange, the head and anterior body with small orange spots; juveniles white with a broad orange bar covering head except snout and chin, and an orange-edged black spot in dorsal fin. Attains about 80 cm. Indo-Pacific. *Scarus pulchellus* Rüppell is a synonym based on the terminal male phase.

## 229 Bumphead Parrotfish

*Bolbometopon muricatum* (Cuvier and Valenciennes), 1840

Pectoral rays 15 or 16; median predorsal scales 2 to 4; three rows of scales on cheek, the lower row with 1 or 2 scales; each upper pharyngeal bone with three rows of molariform teeth, the outer row rudimentary; outer surface of dental plates granular (smooth on species of *Scarus* and *Hipposcarus*); no canine teeth on dental plates; body deep, the depth 2.05 to 2.5 in standard length; dorsal profile of head steep, adults developing a very large hump dorsoanteriorly to eye; caudal fin of adults slightly double emarginate; adults dull green to blue-green, the anterior part of head pink; juveniles brown with two longitudinal rows of whitish spots on dorsal half of body. Reaches at least 120 cm; one of 117.2 cm weighed 46 kg. East Africa to the Line Islands in the central Pacific. Feeds in part on live coral and in part on benthic algae. Often seen in aggregations; a wary fish.

## 230 Bullethead Parrotfish

*Scarus sordidus* Forsskål, 1775

Pectoral rays 14 to 16 (nearly always 15); median predorsal scales 4; two rows of scales on cheek; lips covering less than half of dental plates; none to two small canine teeth posteriorly on side of upper dental plate, none on lower; head bluntly rounded anteriorly, the dorsal and ventral profiles about equally convex; caudal fin truncate to slightly rounded; initial phase dark brown, the head light red ventrally and on lips, often with two longitudinal rows of five or six whitish spots on body; a broad whitish bar may be present on posterior caudal peduncle and caudal fin base containing a large circular blackish spot; dental plates pale salmon pink; terminal males green, the edges of the scales salmon pink except caudal peduncle and scaled basal part of caudal fin which are solid green; head green to blue-green dorsally, the cheek orange-yellow, the chin pink with broad transverse blue-green bands; dental plates green. Largest specimen examined, 32 cm. Indo-Pacific. A common species with 13 synonyms of which the most recent is *Callyodon bipallidus* Smith.

## 231 Purplestreak Parrotfish

*Scarus genazonatus* Randall and Bruce, 1982

Pectoral rays 15 or 16 (usually 15); median predorsal scales 4; two rows of scales on cheek; lips covering less than half of dental plates; one or two prominent canine teeth posteriorly on each side of upper dental plate, none on lower; head bluntly rounded anteriorly; caudal fin truncate; initial phase brown, paler on caudal peduncle, with an orange-red bar on each scale; dental plates white; terminal males blue-green with a salmon bar on scales of body except ventrally; head salmon with blue-green markings, the most prominent a stripe beneath eye (broadens posteriorly); below this is a broad stripe of deep purple; dental plates white. Largest specimen, 31 cm. Red Sea and the Gulf of Aden.

## 232 Steepheaded Parrotfish

*Scarus gibbus* Rüppell, 1829

Pectoral rays 15 to 17 (usually 16); median predorsal scales usually 4; three rows of scales on cheek, the lower row of 1 to 8 scales; one fourth or less of dental plates covered by lips; one or two canine teeth on side of upper dental plate of large adults, none on lower; dorsal profile of snout steep (approaching the vertical in large terminal males); caudal fin of adults lunate; initial phase yellow, shading to green above anal fin, with a light red bar on each scale; head below level of mouth abruptly blue-green; terminal males with upper three-fourths of body green suffused with purple, the edges of the scales light red, the lower fourth blue-green; upper half of head purplish, the lower half deep blue-green. Reaches about 70 cm. Indo-Pacific. Based on colour there are three populations of this species: the Red Sea, the Indian Ocean (where the initial phase is mainly red) and the western and central Pacific (where the initial phase is dominantly green like the terminal males). The Pacific form was named *Scarus microrhinos* by Bleeker.

## 233 Bluebarred Parrotfish

*Scarus ghobban* Forsskål, 1775

Pectoral rays 15 or 16 (rarely 16); median predorsal scales usually 6; three rows of scales on cheek, the lowermost with 1 or 2 scales; lips covering more than half of dental plates; large adults with one to three (usually two) canines posteriorly on upper dental plate, none on lower; posterior nostril oval and large; caudal fin varying from slightly emarginate in small initial-phase fish to lunate on large terminal males; initial phase with centres of scales bluish, the edges pale orange-yellow; five narrow irregular blue bars on body; head yellowish, the lips salmon pink; terminal males green dorsally, the scales narrowly edged in salmon pink; side of body with progressively less green and more salmon ventrally; a faint blackish bar sometimes present in middle of body; head green dorsally, light orangish below, with a broad irregular band of green from corner of mouth across lower cheek; dental plates pale salmon. Attains at least 75 cm. Indo-Pacific. A common species which penetrates silty environments more readily than other scarids. Nineteen synonyms, of which the most recent is *S. fehlmanni* Schultz.

## 234 Rusty Parrotfish
*Scarus ferrugineus* Forsskål, 1775

Pectoral rays 15; median predorsal scales 6 or 7 (usually 6); three rows of scales on cheek, the lower row with 2 to 4 scales; lips covering two-thirds or more of dental plates; no canine teeth on dental plates of initial-phase fish, none to two on upper plate of terminal males; caudal fin of initial phase slightly rounded to truncate, of terminal males double emarginate; initial phase reddish brown to brown with dark brown bars, shading to yellow on caudal peduncle and fin; terminal males with posterior head and anterior body orangish yellow, the scale centres gradually becoming more blue-green in middle of body, the caudal peduncle largely green; edge of upper lip salmon pink; above this a very broad band of blue-green which joins a broader band on chin and passes to eye; dental plates of both phases blue-green; juveniles similar to initial phase. Reaches 41 cm. Red Sea and the Gulf of Aden. *S. aeruginosus* Cuvier and Valenciennes and *S. marshalli* Schultz are synonyms based on the initial and terminal phases, respectively.

## 235 Palenose Parrotfish
*Scarus psittacus* Forsskål, 1775

Pectoral rays 13 or 14 (usually 14); median predorsal scales usually 4; two rows of scales on cheek; lips covering three-fourths or more of dental plates; initial-phase fish usually with a canine on upper dental plate, and large terminal males usually with one lower and two upper canines; caudal fin of adults varying from slightly to deeply emarginate; initial phase reddish brown, shading to orange-red on chest and abdomen; snout paler than rest of head; a small black spot at upper base of pectoral fin, and a dark brown spot basally on first membrane of dorsal fin; terminal males with scales of body about half green and half salmon pink, the green forming four or five series of spots on side of caudal peduncle and three stripes on abdomen; head orangish suffused with green, with blue-green bands, the snout lavender-grey; dental plates of both phases white. A small species, but occasional individuals may reach 30 cm. Indo-Pacific. Ten synonyms, among them *S. taeniurus* Cuvier and Valenciennes, *S. venosus* Cuvier and Valenciennes, *S. forsteri* Cuvier and Valenciennes, and *Xanothon carifanus* Smith.

## 236 Bridled Parrotfish

*Scarus frenatus* Lacepède, 1802

Pectoral rays 14 or 15 (rarely 15); median predorsal scales 6 or 7 (usually 7); three rows of scales on cheek, the lower row with 2 to 4 (rarely 2) scales; lips covering three-fourths or more of dental plates; none to two canine teeth posteriorly on upper dental plate in both phases, none on lower; caudal fin of adults varying from truncate to deeply emarginate; initial phase brownish yellow to light reddish brown with five dark brown stripes on side of body following centres of scale rows; caudal peduncle pale reddish brown without stripes; fins light red; dental plates white; terminal males green on upper head and anterior two-thirds of body, with numerous small orange-red spots and irregular lines; posterior third of body solid green; a broad green stripe across head just below eye, dividing to a branch to front of snout and to two which cross chin; dental plates blue-green. Largest specimen examined, 47 cm. Indo-Pacific. *S. sexvittatus* Rüppell and *S. randalli* Schultz are synonyms based on the initial phase; *Callyodon vermiculatus* Fowler and Bean is a synonym described from the terminal male.

## 237 Greenband Parrotfish

*Scarus collana* Rüppell, 1835

Pectoral rays 13 to 15 (usually 14); median predorsal scales 4; two rows of scales on cheek; snout short, 2.25 to 2.6 in head, but somewhat acute; four-fifths or more of dental plates covered by lips; no canine teeth on side of dental plates but two to eight small canines posteriorly on margin of upper plates; caudal fin of initial phase emarginate, of large terminal males lunate; initial phase yellowish grey-brown, shading to pale red ventrally, with three indistinct whitish stripes on abdomen; terminal males light green, the anterior scales rimmed with light salmon pink, the posterior scales half salmon (on caudal peduncle the green and salmon form alternating stripes); head orangish with green bands radiating from eye, an anterior one broadening to cover most of front of snout. Largest specimen, 33 cm. Red Sea. The typical habitat is small coral heads or dead coral rock on silty sand. *S. ghardaqensis* Bebars is a synonym.

## 238 Purple-Brown Parrotfish

*Scarus fuscopurpureus* (Klunzinger), 1871

Pectoral rays 14 or 15 (usually 14); median predorsal scales 4; two rows of scales on cheek; about three-fourths of dental plates covered by lips; large initial-phase fish with two small canine teeth posteriorly on upper dental plate near margin, none on lower; terminal males with one lower and two upper canines; caudal fin varying from slightly rounded to truncate on small initial-phase fish to lunate on large terminal males; initial phase reddish to purplish brown, the scale centres sometimes dull greenish; a dull blue-green band at front of upper lip becoming submarginal to orange at side of lip and continuing to eye; chin orangish with two faint transverse blue-green bands; terminal males green, the scales edged in reddish anteriorly; posteriorly the green gradually diminishes to a single spot per scale; a pale pink or yellow near-vertical bar often present on side of body in line with first soft rays of dorsal and anal fins; head greenish suffused with salmon with essentially the same blue-green markings as on initial phase, but more pronounced; dental plates of both phases

white. Attains 38 cm. Red Sea. Closely related to the Indian Ocean species *S. russelii* Cuvier and Valenciennes.

## 239 Swarthy Parrotfish

*Scarus niger* Forsskål, 1775

Pectoral rays 13 to 15 (usually 14); median predorsal scales 6 to 8 (usually 7); three rows of scales on cheek, the lower row with 2 to 5 scales; three-fourths or more of dental plates covered by lips; usually no canines on upper dental plate of initial-phase fish (but there may be one or two) and usually two on upper dental plate of terminal males; caudal fin of initial phase slightly rounded, of terminal males double emarginate with lobes projecting; initial phase brownish red, the scales crossed with three to five horizontal dark brown lines (which may be broken to spots); head with irregular dark green bands on snout, chin, and extending anteriorly and posteriorly from eye; dental plates bluegreen; terminal males deep green, the scales edged dark reddish; green bands on head as in initial phase; a small yellow spot within a green band at upper end of gill opening; pectoral fins deep salmon pink; dental plates blue. Largest specimen examined, 39 cm. Indo-Pacific. In the Pacific the initial phase looks much like the terminal phase. *Pseudoscarus madagascariensis* Steindachner is a synonym based on the initial phase.

# **Butterflyfishes** (Chaetodontidae)

The butterflyfishes, another family of the Perciformes, are among the most colourful of reef fishes. They have deep, compressed bodies and small protractile mouths with brush-like teeth in the jaws (none on roof of mouth). The scales are ctenoid and cover the head, body and median fins. There is a single dorsal fin with VI to XVI stout spines and no notch between the spinous and soft portions; the membranes of the anterior spines are deeply incised; the anal fin has III to V stout spines; there is a scaly axillary process at the upper base of the pelvic fins; the caudal fin varies in shape from rounded to slightly emarginate. These fishes have a distinctive late post-larval stage called the tholichthys larva which has large bony plates on the head and anterior body. The family, in general, is diurnal; many of the species feed on the polyps of corals or other coelenterates. Other food items include algae, polychaete worms, crustaceans and tube-feet of sea urchins. Some species are primarily zooplankton-feeders. A few

form aggregations, but most are solitary or occur in pairs. Some have rather small territories on the reef whereas others wander over large areas. Fourteen butterflyfishes are known from the Red Sea of which seven are endemic (or range no farther than the Gulf of Aden).

## 240 Threadfin Butterflyfish

*Chaetodon auriga* Forsskål, 1775

Dorsal rays XIII,23 to 25, the fourth to sixth dorsal rays prolonged into a filament which may extend beyond caudal fin; anal rays III,19 to 22; lateral line ending beneath rear of dorsal fin (true of *Megaprotodon*, *Gonochaetodon*, and other species of *Chaetodon*); pectoral rays 15 to 17; snout moderately prolonged; caudal fin slightly rounded; white with two series of diagonal blackish lines at right angles, shading posteriorly to orange-yellow; a black bar through eye (very broad below eye); a black spot sometimes present posteriorly on dorsal fin. Reaches 20 cm. Indo-Pacific. Feeds on polychaete worms, coral polyps, and algae.

## 241 Striped Butterflyfish

*Chaetodon fasciatus* Forsskål, 1775

Dorsal rays XII,23 to 25; anal rays III,17 or 18; pectoral rays 15 or 16; snout slightly prolonged; caudal fin rounded; deep yellow-orange with 11 diagonal dark brown bands on body, a broad black bar through eye (ending at corner of preopercle) with a short broad diagonal white band above it extending to upper end of gill opening. Attains 22 cm. Red Sea and the Gulf of Aden. A very close relative of the Indo-Pacific *C. lunula* (Lacepède) which does not occur in the Red Sea. A hybrid of *C. fasciatus* and *C. auriga* was collected in the Gulf of Aqaba.

## 242 Lined Butterflyfish

*Chaetodon lineolatus* Cuvier and Valenciennes, 1831

Dorsal rays XII,25 to 27; anal rays III,20 to 22; pectoral rays 17 or 18; snout moderately prolonged, its length 2.3 to 2.6 in head; caudal fin rounded; white with vertical black lines on body; a broad diagonal black band beneath posterior half of dorsal fin, extending across caudal peduncle, narrowing and ending on anal fin base; a broad black bar through eye containing a middorsal white spot above eye; median fins largely yellow. The largest species of the genus; attains 30 cm. Indo-Pacific. Occurs in pairs or as solitary fish.

## 243 Blackback Butterflyfish

*Chaetodon melannotus* Bloch and Schneider, 1801

Dorsal rays XII,19 to 21; anal rays III,16 to 18; pectoral rays 15 or 16 (usually 15); snout relatively short, 2.9 to 3.4 in head; caudal fin slightly rounded; body white with diagonal blackish lines and a broad dorsal blackish area (larger at night and containing two whitish spots); caudal peduncle and basal three-fifths of fin yellow with a black bar on dorsal half of peduncle and a black spot below; anterior half of head yellow with a narrow black bar through eye, the yellow continuing as a narrow band ventrally on body; dorsal, anal, and pelvic fins yellow. Reaches 15 cm. East Africa to the Mariana Islands and Samoa. Not common in the Red Sea.

## 244 Exquisite Butterflyfish

*Chaetodon austriacus* Rüppell, 1836

Dorsal rays XIII,20 or 21; anal rays III,19 or 20; pectoral rays 14 or 15; oval-shaped, the depth of body 1.6 to 1.8 in standard length; snout short, 3.5 to 4.0 in head; caudal fin rounded; orange-yellow with dark lines (blackish dorsally, orangish ventrally) following longitudinal scale rows; two diagonal black bars on head; chin and upper lip black; dorsal fin whitish with a broad black submarginal band posteriorly; anal and caudal fins largely black. Reaches 14 cm. Red Sea. Feeds on coral polyps. One of a complex of three closely related species; the others *C. melapterus* Guichenot, which ranges from the Gulf of Aden to the Arabian Gulf (one site record in the southern Red Sea), and the Indo-Pacific *C. trifasciatus* Mungo Park.

## 245 Paleface Butterflyfish

*Chaetodon mesoleucos* Forsskål, 1775

Dorsal rays XIII,22 to 24; anal rays III,18 to 20; pectoral rays 15 or 16; snout protruding, its length 2.4 to 2.8 in head; caudal fin truncate with slightly rounded corners; head and anterior body pale grey with a faint blackish bar through eye; rest of body brown (bluish anteriorly) with about 15 black lines following vertical scale rows (the scale edges dark brown more posteriorly on body); caudal fin dark brown with a curved white band, which becomes yellow dorsally and ventrally, and a clear posterior border. Reaches 13 cm. Red Sea and the Gulf of Aden.

137

## 246 Crown Butterflyfish

*Chaetodon paucifasciatus* Ahl, 1923

Dorsal rays XIII,20 to 23; anal rays III,16 to 18; pectoral rays 14 to 16; snout not prolonged, its length 2.7 to 3.1 in head; caudal fin slightly rounded; whitish with chevron-like dark bars on anterior three-fourths of body, yellow spots dorsally between bars and black dots behind; posterior fourth of body orange-red, this colour extending broadly into rear part of dorsal fin and narrowly into anal fin; a white-edged orange-yellow bar through eye and a pale-edged black mark middorsally on nape; a spindle-shaped orange-red bar in caudal fin. Attains 14 cm. Red Sea. Related to the Indo-Pacific *C. mertensii* Cuvier and Valenciennes. Often seen in pairs or small groups. Feeds on the polyps of corals and gorgonians, worms, small crustaceans and algae.

## 247 Masked Butterflyfish

*Chaetodon semilarvatus* Cuvier and Valenciennes, 1831

Dorsal rays XII,25 to 27; anal rays III,20 to 22; pectoral rays 16; body very deep, the depth 1.3 to 1.5 in standard length; snout short, 2.9 to 3.4 in head; caudal fin slightly rounded; deep yellow with about 13 narrow orange bars on body following scale rows; a large bluish black spot posteroventrally on head, just enclosing eye. To about 23 cm. Red Sea and the Gulf of Aden. Usually seen in pairs, occasionally in small groups. Spends long periods during the day relatively immobile beneath coral ledges.

## 248 Chevron Butterflyfish

*Megaprotodon trifascialis* Quoy and Gaimard, 1825

Dorsal rays XIV (rarely XIII or XV), 14 to 16; anal rays IV (rarely V),13 to 15; pectoral rays 15; body relatively elongate, the depth 1.7 to 2.1 in standard length; snout not long, its length 2.9 to 3.4 in head; soft portions of dorsal and anal fins angular, the posterior edges nearly vertical when fins fully extended; caudal fin truncate to slightly rounded; whitish, a little dusky dorsally, with chevron-like, vertically oriented, blackish lines on body; a broad white-edged black bar on head enclosing eye; at night the dorsal part of the body becomes blackish with two elliptical white spots on upper side, one in front of the other; juveniles with a black bar posteriorly on body which extends broadly into rear part of dorsal and anal fins (see underwater photo in family account). Attains 17 cm. Indo-Pacific. Defends a relatively small territory of coral (often plate-like *Acropora*); feeds on the polyps (but without killing the coral). Sometimes classified in the genus *Chaetodon*. Often identified as *M. strigangulus* (Gmelin), but this name is invalid.

## 249 Orangeface Butterflyfish

*Gonochaetodon larvatus* (Cuvier and Valenciennes), 1831

Dorsal rays XI or XII (usually XI),24 to 27; anal rays III,21 or 22; pectoral rays 15 or 16; body very deep, the depth 1.3 to 1.45 in standard length; snout not long, its length 3.2 to 3.9 in head; soft portions of dorsal and anal fins very elevated, giving an overall triangular shape to the fish; caudal fin truncate to slightly rounded; head (except posterior part of operculum), nape and chest dark orange without a black bar through eye; rest of head and most of body bluish grey with chevron-shaped vertical yellow lines; caudal peduncle, posterior dorsal fin and most of caudal fin black. Attains 12 cm. Red Sea and the Gulf of Aden. Feeds principally on coral polyps; seems to maintain a territory of *Acropora* coral. Often seen in pairs. Some authors prefer to classify this fish in the genus *Chaetodon*.

## 250 Pennantfish
*Heniochus diphreutes* Jordan, 1903

Dorsal rays XII (rarely XIII),23 to 25, the fourth dorsal spine extremely elongate (often longer than standard length); anal rays III,17 to 19; pectoral rays 16 to 18; lateral line complete (true of other *Heniochus*); body very deep, the depth 1.2 to 1.4 in standard length; snout not long, its length 3.2 to 3.7 in head; caudal fin truncate; white with two broad black bands, one from front of dorsal fin to abdomen and pelvic fins and the other from middle of spinous portion of dorsal fin to rear of anal fin; snout and interorbital space largely blackish; caudal fin and posterior dorsal fin mainly yellow. Reaches 20 cm. Known from the Red Sea, Natal, Maldive Islands, western Australia, New South Wales, Japan and Hawaii (most localities subtropical to warm temperate). Usually seen in aggregations well above the substratum where it feeds on zooplankton; the author has observed it cleaning other fishes. Only recently distinguished from *H. acuminatus* (Linnaeus) which has XI dorsal spines, is more tropical in distribution (not known from the Red Sea) and is bottom-oriented.

## 251 Red Sea Bannerfish
*Heniochus intermedius* Steindachner, 1843

Dorsal rays XI,25 or 26, the fourth spine very elongate (sometimes longer than standard length); anal rays III,17 or 18; pectoral rays 15 or 16 (rarely 16); body deep, the depth 1.3 to 1.4 in standard length; snout somewhat prolonged, its length 2.5 to 3.3 in head; a bony tubercle developing in adults in front of upper edge of eye (each tubercle angling outward); caudal fin truncate to slightly rounded; colour basically the same as in *H. diphreutes*, but the first broad blackish band begins on the nape and passes over most of the operculum (only a diffuse part extending to front of dorsal fin); similarly, the second dark band extends only faintly into middle of dorsal fin. Attains about 20 cm. Red Sea and the Gulf of Aden. Unlike *H. diphreutes*, this species is closely tied to coral reefs and is a benthic feeder.

# Angelfishes (Pomacanthidae)

The angelfishes were once grouped with the butterflyfishes in the same family. They share a number of characteristics such as deep compressed bodies, ctenoid scales which extend well out onto the median fins, a single unnotched dorsal fin and a small mouth with brush-like teeth. They differ from butterflyfishes significantly, however, in having a long spine at the angle of the preopercle (as well as lesser spines on the preopercle, interopercle and preorbital); they lack a scaly axillary process at the base of the pelvic fins; the scales are more strongly ctenoid and have distinct ridges on the exposed part, and adults may have auxiliary scales; the postlarvae lack bony plates on the head and anterior body. The author has encountered seven pomacanthid fishes in the Red Sea, three in the genus *Pomacanthus* and one each in the genera *Holocanthus*, *Centropyge*, *Pygoplites* and *Genicanthus*. Angelfishes are diurnal; the species of *Pomacanthus*, *Holacanthus* and

*Pygoplites* feed mainly on sponges as adults; those of *Centropyge* are grazers on algae and detritus, and the species of *Genicanthus* feed principally on zooplankton. The young of *Pomacanthus* are very different in colour from adults.

141

## 252 Emperor Angelfish
*Pomacanthus imperator* (Bloch), 1787

Dorsal rays XIII or XIV (usually XIV),19 to 21; anal rays III,19 to 21; pectoral rays 19 or 20 (usually 20); lateral line complete; depth of body 1.6 to 1.8 in standard length; posterior margin of preopercle finely serrate; soft portion of anal fin rounded; middle soft rays of dorsal fin of large individuals produced into a filament; caudal fin rounded; body of adults with alternating slightly diagonal stripes of purple and yellow; throat, chest, anterior abdomen and a dorsal extension thereof, including pectoral base and gill opening, purplish black, this region edged with blue anteriorly; a blue-edged black band across interorbital, through eye to edge of preopercle; caudal fin yellow; juveniles deep blue (almost black), with numerous narrow blue and some broader white bands which are vertical anteriorly but progressively more curved posteriorly, one forming a complete circle anterior to caudal peduncle. Reaches 40 cm. Indo-Pacific. Usually found in outer coral reef areas.

## 253 Yellowbar Angelfish
*Pomacanthus maculosus* (Forsskål), 1775

Dorsal rays XII or XIII (usually XII),21 to 23; anal rays III,19 or 20; pectoral rays 18 to 20; lateral line complete; depth of body 1.6 to 1.8 in standard length; posterior margin of preopercle usually finely serrate, the ventral margin with a few small spines in addition to large one at angle; soft portion of dorsal and anal fins of adults elevated and angular, the middle rays produced into a long posteriorly directed filament (dorsal filament developing first); caudal fin rounded; adults blue with a broad irregular yellow bar in middle of body and some dark curved markings dorsoposteriorly on head and body; caudal fin irregularly marked with pale blue and yellow; juveniles deep purplish with slightly curved vertical bright blue and a few white lines, the latter broader; yellow bar developing at a length of about 5.5 cm. Reaches nearly 50 cm. Red Sea to the Arabian Gulf and south to Zanzibar. More often encountered on silty reefs in calm water than in well developed coralliferous areas.

142

# 254 Arabian Angelfish

*Pomacanthus asfur* (Forsskål), 1775

Dorsal rays XII,19 to 21; anal rays III,18 or 19; pectoral rays 17 or 18 (usually 17); lateral line complete; depth of body 1.5 to 1.7 in standard length; posterior margin of preopercle usually finely serrate (serrae may be largely absent in large individuals), the ventral margin with a few small spines; preorbital serrate; soft portions of dorsal fins prolonged into long filaments that extend posterior to caudal fin (except juveniles); pelvic fins very long; caudal fin rounded; head black; anterior body, including chest and nape deep blue, the edges of the scales narrowly black; a broad yellow bar on body centred above anus, extending into dorsal fin between bases of sixth to about the twelfth spines; body posterior to yellow bar bluish black; posterior caudal peduncle and caudal fin bright yellow, the posterior margin narrowly white with a narrow black submarginal line; juveniles coloured like those of *P. maculosus*. Reaches about 35 cm. Red Sea and the Gulf of Aden; one record from Zanzibar.

# 255 Multispine Angelfish

*Centropyge multispinis* (Playfair and Günther), 1867

Dorsal rays XIII to XV (usually XIV),15 to 17; anal rays III,17 or 18; pectoral rays 15 to 17 (rarely 15); lateral line ending beneath soft portion of dorsal fin; depth of body 1.75 to 2.0 in standard length; margin of preopercle coarsely serrate, the ventral edge with one to a few small spines in addition to a very large one at angle; preorbital, subopercle, and interopercle coarsely serrate; soft portions of dorsal and anal fins rounded; caudal fin rounded; yellowish brown to brown with irregular vertical dark brown lines on body and a large deep blue and black spot just behind upper end of gill opening; median fins dark brown with pale blue distal margins; pelvic fins dark brown, the first ray streaked with blue. Reaches 12 cm. Indian Ocean.

143

## 256 Yellow-Ear Angelfish

*Holacanthus xanthotis* Fraser-Brunner, 1950

Dorsal rays XIV,17 to 19; anal rays III,17 or 18; pectoral rays 16 or 17; depth of body 1.5 to 1.7 in standard length; lateral line ending beneath soft portion of dorsal fin; posterior margin of preopercle finely serrate, the ventral margin with a few small spines; pre-orbital serrate; soft portions of dorsal and anal fins rounded; caudal fin slightly rounded, the uppermost branched ray of adults prolonged; large central region of body pale yellowish grey, the edges of the scales narrowly blackish; head and anterior body dark brown to black; a bright yellow spot about as large as pupil above upper end of gill opening; edge of large spine at corner of preopercle blue; black on posterior part of body (caudal peduncle and small region anterior to it), a band along back, dorsal fin except margin, and anal fin except base and a narrow margin; margin of dorsal fin white, of anal fin blue; caudal fin bright yellow. Reaches about 20 cm. Red Sea and the Gulf of Aden. Closely related to the Indian Ocean *H. xanthurus* Bennett. Often classified in *Apolemichthys*.

## 257 Royal Angelfish

*Pygoplites diacanthus* (Boddaert), 1772

Dorsal rays XIV,17 to 19; anal rays III,17 to 19; pectoral rays 16 or 17 (usually 17); lateral line ending beneath soft portion of dorsal fin; depth of body 1.7 to 2.1 in standard length; posterior margin of preopercle serrate, the ventral margin with a few small spines; pre-orbital with a few serrae; soft portion of dorsal and anal fins rounded; caudal fin rounded; orange with eight black-edged blue to bluish white bars on body, the dorsal ends of which narrow and angle posteriorly into dorsal fin; most of soft portion of dorsal fin deep purple; a blue-edged black bar above eye; posterior margin of preopercle, and opercle and preopercular spine blue; anal fin striped with orange-red and blue; caudal and paired fins yellow; juveniles similar in colour to adults, differing chiefly in having a large deep blue ocellus in soft portion of dorsal fin. Attains 25 cm. Indo-Pacific.

## 258 Zebra Angelfish
*Genicanthus caudovittatus* (Günther), 1860

Dorsal rays XIV,15 to 17; anal rays III,17 to 19; pectoral rays 16; lateral line complete, but descending portion beneath soft dorsal fin poorly developed; depth of body 2.0 to 2.25 in standard length; teeth short, their length contained about 5 times in eye diameter of adults (compared to 2 to 3 times in *Holacanthus*); posterior margin of preopercle serrate, the ventral edge with a few small spines; preorbital strongly serrate and notched; soft portions of dorsal and anal fins angular; caudal fin lunate, the lobes of males greatly prolonged; females pale lavender-grey, the edges of the scales darker than centres, with a diagonal dark bar above eye and submarginal black bands in caudal fin lobes, the upper continuing to below base of soft portion of dorsal fin; males bluish white, the upper head and body with numerous dark brown bars; a black spot midventrally on chest; a large black area centrobasally in dorsal fin, the rest of spinous portion largely yellow; soft portion, caudal, and anal fins light bluish grey with small yellow spots. Reaches 25 cm. Western Indian Ocean, generally at depths greater than 35 m. Males develop as a result of sex change of females.

# Surgeonfishes (Acanthuridae)

Along with the Zanclidae and Siganidae, the surgeonfishes constitute the suborder Acanthuroidei of the order Perciformes. They are readily distinguished by their possession of one or more spines or tubercles laterally on the caudal peduncle. They have deep compressed bodies; the eye is high on the head and the small nonprotractile mouth low (the preorbital bone is very deep); the teeth in the jaws are in one row, usually denticulate on the edges; the scales are small and ctenoid; the lateral line is complete; the dorsal fin has IV to IX spines with no notch between spinous and soft portions; the digestive tract is long; the species of *Ctenochaetus* and some *Acanthurus* have a thick gizzard-like stomach. The family is divisible into three subfamilies, two of which are represented by species in the Red Sea: the Acanthurinae (includes the genera *Acanthurus*, *Ctenochaetus*, and *Zebrasoma*) and the Nasinae (genus *Naso*). The species of Acanthurinae (sometimes called tangs) have a single sharp spine on the side of the peduncle which is hinged near the back and folds into a groove; they have III anal spines and I,5 pelvic rays. The species of *Naso* (called unicornfishes though not all have a horn on the forehead) have one or two (usually two) fixed bony plates on the peduncle which develop a sharp keel with age; their anal fin has II spines and the pelvic rays are I,3. The surgeonfishes are able to slash other fishes (or humans who do not handle them carefully) with their sharp caudal spines by a side sweep of the tail. With this damaging capability they are able to ensure dominance over many other reef fishes. Some species have bright hues on or around the caudal spines to serve as warning colouration. Most of the species graze on benthic algae, but a few are zooplankton-feeders, and those of the genus *Ctenochaetus* are detritus-feeders. At night they sleep in the reef. The late postlarval stage (termed the 'acronurus' for the Acanthurinae) is orbicular with vertical ridges on the body (no scales) and transparent except for the abdomen which is silvery; at night it can be dipnetted using a light at the surface. The author has observed and collected 11 species of surgeonfishes in the Red Sea. All are discussed below except *Acanthurus bleekeri* Günther which was seen only in the south (underwater photo shows four being cleaned by juvenile *Thalassoma lunare*).

146

## 259 Sailfin Surgeonfish

*Zebrasoma veliferum* (Bloch), 1797

Dorsal rays IV,27 to 31; anal rays III,22 to 24; pectoral rays 15 to 17; teeth spatulate, denticulate, close-set, up to 16 in upper jaw and 18 in lower; body deep, the depth 1.8 to 2.0 in standard length; snout produced; dorsal and anal fins extremely elevated, the longest dorsal ray 2.1 to 2.5 in standard length; caudal fin truncate to slightly rounded; light grey-brown with brown bars on head and body, the body with vertical yellow lines giving way to small yellow spots ventrally; head and chest with small whitish spots; juveniles with alternating bars of yellow and white on body, a broad black bar across caudal peduncle, a narrower one in front of it, and two black bars on head (see underwater photo in family account). Attains 40 cm. Indo-Pacific. In the Pacific this species has more dorsal rays (29 to 33) and anal rays (23 to 26), and the colour is a little different. Some

authors prefer to regard the Indian Ocean-Red Sea form as a distinct species, *Z. desjardinii* (Bennett).

## 260 Yellowtail Surgeonfish

*Zebrasoma xanthurum* (Blyth), 1852

Dorsal rays V,24 or 25; anal rays III,19 or 20; pectoral rays 15; teeth spatulate, close-set, denticulate, up to 20 in upper jaw and 22 in lower; adults with a velvet-like path of setae in front of caudal spine; body deep, the depth 1.7 to 1.85 in standard length; snout produced; dorsal and anal fins moderately elevated, the longest dorsal ray 3.4 to 3.7 in standard length; caudal fin slightly rounded; blue with dark dots on head, anterior body and abdomen; caudal fin and posterior part of pectoral fins bright yellow. Largest specimen, 22 cm. Red Sea to the Arabian Gulf. The type locality was given as Ceylon, but this is probably an error.

## 261 Black Surgeonfish

*Acanthurus nigricans* (Linnaeus), 1758

Dorsal rays IX,25 or 26; anal rays III,23 to 25; pectoral rays 16 or 17; teeth spatulate, denticulate, close-set, up to 20 in upper jaw and 22 in lower; depth of body 1.75 (in juveniles) to 2.3 (in large adults) in standard length; a gizzard-like stomach; caudal fin of juveniles emarginate, of adults lunate; adults dark brown with a horizontal black band above upper end of gill opening (extending much more posteriorly than anteriorly); a white bar at base of caudal fin; distal part of pectoral fin yellowish; juveniles lack the dark band on the shoulder. Reaches at least 40 cm. Red Sea and the Gulf of Aden. *A. gahhm* (Forsskål) is a synonym. Not to be confused with the Indo-Pacific *A. nigricauda* Duncker and Mohr which does not occur in the Red Sea; it has a dark band

on the shoulder but also a black line extending anteriorly from the caudal spine.

## 262 Brown Surgeonfish

*Acanthurus nigrofuscus* (Forsskål), 1775

Dorsal rays IX,24 to 27; anal rays III,22 to 24; pectoral rays 16 or 17; teeth spatulate, denticulate, close-set, up to 14 in upper jaw and 16 in lower; depth of body 1.9 to 2.3 in standard length; caudal fin lunate; yellowish brown with pale blue dots on scales of body forming fine irregular longitudinal lines; head and chest with small yellow-orange spots; lips blackish; a black spot at rear base of dorsal and anal fins; caudal fin with a narrow white margin and black submarginal line. Maximum length, 21 cm. Indo-Pacific.

# 263 Sohal

*Acanthurus sohal* (Forsskål), 1775

Dorsal rays IX,30 or 31; anal rays III,28 or 29 (usually 29); pectoral rays 17; teeth spatulate, denticulate, close-set, up to 16 in upper jaw and 18 in lower; depth of body 2.0 to 2.2 in standard length; caudal spine very large, its length about 2 in head; caudal fin very lunate; pale grey, whitish ventrally, with narrow blackish stripes on head above level of lower edge of eye and along side of body (stripes very narrow and faint below eye and on back); a patch of orange beneath pectoral fins; sheath and socket of caudal spine bright orange; median and pelvic fins blackish with blue margins. Attains

40 cm. Red Sea to the Arabian Gulf. The typical habitat is outer edge of reef flats exposed to surge. A very aggressive territorial species.

# 264 Lined Bristletooth

*Ctenochaetus striatus* (Quoy and Gaimard), 1825

Dorsal rays VIII,27 to 31; anal rays III,24 to 28; pectoral rays 16 or 17; teeth elongate, flexible, the tips expanded and incurved with denticulations on the lateral edge (six on upper teeth and four on lower), and numerous (up to 45 in upper jaw and 52 in lower); depth of body 1.9 to 2.3 in standard length; caudal fin lunate; dark olive brown with numerous fine pale blue longitudinal lines on body; head and nape with small orange spots; a small black spot at rear base of dorsal fin; pectoral fins with brownish yellow rays and clear membranes. Largest specimen, 26 cm. A common Indo-Pacific species.

# 265 Orangespine Unicornfish

*Naso lituratus* (Bloch and Schneider), 1801

Dorsal rays VI,28 to 30; anal rays II,28 to 30; pectoral rays 16 or 17; teeth of juveniles pointed, compressed, with serrate edges, of adults smooth-edged incisors with rounded tips, about 30 to 35 in jaws; depth of body 1.9 to 2.4 in standard length; no rostral prominence on forehead; caudal spines large, forward-curved; caudal fin lunate, the large males developing a long filament from each lobe; grey-brown with a narrow curved yellow band from corner of mouth to eye, snout in front of yellow band black; a yellow area behind and above eye; lower lip and edge of upper lip orange; caudal spines and an area around each bright orange; dorsal fin yellow with a broad black band at base; anal fin orange-brown; caudal fin grey-brown with narrow black upper and lower margins and a broad black posterior submarginal band. Reaches 45 cm. Indo-Pacific. In the Pacific this species

has a broader black basal part of the dorsal fin and the outer part is white instead of yellow; the anal fin is orange, and the caudal peduncle has a yellow posterior border without a submarginal black band. Some authors have classified *lituratus* in the genus *Callicanthus*.

149

## 266 Bluespine Unicornfish

*Naso unicornis* (Forsskål), 1775

Dorsal rays VI,27 to 30; anal rays II,27 to 30; pectoral rays 17 or 18; teeth pointed, compressed, with fine serrae on edges (may disappear with age), 50 to 60 in jaws of adults; depth of body 1.8 to 2.5 in standard length (younger individuals deeper bodied); adults with a bony prominence projecting anteriorly from in front of eyes but not projecting anterior to mouth; dorsal profile of snout to base of horn forming an angle of about 45°; caudal spines large, forward-curved; caudal fin slightly emarginate in young, the adults developing a long filament from each lobe; light olive to yellowish grey, the caudal spines and a small area around each blue; dorsal and anal fins with alternating narrow bands of light blue and brownish yellow. Largest collected by author, 70 cm. Indo-Pacific.

Will penetrate very shallow water in the quest for benthic algae. This and the preceding species feed mainly on leafy algae such as *Sargassum*.

## 267 Sleek Unicornfish

*Naso hexacanthus* (Bleeker), 1855

Dorsal rays VI,27 to 29; anal rays II,28 to 30; pectoral rays 17 or 18 (usually 17); teeth pointed, compressed, finely serrate on edges, up to 60 or more in jaws of large adults; body somewhat elongate, the depth 2.6 to 3.0 in standard length (the adults more elongate); no rostral prominence on forehead; caudal spines of young weakly keeled, only the large adults develop large forward-projecting spines; caudal fin slightly emarginate to truncate; grey-brown, shading to yellowish ventrally (in life the colour can vary from dark brown to pale blue); opercular membrane dark brown. Attains about 75 cm. Indo-Pacific. Not common in less

than 15 to 20 m; often seen in aggregations near drop-offs to deep water. Feeds on the larger animals of the zooplankton.

## 268 Spotted Unicornfish

*Naso brevirostris* (Cuvier and Valenciennes), 1835

Dorsal rays VI,27 to 29; anal rays II,27 to 30; pectoral rays 15 or 16 (usually 16); teeth pointed, the edges finely serrate, about 50 in jaws; depth of body 2.4 to 2.7 in standard length; adults with a long bony projection anterior to eyes extending well in front of mouth; dorsal profile of snout to base of horn nearly vertical; caudal spines slow to develop and not as large as the preceding three species; caudal fin truncate to slightly rounded; brownish grey, darker dorsally, with a bluish cast; numerous small dark brown spots on head and body (more evident ventrally); caudal fin whitish. Reaches 60 cm. Indo-Pacific. Juveniles and subadults (without long horns) feed on

benthic algae; adults feed mainly on zooplankton.

# Rabbitfishes (Siganidae)

The rabbitfishes are unique in having pelvic fins which consist of a spine at each end and three soft rays between. All members of the family have XIII,10 dorsal rays (in addition, an anterior recumbent spine which is largely or completely embedded) and VII,9 anal rays. The spines are venomous; wounds inflicted by them are very painful though not as serious as those from the spines of some of the scorpionfishes. The venom glands lie in the outer third of an anterolateral groove on each side of the spines. The body of siganids is ovate and compressed, the caudal peduncle narrow, without spines; the caudal fin varies in shape from truncate to deeply forked. The mouth is small, somewhat ventral, and not protractile; the upper lip is notably broader than the lower; the teeth are small, incisiform, bicuspid or tricuspid, and in one series. The skin is smooth, the scales minute and cycloid; the lateral line is complete. The digestive tract is long. These fishes are diurnal and primarily herbivorous, feeding on a wide variety of benthic plants, but some may ingest sessile animals such as sponges or tunicates. Certain species are usually seen in small schools; these tend to range over algal flats or seagrass beds. They are very changeable in colouration and may rapidly assume a mottled pattern when they come to rest on the bottom. Other species are often encountered in pairs; these are more apt to be found on coral reefs. There are 26 species in the family, all in the Indo-Pacific region and all in the genus *Siganus*. Four occur in the Red Sea.

## 269 Rivulated Rabbitfish

*Siganus rivulatus* (Forsskål), 1775

Pectoral rays 16 or 17 (usually 16); a few scales on cheek; depth of body 2.5 to 3.2 in standard length; dorsal spines not long, the longest 1.9 to 2.1 in head; last dorsal spine short, its length contained about 2 times in first dorsal soft rays; caudal fin emarginate; greenish grey dorsally, shading to whitish ventrally, with irregular narrow yellow stripes (these more evident on pale ventral half of body); opercular membrane dark brown; can rapidly assume a dark mottled pattern with scattered small blackish spots. Reaches 30 cm. Red Sea; has moved to the Mediterranean Sea via the Suez Canal. An inshore fish

often seen in schools of 100 or more; feeds on benthic algae. Spawning occurs during or near new moon from June to December; eggs are very small, heavier than seawater, and adhesive.

## 270 Forktail Rabbitfish

*Siganus argenteus* (Quoy and Gaimard), 1825

Pectoral rays 18 (rarely 17 or 19); no scales on cheek; body moderately elongate, the depth 2.3 to 3.0 in standard length; head somewhat pointed; dorsal spines short, the longest 2.0 to 2.3 in head; last dorsal spine very short, its length 2.5 to 2.7 in first dorsal soft ray; caudal fin deeply forked; bluish grey to brown with numerous small yellow spots (sometimes joined to form lengthwise lines) which are usually larger than spaces between spots; opercular membrane dark brown. The night pattern(of sleeping fish) is light brown broadly marked in diagonal zones of dark brown. Largest specimen examined, 37 cm. Indo-Pacific. Usually seen in small aggre-

gations. Spawning in the Red Sea occurs on or near new moon in July and August; the eggs are pelagic.

## 271 Squaretail Rabbitfish

*Siganus luridus* (Rüppell), 1829

Pectoral rays 16 or 17 (usually 17); scales on cheek; depth of body of adults 2.2 to 2.8 in standard length; head not pointed; dorsal spines long, the longest about 1.3 to 1.4 in head; last dorsal spine 1.2 to 1.3 in length of first dorsal soft ray; caudal fin truncate (slightly rounded when fully spread); greyish brown to whitish below (the upper half of body often abruptly darker than the lower) with numerous small whitish spots and short irregular lines; sometimes four large dark blotches along side of body; can assume a colour pattern of dark brown with short white lines set at various angles, mostly on upper half of body (in addition to whitish spots and irregular lines). Reaches 25 cm. Red Sea to Mozambique, Réunion and

Mauritius; has migrated through the Suez Canal to the Mediterranean Sea. A shallow water species which feeds on benthic algae. May be solitary but more often seen in small groups. Spawns in the Red Sea from May to August, the eggs very small, heavier than seawater, and adhesive.

## 272 Stellate Rabbitfish

*Siganus stellatus* (Forsskål), 1775

Pectoral rays 16 or 17 (usually 16); scales on cheek; depth of body of adults 2.0 to 2.3 in standard length; head not pointed; longest dorsal spines 1.8 to 1.9 in head; last dorsal spine relatively long, 1.1 to 1.2 in first dorsal soft ray; caudal fin deeply forked; light grey with numerous small close-set dark brown spots on head, body, and fins; a dull yellow region without spots on nape and back below anterior part of dorsal fin; posterior edge of dorsal and anal fins, dorsal edge of caudal peduncle and margins of caudal fin yellow (broad on dorsal and centroposteriorly on caudal fin). Attains 35 cm. Indian Ocean. Outside the Red Sea this fish is fully spotted over the nape and

dorsoanteriorly on the body, and the yellow on the caudal peduncle and dorsal and caudal fins is whitish. Usually seen in pairs.

# Blennies (Blenniidae)

The blennies are a large family (over 300 species) of small, agile, bottom-dwelling fishes. They are classified in the perciform suborder Blennioidei, along with the Clinidae (scaled blennies), and a few other small families. Their pelvic fins are distinctly anterior to the pectorals, and the number of rays is reduced from the usual I,5 of most perciform fishes to I,2 to I,4 (pelvic fins lost in adult of one species of *Plagiotremus*); these fishes are scaleless and often blunt-headed; they have a single dorsal fin with from III to XVII flexible spines; there may be a deep notch between the spinous and soft portions of the fin, and the last dorsal ray is often connected by a membrane to the caudal fin; all have II anal spines (though one or both may be embedded in females and easily overlooked) which in males may be capped by fleshy tissue believed to secrete an attracting substance at spawning time; the soft rays of the fins are simple except for some species with branched caudal rays; many blennies have tentacles or cirri over the eye,

anterior nostril or on the nape; the mouth is low on the head, the teeth usually numerous, slender, and close-set. One subfamily, the sabretooth blennies, have a pair of enormous curved canine teeth in the lower jaw which are used for defence (these two teeth are venomous in *Meiacanthus*). Many blenniid species, such as those of the genus *Istiblennius*, live inshore on rocky substrata; some are adapted to the surf-swept intertidal zone; they are able to leap from one pool to another (hence the common name rockskipper). The majority of tropical blennies are herbivorous. Those for which reproductive habits are known lay demersal eggs which are guarded by the male parent. Approximately 40 species of Blenniidae occur in the Red Sea of which 16 representatives often seen inshore or on reefs are discussed below. The related family Tripterygiidae is represented by 11 very small benthic species in the Red Sea (hence rarely noticed by snorkelers or divers); they are unique in having three dorsal fins.

## 273 Chestnut Blenny

*Cirripectes castaneus*
Cuvier and Valenciennes, 1836

Dorsal rays XII,13 to 15 (rarely 13 or 15); anal rays II,14 to 16 (rarely 14 or 16); pectoral rays 15 or 16 (rarely 16), the lower rays thickened; body relatively deep, the depth 2.8 to 3.2 in standard length; a branched tentacle over each eye; a transverse band of cirri on nape (15 to 23 cirri on each side); no crest on head; margin of upper lip crenulate; teeth incisiform, flexible in jaws, and numerous (about half as many in lower as upper jaw); a canine posteriorly on each side of lower jaw; caudal fin slightly rounded; females grey-brown with a dark orangish brown reticular pattern on

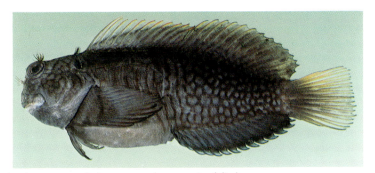

body except abdomen and on postorbital head; males light brown on head and about anterior third of body with narrow dark orangish bars (four on head, slightly diagonal, and about four on body), the posterior two-thirds of body dark brown. Attains 10 cm. East Africa to the western Pacific [east to Belau Islands and Tonga].

## 274 Shortbodied Blenny

*Exallias brevis* (Kner), 1868

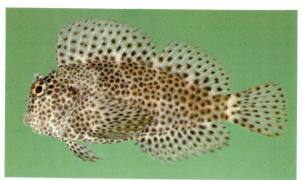

Dorsal rays XII,12 or 13 (usually 13), the fin deeply notched between spinous and soft portions; anal rays II,13 or 14; pectoral rays 14, the lower rays thickened; body relatively deep, the depth 2.6 to 2.8 in standard length; a branched tentacle over each eye; a transverse band of cirri across nape; a pair of tiny barbels on chin; no fleshy crest on head; edge of upper lip with a series of papillae; lower lip a series of fleshy ridges; teeth incisiform, very numerous, those in upper jaw movable, those in lower jaw nearly fixed; no canine teeth; caudal fin slightly rounded; whitish with numerous dark spots which tend to form clumps on body (the spots of females dark brown, those posteriorly on males orange-red; modified anal spines of males deep blue). Largest specimen examined, 14.5 cm (but none nearly this large seen in Red Sea). Indo-Pacific. Feeds on coral polyps.

## 275 Rockskipper

*Istiblennius edentulus* (Bloch and Schneider), 1801

Dorsal rays XIII,19 to 21, the fin deeply notched between spinous and soft portions; anal rays II,21 to 23; pectoral rays 14, the lower rays thickened; depth of body 3.6 to 5.0 in standard length; supraorbital tentacle slender, unbranched, its length more than half eye diameter; a single cirrus on each side of nape; males with a well-developed median dorsal crest posteriorly on head; margins of lips smooth; incisiform teeth in jaws slender, flexible and very numerous; no inner posterior canine in lower jaw; caudal fin rounded; olivaceous, often with six or seven dark double bars on body. Reaches 17 cm. Indo-Pacific. A common species; found along rocky shores.

## 276 Red-Dotted Blenny

*Istiblennius periophthalmus* (Cuvier and Valenciennes), 1836

Dorsal rays XIII,19 to 21, the fin deeply notched between spinous and soft portions, the first spine as long as the second; anal rays II,20 to 22; pectoral rays 14, the lower rays only slightly thickened; depth of body 4.2 to 6.0 in standard length; supraorbital tentacle unbranched, its length more than half eye diameter; a single cirrus on each side of nape; no crest on head (large males with a low middorsal ridge); margin of upper lip crenulate; incisiform teeth in jaws slender, flexible and very numerous, the lower jaw with a posterior inner canine on each side; caudal fin slightly rounded; white with seven faint dark bars on body which bifurcate on ventral half; two longitudinal rows of small, oblong dark-edged pale blue spots on side of body (spots within dark bars); numerous orange-red dots on head, anteriorly on body and dorsal fin, becoming black posteriorly on body; a dark blue spot dorsally on opercle; a diagonal orange-red line passing through posterior part of eye and another just behind eye. Reported to 15 cm (but does not approach this size in the Red Sea). Indo-Pacific; in Oceania where the colour is different (red and black dots are lacking), it has been called *I. paulus* (Bryan and Herre). A common reef flat species which quickly hides in a small hole when approached.

## 277 Leaping Blenny

*Alticus kirkii* (Günther), 1868

Dorsal rays XVI or XVII,20 to 22, the fin much higher in males and more conspicuously notched; anal rays II,25 to 27; pectoral rays 14, the lower rays thickened; lateral-line pores small and difficult to detect; body elongate, the depth 5.5 to 7.2 in standard length; supraorbital tentacle small, simple or with a few branches; no cirri on nape; a median crest on head, commencing in interorbital space, better developed on males (often pointed posteriorly); margin of upper lip crenulate; mouth ventral, the teeth incisiform, slender, flexible, and very numerous, no canines; a few small

teeth on vomer; caudal fin rounded; brown to tan with double dark bars which join dorsally; dorsal fin with alternating diagonal lines of dark brown and pale tan; anal fin with a narrow black submarginal band, the tips of the rays whitish. Reaches 9 cm. Western Indian Ocean. Occurs on rocky shores, often out of water; has phenomenal leaping ability.

## 278 Jewelled Blenny

*Salarias fasciatus* (Bloch), 1786

Dorsal rays XII,18 to 20, the fin without a notch (though the soft rays may be a little higher than the last few spines); anal rays II,19 to 21, the three anterior rays of males often elongate; pectoral rays 14, the lower rays slightly thickened; depth of body 2.8 to 4.2 in standard length, the abdomen frequently distended; supraorbital tentacle and nuchal cirrus with several branches; no crest on head; margins of lips smooth; teeth incisiform, slender, flexible, and very numerous; males with a small inner posterior canine tooth; caudal fin rounded; olivaceous to brown with dark bars, the abdomen whitish; numerous, round to oblong, dark-edged, white to pale blue

spots on head and body; some small, dark-edged, bright blue spots, particularly dorsoposteriorly on body; dark brown dots and lines may be present dorsoanteriorly on body. Attains 14 cm. East Africa to Samoa and the Mariana Islands. Often encountered on reef flats, particularly with heavy algal cover, generally in 0.5 to 3 m.

## 279 Smoothfin Blenny

*Escenius frontalis* (Cuvier and Valenciennes), 1836

Dorsal rays XI to XIII (usually XII),17 to 21, the fin without a notch; anal rays II,18 to 21; pectoral rays 14 to 16 (usually 15), the lower rays of this and other *Ecsenius* not thickened; segmented caudal rays 13 (rarely 14); anterior profile of head convex, the snout overhanging mouth; a cirrus at hind edge of anterior nostril, none over eye or on nape (true of all *Ecsenius*); no crest on head (same for all *Ecsenius*); margins of lips smooth (also true of all *Ecsenius*); teeth in jaws incisiform, slender, flexible, and very numerous, usually with an inner canine posteriorly in lower jaw; caudal fin rounded; apparently a polymorphic species with three colour forms: one is bluish on the head and anterior body, shading to orange-yellow posteriorly and on caudal fin; the second is dark brown

to black with a white caudal fin (this form described as *E. albicaudatus* by Lotan); the third is brown with a pale-edged black stripe dorsally on body (named *Salarias nigrovittatus* by Rüppell). Attains 8 cm. Red Sea and the Gulf of Aden (the *nigrovittatus* form only in the southern Red Sea and the Gulf of Aden).

## 280 Midas Blenny

*Ecsenius midas* Starck, 1969

Dorsal rays XIII or XIV (usually XIII),18 to 21, the fin without a notch; anal rays II,21 to 23; pectoral rays 13; segmented caudal rays 13 to 15 (usually 14); body relatively elongate, the depth about 5 in standard length (3.8 to 4.6 for other *Ecsenius* herein); anterior profile of head convex, the snout overhanging mouth; teeth incisiform, slender, fixed in jaws, and not numerous (26 to 34 in upper jaw compared to 105 to 148 in other *Ecsenius*; 13 to 18 in lower jaw compared to 30 to 64 for other *Ecsenius*); a large recurved canine tooth at posterior end of row of incisiform teeth on each side of lower jaw; caudal fin lunate; two common colour forms, one orange-yellow, the other dark bluish grey, both with a large black spot around and in front of anus. To 13 cm. Indo-Pacific. Occurs to at least 30 m. The yellow phase often observed schooling above coral reefs with *Anthias squamipinnis* which it resembles in colour. Reported to feed on zooplankton.

## 281 Nalolo

*Ecsenius nalolo* Smith, 1959

Dorsal rays XII (rarely XIII),13 or 14, the fin deeply notched between spinous and soft portions; anal rays II,14 to 17 (usually 15 or 16); pectoral rays 12 or 13 (rarely 12); segmented caudal rays 12 to 14 (usually 13); anterior profile of head convex, the snout overhanging mouth; teeth incisiform, slender, flexible, and very numerous, usually with an inner canine posteriorly on each side of lower jaw; caudal fin truncate; light brown with diffuse white spots about the size of pupil or a little larger, becoming white on abdomen; a small black spot behind eye followed by a black line which extends to upper end of gill opening; a diagonal black line from chin to operculum; a wavy, near-horizontal, black line at pectoral base; cheek with yellow dots. Attains 6.5 cm. Western Indian Ocean.

## 282 Aron's Blenny

*Ecsenius aroni* Springer, 1971

Dorsal rays XIII (rarely XII),17 or 18, the fin deeply notched between spinous and soft portions; anal rays II,19 or 20; pectoral rays 14 (rarely 15); segmented caudal rays 13; anterior profile of head convex, the snout overhanging mouth; teeth incisiform, slender, flexible, and very numerous, with an inner canine posteriorly on each side of lower jaw; caudal fin truncate, the third and eleventh segmented rays prolonged as filaments; yellowish brown, becoming whitish ventrally on head and abdomen, with a vertically elongate black spot at base of caudal fin; often an orange-yellow line along base of dorsal fin. A small species; reaches only 5.5 cm. Red Sea. More secretive and deeper-dwelling (to at least 35 m) than most other *Ecsenius*.

## 283 Red Sea Mimic Blenny

*Ecsenius gravieri* (Pellegrin), 1906

Dorsal rays XII to XIV (usually XIII),16 to 18 (rarely 16), notched between spinous and soft portions; anal rays II,18 to 21 (usually 19 or 20); pectoral rays 14 or 15 (usually 14); segmented caudal rays 13; anterior profile of head convex, the snout overhanging mouth; teeth incisiform, slender, flexible and very numerous, usually with an inner canine tooth posteriorly on each side of lower jaw; caudal fin truncate, the third and eleventh segmented rays prolonged as filaments; blue on head and anteriorly on body, shading to light yellow posteriorly, with a horizontal black line from eye, across head and along upper side of body, breaking into spots and/or dashes posteriorly; a longitudinal series of blackish spots, one per membrane, in about middle of spinous portion of dorsal fin; dorsal and ventral edges of caudal fin dusky. Reaches 8 cm. Red Sea to the Gulf of Aden. A mimic of *Meiacanthus nigrolineatus* Smith-Vaniz, a sabretooth blenny with venomous fangs. The mimic not only closely matches the model in colour but has adopted the same mode of swimming just off the bottom. In the southern Red Sea the model is less colourful; the mimic there is the same colour. A second Red Sea mimicking blenny of *M. nigrolineatus*, *Plagiotremus townsendi* (Regan), is not as impressive due to its more slender body, imperfect colour and behaviour.

## 284 Blackline Blenny

*Meiacanthus nigrolineatus* Smith-Vaniz, 1969

Dorsal rays IV or V (rarely V),23 to 26 (usually 25), the fin not notched; anal rays II,14 to 16; pectoral rays 26 to 28; segmented caudal rays 11 to 13 (rarely 13); depth of body 3.7 to 4.3 in standard length; dorsal profile of snout evenly convex, rising above mouth initially at an angle of about 60° (hence not anterior to mouth); a very large recurved canine tooth on each side of lower jaw, these teeth with a deep groove on their anterior surface and a venom gland at their base; jaws otherwise with 14 to 23 narrow, slightly flexible, incisiform teeth; caudal fin emarginate to lunate; head and anterior body bluish, the head and chest with pale blue dots, shading posteriorly to light yellow with a black line from eye to upper caudal base (broken into spots or dashes posteriorly); a black spot on each membrane of dorsal fin beginning on outer half of fin anteriorly and becoming progressively smaller and lower in fin posteriorly; a submarginal dusky band in each lobe of caudal fin; individuals from the southern Red Sea are more darkly pigmented. Largest specimen, 9.5 cm. Red Sea and the Gulf of Aden. Predaceous fishes learn to avoid this species due to its venomous bite; as discussed above, it is mimicked by two other Red Sea blennies.

## 285 Scale-Eating Blenny

*Plagiotremus tapeinosoma* (Bleeker), 1857

Dorsal rays VII to IX (usually VIII),34 to 39, the fin not notched; anal rays II,28 to 33; pectoral rays 11 to 13 (usually 12); segmented caudal rays 11; body elongate, the depth 6.8 to 9.2 in standard length; mouth ventral, the conical snout strongly overhanging; slender, incisiform, fixed teeth in jaws, except for a very large recurved canine posteriorly on each side of lower jaw (not associated with a venom gland); caudal fin emarginate; reddish to yellowish brown on back, pale blue to whitish ventrally, with two black stripes, the upper consisting of a series of contiguous black spots, ending in a black streak in middle of caudal fin; lower stripe narrow, but solid, passing through ventral edge of pectoral base to lower edge of caudal peduncle; a narrow white line dorsally on head and body. Reaches 14 cm. Indo-Pacific. Makes rapid attacks on fishes to feed on epidermal tissue, small scales, and mucus.

## 286 Bluestriped Blenny

*Plagiotremus rhinorhynchos* (Bleeker), 1852

Dorsal rays X to XII,32 to 36, the fin not notched; anal rays II,29 to 33; pectoral rays 11 to 13 (usually 12); segmented caudal rays 11; body elongate, the depth 6.6 to 8.0 in standard length; mouth ventral, the conical snout strongly over-hanging; teeth in jaws slender, incisiform and fixed except for a very large recurved canine posteriorly on each side of lower jaw; caudal fin emarginate to forked; usual colour dark brown with two blue stripes, the median fins orangish; the ground colour, however, can be yellow, orange-red, or black. Attains 12 cm. Indo-Pacific. Like other *Plagiotremus*, it feeds on epidermal tissue of fishes. Its blue-and-black-striped phase resembles the pattern of the cleaner wrasse *Labroides dimidiatus*. In spite of the more slender body of the blenny (partially overcome by erecting its dorsal and anal fins), some fishes probably mistake it, at least initially, for the wrasse, thus enab-ling the blenny to be close enough for one of its rapid attacks.

## 287 Lance Blenny

*Aspidontus dussumieri* (Cuvier and Valenciennes), 1836

Dorsal rays IX to XI,29 to 33, the fin not notched; anal rays II,26 to 30; pectoral rays 13 to 15; segmented caudal rays 11; body elongate, the depth 6.7 to 8.4 in standard length; snout rounded, slightly anterior to mouth; teeth in jaws slender, incisiform and fixed except for a very large recurved canine posteriorly on each side of lower jaw (not associated with a venom gland) and a small canine pos-teriorly on upper jaw; caudal fin slightly rounded, becoming lanceolate (middle two rays elongate in large adults); whit-ish with a black stripe from eye to midbase of caudal fin; a pale-edged black spot anteriorly in dorsal fin; Red Sea individuals have a second narrow black stripe ventrally on body. Attains 12 cm. Indo-Pacific. Limited data suggest that this species feeds mainly on algae and detritus.

## 288 Mimic Blenny

*Aspidontus taeniatus* Quoy and Gaimard, 1834

Dorsal rays X to XII,26 to 29, the fin not notched; anal rays II,25 to 28; pectoral rays 13 to 15; segmented caudal rays 11; body moderately elongate, the depth 5.0 to 6.5 in standard length; mouth ventral, the conical snout strongly overhanging; teeth in jaws slender, incisiform and fixed except for a very large recurved canine posteriorly on each side of lower jaw; caudal fin truncate; blue, whitish anteriorly, with a lateral black stripe which commences on snout, passes through eye, and extends to hind border of caudal fin, this stripe progressively broader as it passes posteriorly; a black bar at pectoral base (absent on indi-viduals from the Pacific). Largest speci-men 11.5 cm. Indo-Pacific. An amazing mimic of the cleaner wrasse *Labroides dimidiatus*, not only in colour but also behaviour. Juveniles of the wrasse have a broader black stripe and deeper blue colour; this is matched by blennies of like size; individual variation in adult wrasses is also copied by the blennies that lurk nearby. There is a dual basis to the mimicry: the blenny avoids preda-tion in its guise of the wrasse (which is protected because it removes ecto-parasites from other fishes) and it gets closer to its prey. It feeds in part by tearing pieces from the fins of other fishes (not yet observed in the Red Sea). The author has also observed it eat demersal fish eggs and the tentacles of plume worms. *Blennechis filamentosus* Cuvier and Valenciennes is a synonym based on the prejuvenile stage which has the dorsal fin elevated anteriorly.

# Gobies (Gobiidae)

The gobies represent the largest family of fishes in tropic seas and many are found in temperate waters as well. It is estimated that about 500 species occur in the Indo-Pacific region, some still undescribed. They are grouped in the suborder Gobioidei of the order Perciformes, along with the sleepers (Eleotridae; mostly freshwater; the genus *Xenisthmus* is marine), wormfishes (Microdesmidae) and a few other small families. They are carnivorous and bottom-dwelling; most rest directly on the substratum or live within burrows, but some hover just above the bottom. The famous mudskippers (genus *Periophthalmus*), which live in the mangrove habitat, spend more time out of the water than in it; they are often classified in a family of their own, the Periophthalmidae. The majority of gobies have the pelvic fins (one weak spine and four or five rays) joined to form a sucking disc (those in the accounts below have such a disc unless otherwise stated). Species that spend most of their time in the water column generally have these fins divided, as do some demersal species such as those of the genera *Eviota*, *Valenciennea*, and *Asterropterix*. Usually there are two dorsal fins (though they may be connected basally), the first of II to VIII (frequently VI) flexible spines; often the last two spines have a broader space between them than the foregoing spines. The second dorsal and anal fins are preceded by a single weak spine. The fins are not scaled except the basal part of the caudal and pectoral fins. The caudal fin is usually rounded, but it may be pointed or lanceolate and, rarely, emarginate. There is no lateral line, but the head is generally well supplied with pores and sensory papillae. The gas bladder is absent except in those living above the bottom. The mouth is moderately large and oblique, the teeth conical, often with some enlarged as canines; most species lack teeth on the roof of the mouth. There are no spines on the opercle, and the preopercular margin is smooth (exceptionally with one to a few short spines). The majority of the species have small cycloid or ctenoid scales on the body, but a few are completely scaleless. The gill membranes are often broadly attached to the isthmus, thus restricting the gill opening to the side of the body. Most gobies are shallow-water fishes, though some have been collected at depths greater than 200 m. Most are marine, but many occur in brackish

environments and some penetrate freshwater. Gobiid fishes are associated with a variety of substrata such as reef, sand, mud and rubble. A number live in close association with other animals, such as within sponges or on gorgonians. Species of several genera are symbiotic with snapping shrimps (Alpheidae). The shrimps build a burrow in sand or mud; the gobies use the burrow as a refuge, but they serve as sentinels; with their superior vision and ability to monitor low frequency vibrations with the lateralis system of their head, they can detect approaching predators far sooner than their crustacean partners. The shrimps spend much time removing sediment

from the burrow or adjusting the bits of dead coral or shell with which they line the burrow entrance; however, they do not leave it unless the goby is at the entrance; when outside they generally make physical contact with the guarding fish with one of their antennae. Nearly all of those species of Gobiidae for which reproductive habits are known lay demersal eggs which are guarded by the male parent. The author once frightened a male *Gnatholepis* from its egg mass on a rock near sand, but before the fish departed, it flipped sand over the eggs with its tail. Gobies are small fishes. Indeed, their ranks include the smallest known vertebrate, *Trimmatom nanus* Winterbottom and Emery from the Chagos Archipelago (matures at 8 mm standard length). The Indo-Pacific goby genus *Eviota*, characterized by a fringe along the lateral edge of the last pelvic ray, contains numerous tiny species, six of which are known from the Red Sea. Similarly, the genus *Trimma* includes many very small species; these are colourful and hover above the bottom, often in caves. This genus is in great need of revision, as are many others of the family. Over 75 species of gobies occur in the Red Sea. The 16 selected below are among those most often seen by snorkelers or divers due to their size, colour, and abundance.

## 289 Ornate Goby

*Istigobius ornatus* (Rüppell), 1830

Dorsal rays VI–I,10 or 11; anal rays I,8 or 9; pectoral rays 18 to 20, the upper rays free from membranes; scales on body ctenoid; scale rows between upper end of gill opening and caudal fin base 28 or 29; scales dorsally on head extending to interorbital space; no scales on opercle or cheek; ventral end of gill opening extending to below front of opercle; depth of body about 5 in standard length; conical teeth in bands in jaws, the outer row at the front as small canines; caudal fin rounded, slightly longer than head; whitish with three or four longitudinal rows of broken dark brown lines on back, a row of small blackish spots (some joined as short lines) on midside and one

on lower side; orange-red and pale blue spots and short lines on cheek and opercle. Attains 10 cm. Indo-Pacific. Usually found in estuarine environments. Often classified in *Acentrogobius*. The related but less colourful *I. decoratus* (Herre) (see underwater photo at the top of the previous page) is abundant on sandy bottoms around shallow Red Sea reefs.

## 290 Eyebar Goby

*Gnatholepis anjerensis* (Bleeker), 1850

Dorsal rays VI–I,10 or 11 (usually 11); anal rays I,10 or 11 (usually 11); pectoral rays 15 to 17; scales on body ctenoid; scale rows between upper end of gill opening and caudal fin base 28 or 29; scales dorsally on head extending nearly to posterior edge of eyes; cheek and opercle scaled; ventral end of gill opening extending to below posterior part of opercle; depth of body about 4.5 in standard length; slender conical teeth in about four rows at front of jaws, narrowing to one posteriorly, the outer row at front of lower jaw and entire length of upper jaw enlarged as slender curved canines; caudal fin rounded, slightly longer than head; light brown dorsally, mottled and finely spotted with darker brown, whitish below, with seven indistinct dark spots in a longitudinal row on lower side, the first (and largest, usually

larger than eye) beneath pectoral fin, and the last (smallest, size of pupil or smaller) at midbase of caudal fin; a blackish blotch at upper end of gill opening usually containing a small yellow spot (sometimes more); a bluish black line passing ventrally from lower edge of eye; a diagonal orange line on opercle and one or two horizontal orange lines on pectoral base. To 8 cm. Indo-Pacific. Abundant on sand around reefs; collected by the author in the Red Sea in the depth range of 1 to 46 m. *Gobius cauerensis* Bleeker is a synonym.

## 291 Ninebar Goby

*Cryptocentrus cryptocentrus* (Cuvier and Valenciennes), 1837

Dorsal rays VI–I,10; anal rays I,9; pectoral rays 16 or 17; scales cycloid; scale rows from upper end of gill opening to caudal fin base 83 to 95; head scaleless; ventral end of gill opening extending to below posterior border of preopercle; body elongate, the depth 5.0 to 6.0 in standard length; conical teeth in several rows in jaws, the outer row of upper jaw has slender canines except for two pairs at front of jaw which are longer and stouter; outer row of teeth at front of lower jaw as slender canines, and two strong recurved canines in inner row on side of jaw; tongue bi-lobed; caudal fin rounded, longer than head; nine broad dark brown bars on body, the interspaces narrow pale yellowish lines; blue dots on head and body; a reddish bar from eye to mouth and a few red-edged small blackish spots on head and anterior body. Reaches 13 cm. Western Indian Ocean. Lives in association with alpheid shrimps.

## 292 Luther's Goby

*Cryptocentrus lutheri* Klausewitz, 1960

Dorsal rays VI–I,11; anal rays I,10; pectoral rays 17 or 18; scales cycloid; scale rows from upper end of gill opening to caudal fin base 95 to 101; scales dorsally on head extending forward nearly to posterior margin of eyes; ventral end of gill opening extending nearly to posterior border of preopercle; body moderately elongate, the depth 4.7 to 5.2 in standard length; small conical teeth in several rows in jaws; an outer row of slender incurved canines at side of upper jaw and two pairs of stronger incurved canines anteriorly; front of lower jaw with slender incurved canines, one at the end of this series enlarged and recurved; tongue rounded; caudal fin round, its length about equal to head; body with eight dark bars broader than interspaces, the first two passing beneath pectoral fin; head and body with bright blue spots, few on side and ventral part of body. Largest specimen, 11 cm. Red Sea to the Arabian Gulf. Lives symbiotically with alpheid shrimps.

## 293 Blue-and-Red-Spotted Goby

*Cryptocentrus caeruleopunctatus* (Rüppell), 1830

Dorsal rays VI–I,10; anal rays I,9; pectoral rays 16 or 17; scales ctenoid; rows of scales from upper end of gill opening to caudal fin base 80 to 93; head scaleless; ventral end of gill opening extending slightly anterior to posterior border of preopercle; body moderately elongate, the depth 4.7 to 5.5 in standard length; dentition similar to that of *C. cryptocentrus*; tongue bi-lobed; caudal fin rounded, longer than head; body with eight or nine diagonal dark bands much broader than pale interspaces; a blue-edged black spot nearly as large as eye on back below each dorsal fin, and numerous blue dots on body, many of which lie in diagonal pale interspaces; head, anterior body and dorsal fins with blue-edged red spots; males darker in general, the caudal fin blackish with a red posterior border and light yellow submarginal band; also the first dorsal fin is higher. Reaches 13 cm. Red Sea. Symbiotic with alpheid shrimps. Related to the Indo-Malayan *C. leptocephalus* Bleeker.

## 294 Prawn Goby

*Ctenogobiops maculosus* (Fourmanoir), 1955

Dorsal rays VI–I,11; anal rays I,11; pectoral rays 18 or 19; scales of body ctenoid; rows of scales from upper end of gill opening to caudal fin base 54 to 63; head scaleless; ventral end of gill opening extending to below middle of preopercle; depth of body 4.5 to 5.2 in standard length; upper jaw with an outer row of slender incurved canine teeth, one or two pairs at front of jaw enlarged, and smaller teeth medially in about two irregular rows (some inner teeth enlarged to canine proportions anteriorly); lower jaw with slender incurved canines only anteriorly, a band of smaller teeth medial to these, continuing as a single row on side of jaw, and one or two large recurved canines medial to small teeth in about middle of side of jaw; tongue bi-lobed; caudal fin rounded, its length equal to or slightly shorter than head; upper half of body with three longitudinal rows of oblong yellowish brown spots and a fourth row of two spots beneath pectoral fin; three diagonal rows of brownish yellow lines on cheek and postorbital head. Reaches 7 cm. Red Sea; a common species on sand in 1 to 15 m. Symbiotic with alpheid shrimps.

## 295 Steinitz' Goby

*Amblyeleotris steinitzi* (Klausewitz), 1974

Dorsal rays VI–I,12; anal rays I,12; pectoral rays 18; scales on body ctenoid except anteriorly; rows of scales between gill opening and caudal fin base 74 to 78; head scaleless; gill opening extending anterior to middle of preopercle; depth of body 4.7 to 5.4 in standard length; several rows of teeth in jaws, the outer row enlarged; a pair of canines anteriorly in upper jaw and two in inner row on side of lower jaw; tongue truncate; caudal fin rounded, slightly longer than head; pelvic fins nearly completely separated (united at base by a narrow membrane), reaching origin of anal fin; white with five dusky red bars narrower than interspaces, the first four slightly diagonal, the fifth (on caudal peduncle) vertical; dorsal fins blue with dark-edged orange-yellow dots; snout may or may not be blackish (in life the blackish colour disappears when the fish is frightened). Attains about 8 cm. Indo-Pacific. Symbiotic with alpheid shrimps.

## 296 Magnus' Goby

*Amblyeleotris sungami* (Klausewitz), 1969

Dorsal rays VI–I,13; anal rays I,13; pectoral rays 19; scales on body ctenoid, becoming cycloid on about anterior third; rows of scales from upper end of gill opening to caudal fin base 100–106; head scaleless; ventral end of gill opening extending anterior to below middle of preopercle; depth of body 5.6 to 6.2 in standard length; dentition similar to *A. steinitzi*; caudal fin somewhat pointed, distinctly longer than head; pelvic fins nearly completely separated (united at base by a narrow membrane), reaching origin of anal fin; white with five orange bars, the first four diagonal, the fifth on caudal peduncle vertical; a faint sixth orangish bar basally in caudal fin; whitish interspaces and head with numerous pale blue spots and irregular markings and a few orange-yellow dots within blue spots dorsally on head and anterior body and basally in dorsal fins; snout may be dusky. Attains about 10 cm. Red Sea, but similar specimens from elsewhere in the Indo-Pacific will probably be identified as *sungami*. Symbiotic with alpheid shrimps. The scientific name is derived from the name of the first collector, Professor Magnus, spelled backwards.

## 297 Halfspotted Goby

*Asterropterix semipunctatus* Rüppell, 1830

Dorsal rays VI–I,10 or 11 (usually 10); anal rays I,9; pectoral rays 16; scales ctenoid; scale rows from upper end of gill opening to caudal fin base 24 to 26; head fully scaled except interorbital and snout; lower part of posterior margin of preopercle with four to six short spines; ventral end of gill opening extending slightly anterior to posterior margin of head; body moderately deep, the depth 3.0 to 3.4 in standard length, and compressed; small teeth in several rows in jaws, the outer row enlarged as slender canines, the largest a recurved one at end of outer series in lower jaw; third dorsal spine prolonged; caudal fin rounded, shorter than head; pelvic fins fully sep- arated; dark grey-brown, blotched with darker grey-brown (the darkest spots are two on upper half of caudal fin base), with numerous bright blue dots on lower half of head and body. Attains 5 cm. Indo-Pacific. Lives in silty dead-reef areas, often in very shallow water.

## 298 Roundfin Goby

*Bathygobius cyclopterus* (Cuvier and Valenciennes), 1837

Dorsal rays VI–I,9; anal rays I,8; pectoral rays 19 or 20, the upper five rays free from membranes; scales on body ctenoid except anteriorly; scale rows from upper end of gill opening to caudal fin base 38 to 41; scales dorsally on head extending slightly anterior to posterior margin of preopercle; head otherwise scaleless except for two or three rows of scales dorsally on opercle; ventral end of gill opening ending beneath front part of opercle; depth of body 4.0 to 5.0 in standard length; head depressed and broad, nearly as wide as long; several rows of teeth in jaws, the outer row enlarged as slender canines; caudal fin rounded, shorter than head; posterior margin of fleshy frenum across base of pelvic disc with three pronounced point- ed lobes; colour variable, but generally mottled brown, sometimes with faint broad dark bars. Reaches 7 cm. East Africa to Samoa and the Marshall Islands. Found along sandy-rocky shores, often in tidepools. The related *B. fuscus* (Rüppell) has modally 18 pectoral rays (the upper three free) and a pelvic frenum without lobes. *Mapo crassiceps* Jordan and Seale is a synonym.

## 299 Sixspot Goby

*Valenciennea sexguttata* (Cuvier and Valenciennes), 1837

Dorsal rays VI–I,12; anal rays I,11 to 13 (usually 12); pectoral rays 19 or 20; scales ctenoid; scale rows from upper end of gill opening to caudal fin base 85 to 91; head scaleless; ventral end of gill opening extending to below middle of opercle; body elongate, the depth 5.0 to 5.7 in standard length; a single row of slender incurved teeth in upper jaw; lower jaw with three rows of similar teeth an- teriorly and a single row of smaller teeth posteriorly; caudal fin rounded to some- what pointed, its length varying from slightly shorter to slightly longer than head; pelvic fins completely separated; whitish, sometimes with two pale red stripes on side of body connected by narrow bars of the same colour; six to eight small blue spots on cheek and opercle; tip of first dorsal fin with a small black spot. Reaches 14 cm. East Africa to Samoa and the Marshall Islands. Builds a burrow in sand under rocks by transport- ing mouthfuls of sand to the exterior; usually seen in pairs.

## 300 Maiden Goby

*Valenciennea puellaris* (Tomiyama), 1956

Dorsal rays VI–I,11 or 12 (usually 12); anal rays I,11 or 12 (usually 12); pectoral rays 19 to 21; scales ctenoid (except anteriorly); rows of scales from upper end of gill opening to caudal fin base 85 to 92; head scaleless; ventral end of gill opening extending to below middle of opercle; depth of body 4.5 to 5.6 in standard length; dentition similar to *V. sexguttata*; caudal fin rounded, its length varying from slightly shorter to slightly longer than head; pelvic fins completely separated; white with diagonal orange-yellow bars or elongate spots on back

(with small fainter spots between) and an orange-yellow band faintly edged in pale blue on side of body (which may contain more intense spots of orange); oblong pale blue spots on cheek and opercle. Reaches 14 cm. East Africa to the Samoa Islands. Habits as in preceding species.

## 301 Smallscale Hover Goby

*Ptereleotris microlepis* (Bleeker), 1856

Dorsal rays VI–I,25 or 26; anal rays I,24 or 25; pectoral rays 22 or 23; scales cycloid and partially embedded; scale rows from upper end of gill opening to caudal fin base 154 to 162; head scaleless; ventral end of gill opening extending to below front part of opercle; body very elongate, the depth 6.0 to 6.7 in standard length; mouth highly oblique, the lower jaw strongly projecting; upper jaw with an outer row of canine teeth and an inner band of small conical teeth; lower jaw with two rows of canines anteriorly, narrowing to a single row of small teeth posteriorly; tongue very slender; caudal fin emarginate; pelvic fins completely separated; bluish white, sometimes with two faint pale orange longitudinal lines posteriorly on side of body; a narrow, blue-edged, black bar on

lower half of pectoral fin base; cheek and opercle with irregular, iridescent light blue markings. Reaches 12 cm. Indo-Pacific. Collected by the author in the Red Sea in the depth range of 2 to 49 m. Found in sandy areas, often near reefs. May rise a metre or more above the bottom to feed on zooplankton but never ventures far from a burrow into which it can dart head-first with the approach of a predator; several individuals may share the same burrow.

## 302 Tailspot Goby

*Amblygobius albimaculatus* (Rüppell), 1830

Dorsal rays VI–I,14; anal rays, I,13 or 14 (usually 14); pectoral rays 18 to 20; scales ctenoid; rows of scales from upper end of gill opening to caudal fin base 52 to 56; scales dorsally on head extending to interorbital space; cheeks scaleless; small scales in several rows dorsally on opercle; ventral end of gill opening ending beneath posterior part of opercle (just below pectoral base); depth of body 3.4 to 4.0 in standard length; several rows of conical teeth in jaws, the outer row at front enlarged to canine proportions, the largest a recurved tooth at end of lower series of canines; middle spines of first dorsal fin of adults prolonged; caudal fin rounded, as long as head or slightly shorter; ground colour varying from dark brown or olive to whitish; five

narrow blackish bars on body, a blackish spot at upper end of gill opening and another just above middle of caudal fin base; diagonal pale blue lines on head. Reaches 17 cm. Indian Ocean. Closely related to *A. phalaena* (Cuvier and Valenciennes) of the Pacific. A shallow-water species living in protected sandy or grassy areas around reefs; excavates its own burrow in sand under rocks with its mouth.

## 303 Hector's Goby

*Amblygobius hectori* (Smith), 1956

Dorsal rays VI–I,15 or 16 (usually 16); anal rays I,15 or 16 (usually 16); pectoral rays 15 or 16 (usually 16); scales ctenoid except anteriorly; scale rows from upper end of gill opening to caudal fin base 53 to 55; scales dorsally on head extending nearly to posterior edge of eyes; cheek and opercle scaleless; ventral end of gill opening extending below posterior part of opercle; depth of body 4.3 to 4.9 in standard length; head pointed; slender canine teeth in jaws in two rows anteriorly, the outer enlarged, the largest tooth a recurved canine at end of outer series of lower jaw; first two spines of dorsal fin prolonged; caudal fin rounded, its length slightly shorter than head; upper half of head and body with alternating broad reddish brown and narrow black-edged yellow stripes; a broad bluish grey stripe on lower side of body; ventral part of head and body abruptly bluish white; an ocellated black spot in first dorsal fin, at rear basal part of second dorsal fin, and dorsally at base of caudal fin. Attains 5.5 cm. East Africa to the western Pacific. A solitary reef-dwelling species which swims slightly above the bottom. Often classified in the genus *Seychellea*.

## 304 Citron Goby

*Gobiodon citrinus* (Rüppell), 1838

Dorsal rays VI–I,10 or 11 (usually 10); anal rays I,9; pectoral rays 18; no scales; ventral end of gill opening extending to level of twelfth pectoral ray; body very deep, the depth 2.2 to 2.7 in standard length, and compressed, the width 2.5 to 3.0 in depth; a band of brushlike teeth in jaws with an outer row of slender curved canines which are only slightly longer; lower jaw, in addition, with three to five pairs of recurved canines in a detached inner row; dorsal fins joined at their extreme base by membrane; caudal fin rounded, shorter than head; bright yellow to brown with a small black spot at upper end of opercular membrane, near-vertical blue lines on head and one on pectoral base, and a blue line along base of dorsal and anal fins. Largest collected, 6.6 cm. East Africa to Samoa and the Marshall Islands. Lives on branches of live coral (*Acropora*). Species of the genus *Gobiodon* produce much mucus which contains a toxin; the mucus has a strong bitter taste. Another colourful species, *G. rivulatus* (Rüppell) is shown in an underwater photo in the section on the family.

# Triggerfishes (Balistidae)

The Balistidae is one of eight families of the order Tetraodontiformes (Plectognathi of older literature) which also includes the puffers and trunkfishes. This group is believed to have evolved from acanthurid-like stock. Triggerfishes have relatively deep compressed bodies, the eye set high on the head, the snout long but not protruding; the mouth is small, terminal or with lower jaw slightly projecting, and nonprotrusible; the jaws are short but strong; there are eight long, protruding, close-set, incisiform teeth in the outer row of both jaws and an inner row of six teeth which buttress the ones in front; the gill opening is a short slit above and anterior to base of pectoral fin; there are two dorsal fins, the first of three spines; the first dorsal fin is very strong and may be locked into an erect position with the small second spine; the third dorsal spine is very small, sometimes not projecting above the edge of the groove into which the fin folds; the second dorsal and anal fins are supported only by soft rays; the pelvic fins are replaced by a single spinous knob at the end of a long, depressible pelvic bone; the skin is tough, consisting of nonoverlapping scales with a broad area of small tuber-

165

cles in the centre of each; most species have a patch of enlarged modified scales behind the gill opening. Triggerfishes are usually solitary. They swim by undulating the second dorsal and anal fins, bringing their tail into action only when they wish to move swiftly. When pursued, they often seek refuge in a hole in the reef with a small entrance; inside they wedge themselves by locking the first dorsal spine in an erect position and depressing the pelvic flap. One can depress the first dorsal spine by pressing on the second or 'trigger' spine. At night they retire to a hole (probably their same favourite daytime refuge) to sleep. The majority of species are carnivorous, feeding on a wide variety of animal life from zooplankton to crabs, molluscs, sea urchins, other echinoderms and coral. A few species feed in part on benthic algae. In spite of their small mouths, triggerfishes are able to reduce large prey to pieces with their powerful jaws and chisel-like teeth. Those for which reproductive habits are known lay demersal eggs which are aggressively guarded by the male. Some species excavate a shallow crater in sand, the centre of which contains the egg mass. Divers should be on the alert for the guarding males of the larger balistid fishes, for these fishes will attack if one ventures within a few metres of the nest. Usually they swim rapidly towards the intruder, but turn before contact is made. Occasionally, particularly if one is close to the nest, they will bite. Ten triggerfishes are recorded from the Red Sea, of which seven are discussed below. Omitted are *Melichthys indicus* Randall and Klausewitz (one record from the southern Red Sea), *Abalistes stellatus* Anonymous (not a reef fish) and *Canthidermis maculatus* (Bloch) (a pelagic species). Pectoral ray counts include upper rudimentary ray.

## 305 Orangestriped Triggerfish

*Balistapus undulatus* (Mungo Park), 1797

Dorsal rays III–25 or 26 (rarely 27); anal rays 22 or 23 (rarely 21 or 24); pectoral rays 14 (rarely 13 or 15); scale rows from upper end of gill opening to caudal fin base 37 to 45; no groove anterior to eye; two rows of strong forward-curved spines on caudal peduncle (usually three spines per row); caudal fin slightly rounded; dark brown to dark green with diagonal orange stripes on body; a diagonal band of orange and blue stripes from around mouth to below pectoral fin; black around caudal peduncle spines; a black spot on outer part of first dorsal fin membrane. Reaches 30 cm. Indo-Pacific. The diet is extremely varied, consisting of the tips of branches of live coral (especially *Acropora*), benthic algae (often coralline reds), sea urchins and heart urchins, crabs and other crustaceans, fishes, molluscs, brittle stars, tunicates, polychaete worms, sponges and hydrozoans.

167

## 306 Bluethroat Triggerfish

*Sufflamen albicaudatus* (Rüppell), 1829

Dorsal rays III–26 to 29; anal rays 23 to 26; pectoral rays 14 (rarely 13); scale rows from upper end of gill opening to caudal fin base 46 to 51; a deep groove passing anteriorly from eye; about 12 rows of small spines posteriorly on side of body; caudal fin truncate; brown, the lower part of head and region around mouth purplish blue; lips pale pink, a narrow bar varying in colour from yellow to dark brown extending ventrally across head from posterior edge of eye; caudal fin white with a very large yellowish brown semicircular area covering most of central part of fin. Red Sea to the Gulf of Oman. A close relative of the

Indo-Pacific *S. chrysopterus* (Bloch and Schneider) which differs in lacking a broad white zone across basal part of caudal fin; some authors prefer to regard *albicaudatus* as a subspecies of *chrysopterus*.

## 307 Picasso Triggerfish

*Rhinecanthus assasi* (Forsskål), 1775

Dorsal rays III–25 to 27 (usually 25 or 26); anal rays 22 to 24; pectoral rays 15; scale rows from upper end of gill opening to caudal fin base 36 to 43; no groove in front of eye; three rows of small forward-curved spines posteriorly on body; caudal fin slightly rounded to slightly double emarginate; tan, shading to white ventrally, caudal spines in black bands within an elliptical whitish area; a narrowing blue-edged dark brown bar from eye to gill opening, preceded by a yellow band and a blue line; four narrow blue bands alternating with three of black across interorbital space; lips yellow; a

narrow blue zone adjacent to upper lip, above this a dark brown streak which extends to lower pectoral fin base; anus in a large black spot broadly surrounded by orange. Reaches 30 cm. Red Sea to the Gulf of Oman.

## 308 Titan Triggerfish

*Balistoides viridescens* (Bloch and Schneider), 1801

Dorsal rays III–25 or 26; anal rays 23 or 24; pectoral rays 15; scale rows from upper end of gill opening to caudal fin base 29 to 32; a deep groove passing anteriorly from eye; small spines in four or five rows posteriorly on body; caudal fin rounded; most of body yellowish grey, the centres of the scales dark brown to dark green, becoming whitish posteriorly on body and ventrally on head, the scale centres slightly dusky; top of head dark purplish (sometimes with yellowish spots), this colour enclosing eye and continuing as a narrowing band to front of gill opening; lower lip pink; upper lip and a broad zone above and posterior to it blackish, this zone crossed by a diagonal pale band which is joined by another from chin; rays of second dorsal, anal, and caudal fins blackish submarginally. Largest examined by author, 68 cm; reported to 75 cm. Indo-

Pacific. Stomach and gut contents of five adults consisted of sea urchins (*Diadema* and *Echinometra*), heart urchins, coral (*Acropora* and *Pocillopora*), crabs, bivalve molluscs, gastropod molluscs, chitons, tube worms and some algae and detritus. The author was once bitten by a large male guarding an egg mass.

## 309 Yellowmargin Triggerfish

*Pseudobalistes flavimarginatus* (Rüppell), 1829

Dorsal rays III–24 to 27 (usually 25 or 26); anal rays 23 to 25 (usually 24); pectoral rays 15 or 16 (usually 16); scale rows from upper end of gill opening to caudal fin base 28 to 33; a deep groove passing anteriorly from eye; shallow horizontal grooves on cheek above level of mouth; a broad region above, below and posterior to mouth scaleless in adults; small spines in five or six horizontal rows posteriorly on body; caudal fin rounded in juveniles, becoming lunate in large adults; pale yellowish brown, the scale edges lighter than centres; front of head and chest often yellow-orange; margins of second dorsal, anal, and caudal fins yellowish; juveniles with

numerous small black spots. Attains 60 cm. Indo-Pacific.

## 310 Blue Triggerfish

*Pseudobalistes fuscus* (Bloch and Schneider), 1801

Dorsal rays III–25 to 27; anal rays 22 to 24; pectoral rays 15; scale rows from upper end of gill opening to caudal fin base 35 to 45; a deep groove passing anteriorly from eye; lower part of cheek (between mouth and pectoral fin base) with shallow horizontal grooves; broad region around mouth of adults without scales; no spines posteriorly on side of body; second dorsal and anal fins elevated anteriorly (not true of balistids previously discussed); caudal fin of young rounded, of large adults double emarginate with prolonged lobes; deep blue with a yellow spot on each scale; margins of second dorsal and anal fins and posterior edges of caudal and pectoral fins pale blue; juveniles yellow with wavy bright blue lines. Reaches 55 cm. Indo-Pacific.

## 311 Redtooth Triggerfish

*Odonus niger* (Rüppell), 1837

Dorsal rays III–33 to 36; anal rays 28 to 31; pectoral rays 15; scale rows from upper end of gill opening to caudal fin base 29 to 34; mouth upturned, the chin protruding; two upper teeth prolonged; a long deep groove passing anteriorly from eye; caudal peduncle narrow; about seven longitudinal rows of small spines on posterior half of body; second dorsal and anal fins very elevated anteriorly; caudal fin lunate, the lobes very elongate on large adults; deep purplish blue with blue bands on upper half of head; margins of second dorsal and anal fins, and posterior margin of caudal fin pale blue; teeth red. Reaches 50 cm (including

long caudal lobes). Indo-Pacific. Appears to feed mainly on zooplankton.

# Filefishes (Monacanthidae)

The filefishes are closely related to the triggerfishes (Balistidae), and some authors have preferred to place the two in the same family. On the other hand, some classifications split off the bizarre *Aluterus* and its relatives as a separate family from the rest of the monacanthids. Following a recent major study of the Tetraodontiformes, all the filefishes are here regarded as a single family distinct from the Balistidae. They differ from the triggerfishes in having more compressed bodies, generally a more pointed snout, a longer first dorsal spine, a very small second spine (sometimes absent), and no third spine; the teeth are basically the same but not as strong, and there are six instead of eight in the outer row and four in the inner reinforcing row; the scales, which are not well differentiated, have small setae which gives the skin its coarse texture. Some species have a brushlike patch of longer setae posteriorly on the body (often better developed on males). Males of a few of these fishes have curved spines on the caudal peduncle which are absent or poorly developed in females. Unlike the triggerfishes, most species are able to change their colour to match their surroundings, and some develop small cutaneous projections which further aid them in camouflage. They tend to be secretive, often hiding in seagrass, thick algal cover, or gorgonians. Most are very catholic in their food habits, feeding on a great variety of benthic animal and plant life. Thirteen species occur in the Red Sea, but only the three discussed below are moderately common on reefs. Other species are rare there, such as *Aluterus*

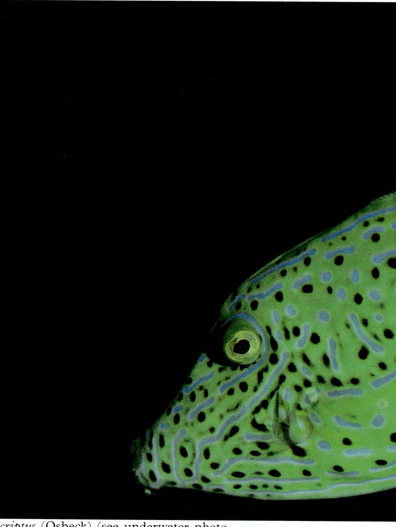

*scriptus* (Osbeck) (see underwater photo of one being approached by the cleaner wrasse, *Labroides dimidiatus*) or occur in different habitats.

## 312 Broom Filefish

*Amanses scopas* (Cuvier), 1829

Dorsal rays II–26 to 29; anal rays 22 to 25; pectoral rays 14; first dorsal spine over front part of eye, about as long as snout; snout short and obtuse, the dorsal and ventral profiles of head forming an angle of nearly 90° when pelvic bone is fully depressed; knob at end of pelvic bone not movable; males with a group of five or six long stout spines lying against the side posteriorly on body; females with a dense mass of long setae, not unlike a toothbrush, posteriorly on side of body; caudal peduncle very deep; caudal fin short and slightly rounded; brown, becoming nearly black on caudal peduncle and fin, with up to 12 narrow dark brown bars on midside of body;

second dorsal, anal, and pectoral fins with yellow rays and clear membranes. Reaches 20 cm. Indo-Pacific.

## 313 Wire-Net Filefish

*Cantherhines pardalis* (Rüppell), 1837

Dorsal rays II–32 to 36; anal rays 29 to 32; pectoral rays 14 (rarely 13 or 15); first dorsal spine over eye, about as long as snout; snout about 3.7 in standard length; dorsal profile of snout concave; knob at end of pelvic bone not movable; no spines posteriorly on side of body, but males with a dense patch of setae on caudal peduncle and extending a short distance anterior to it; caudal peduncle not very deep; caudal fin not long, its length 4.4 to 5.0 in standard length, and rounded; colour can be altered to any of three basic patterns: dark brown, light grey-brown very broadly mottled with dark brown, and grey with numerous orange-brown spots; all three have in common a small white spot at rear base of second dorsal fin. Largest specimen examined, 20.6 cm. Indo-Pacific except Hawaii, where the related *C. sandwichiensis* (Quoy and Gaimard) occurs. The

Atlantic *C. pullus* (Ranzani) is also a close relative.

171

### 314 Harlequin Filefish

*Oxymonacanthus halli* Marshall, 1952

Dorsal rays II–26 to 31 (usually 27 to 29); anal rays 23 to 28 (usually 25 to 27); pectoral rays 11 or 12 (usually 11); body relatively elongate; first dorsal spine over eye, its length about as long as snout; snout strongly produced, about 4.5 in standard length; mouth very small and upturned; knob at end of pelvic bone not movable; no spines posteriorly on side of body, but setae of adults longer there; caudal fin not long, about as long as snout, and rounded; blue with orange spots, the ventral part of pelvic flap and lower part of head green; tip of snout orange; a black bar in outer middle part of caudal fin; males with a large black-edged orange spot posteriorly on pelvic flap (this area dusky olivaceous in females). Attains about 7 cm. Red Sea. Closely related to *O. longirostris* (Bloch and Schneider) which ranges from the Indian Ocean to Samoa and the Marshall Islands; *O. halli* differs slightly in colour and has lower fin-ray counts. Both feed on coral polyps.

# Trunkfishes (Ostraciidae)

The trunkfishes, sometimes called box-fishes, are named for their hard external carapace. It is made up of bony hexagonal plates and covers most of the head and body (leaving gaps for the mouth, nostrils, gill opening, anus, caudal peduncle, and fins); it may be triangular, quadrangular, pentagonal, hexagonal or nearly round in cross-section. The plates comprising the carapace often have small tubercles, thus giving it a rough texture. Some trunkfishes possess very large spines which project from the carapace. Those species in the Indo-Pacific with horns in front of the eyes are called cowfishes (genus *Lactoria*). Ostraciid fishes have a small mouth, which is low on the head, and thick lips. The teeth are conical to incisiform with rounded tips, yellowish brown, and uniserial in the jaws. As in other tetraodontiform fishes, there are no teeth on the roof of the mouth. The gill opening is a near-vertical slit extending dorsally from in front of the pectoral fin base. No spines are present in the fins; there is one dorsal fin posterior in position, and no pelvic fins. As would be expected from their bony armour and boxy shape, they are slow swimmers; they propel themselves primarily by a sculling action of the dorsal and anal fins, but the caudal fin is brought into play if they want to move faster. Trunkfishes are bottom-dwelling. They feed on a wide variety of benthic invertebrate animals, especially sessile forms such as tunicates, sponges and alcyonarians; many also ingest considerable quantities of algae. Though one would think their carapace would provide adequate protection from most pre-

dators, some species, at least, have another defence – a skin poison called ostracitoxin. This is secreted when the fish is under stress. As with the soapfishes, it will kill other fishes in a confined body of water. In high enough concentration it will kill the trunkfishes too. Only four species are recorded from the Red Sea, the three discussed below and the cowfish *Lactoria cornuta* (Linnaeus) which is known only from one specimen from the southern part of the Sea.

## 315 Bluetail Trunkfish

*Ostracion cyanurus* Rüppell, 1828

Dorsal rays 9; anal rays 9; pectoral rays 11 (including rudimentary upper ray); carapace quadrangular in cross-section, broader at base than high, and without spines; jaws with ten upper and eight lower teeth; chin fleshy and protuberant; profile of snout of males convex, of females slightly concave; caudal fin slightly rounded; deep blue with small black spots (absent on snout and cheek of males; spots on side of males larger and

sometimes ocellated); dorsal part of carapace yellow; caudal fin with a broad whitish posterior border. Reaches 15 cm. Red Sea and the Gulf of Aden.

## 316 Cube Trunkfish

*Ostracion cubicus* Linnaeus, 1758

Dorsal rays 9; anal rays 9; pectoral rays 11; carapace quadrangular in cross-section, broader at the base than high, and without spines; jaws with ten upper and eight lower teeth; large adults develop a bump anteriorly on snout; caudal fin rounded; carapace yellow to yellowish brown with white to pale blue spots edged with black or rimmed with small black spots (young with fewer and relatively larger spots); fins yellow. Reaches 45 cm. Indo-Pacific. Elsewhere in the Indo-Pacific region, juveniles have small black spots on the head and body whereas those in the Red Sea have white spots broadly edged with black. The Red

Sea form has been named *O. argus* by Rüppell, but most authors do not believe it should be given specific rank. *O. tuberculatus* Linnaeus is a synonym.

### 317 Thornback Trunkfish

*Tetrosomus gibbosus* (Linnaeus), 1758

Dorsal rays 9; anal rays 9; pectoral rays 11; carapace triangular in cross-section; a large blade-like ridge dorsally on carapace, ending in a flattened spine; ventral ridge of carapace with a series of five posteriorly directed spines (the first below gill opening small); ridge over eye with one spine; jaws with ten upper and eight lower teeth; caudal fin rounded; yellowish grey with pale blue spots (generally one per carapace plate); a broad, diffuse, irregular dark bar across middle of carapace; a few scattered small blackish spots; caudal peduncle with small dark brown spots and a faint reticular network of light blue. Attains

30 cm. East Africa to Indonesia and the Philippines. Sometimes classified in *Rhinesomus*, but this is a synonym of the Atlantic genus *Lactophrys*. Found more in seagrass beds or on algal flats than coral reefs.

# Puffers (Tetraodontidae)

The puffers, or blowfishes, are named for their ability, when provoked, to greatly expand their bodies by drawing water into the abdomen (or air if they are removed from the sea). The water enters a highly distensible diverticulum from the ventral part of the stomach. Other characteristics are a tough scaleless skin (often with small spinules), jaws with beak-like dental plates having a median suture, a small slit-like gill opening just anterior to upper base of pectoral fin, no spines in fins, a single short-based dorsal fin posterior in position, a comparable anal fin below or behind the dorsal, no pelvic fins, and no ribs. Puffers are well known for harbouring a powerful toxin, tetrodontoxin, particularly in the liver and ovaries. Serious illness and death may result from eating these tissues. The degree of toxicity varies greatly with the species, the geographical area, the season and the individual fish. Muscle tissue of puffers is usually safe to eat and considered a delicacy by some people, but even it can show slight toxicity in a few species. The family is divisible into two subfamilies: the Tetraodontinae and the Canthigasterinae. The latter group contains the small, often colourful tobies (or sharpnose puffers), which have a repelling substance in the skin. Twelve puffers are known from the Red Sea, three in the genus *Canthigaster*.

# 318 Crown Toby

*Canthigaster coronata* (Vaillant and Sauvage), 1875

Dorsal rays 9 or 10 (usually 10); anal rays 9 or 10 (usually 9); pectoral rays 16 or 17 (usually 17); a middorsal ridge of skin on back; snout long and produced, its length 1.4 to 1.8 in head; nostril a single small opening on each side of snout; caudal fin slightly to moderately rounded; whitish with a dark brown band across head behind eyes, including posterior part of interorbital space, and three broad dark brown bars on upper third of body separated by pale interspaces narrower than eye; bars narrowing as they pass ventrally, the middle one slightly diagonal and the last on caudal peduncle highly diagonal; small blue spots and lines on head and body, including several lines radiating from eye. Attains 13 cm. East Africa to Micronesia and the

Hawaiian Islands. Not common in less than 15 m, and occurs to at least 80 m. Feeds on algae, small molluscs, crabs, polychaete worms, sipunculid worms, bryozoans, tunicates, foraminifera and small crustaceans. *C. cinctus* Jordan and Evermann is a synonym.

# 319 Pearl Toby

*Canthigaster margaritata* (Rüppell), 1829

Dorsal rays 8 or 9 (usually 8); anal rays 8 or 9 (usually 8); pectoral rays 16 to 18 (usually 17); a middorsal ridge of skin on back; snout long and produced, its length 1.4 to 1.6 in head; nostril a single small opening on each side of snout; caudal fin slightly rounded; pale yellowish, slightly dusky on back, the head, body, and caudal fin with numerous small dark-edged blue spots; short blue lines radiating from eye; a blackish spot below base of dorsal fin; a dark-edged longitudinal blue line ventrally on body. Largest specimen, 12.3 cm. Red Sea. Closely related to the Indo-Pacific *C. solandri* (Richardson).

# 320 Pygmy Toby

*Canthigaster pygmaea* Allen and Randall, 1977

Dorsal rays 8 to 10; anal rays 9 or 10; pectoral rays 14 to 16; a middorsal ridge of skin on back; snout moderately long and produced, 1.6 to 1.9 in head; nostril a single small opening on each side of snout; caudal fin slightly rounded; light brown with numerous small blue spots on body and vertical blue lines on head except some extending posteriorly and dorsally from eye; a dark area behind eye and a blackish spot at base of dorsal fin; fins without blue spots except a few at extreme base. A small species; largest specimen, 5.6 cm. Red Sea. Collected in the depth range from 2 to 30 m. A very secretive fish; comes into the open only briefly to move from one hole of the reef to the next.

### 321 Masked Puffer

*Arothron diadematus* (Rüppell), 1829

Dorsal rays 10; anal rays usually 10; pectoral rays 18 or 19; body orbicular; no ridge of skin on back; snout short and obtuse; nasal organ consisting of two short tentacles from a common base; small spinules present on head and body except snout and caudal peduncle; caudal fin rounded; light olivaceous, often mottled with brown, a broad irregular black area around mouth separated by a broad white zone from a black band across eyes which has a narrow irregular connection to a large dark brown area around pectoral base and gill opening; dorsal, anal, and pectoral fins black basally, the rays black and outer membranes clear; caudal rays whitish, the membranes blackish. Attains

30 cm. Red Sea. Very closely related to and considered by some authors conspecific with the Indo-Pacific *A. nigropunctatus* (Bloch and Schneider).

### 322 Bristly Puffer

*Arothron hispidus* (Linnaeus), 1758

Dorsal rays 10 or 11; anal rays 10 or 11; pectoral rays 17 to 19; no ridge of skin on back; snout short and obtuse; bony rim of orbit extending above interorbital level; nasal organ consisting of two short fleshy tentacles arising from a basal stem; scattered small spinules present on head and body except snout and posterior caudal peduncle; caudal fin rounded; olive to brown with numerous small white spots, shading to white ventrally; diffuse dark bars usually present, more evidence on side than dorsally; base of pectoral fin and gill opening in a black area surrounded by concentric white rings; white rings around eye; basal third of dorsal and basal half of pectoral fins brown with small white spots; caudal fin light grey, partially spotted with white. Attains 50 cm. Indo-Pacific. Feeds on

algae and detritus, molluscs, tunicates, sponges, corals, zoanthid anemones, crabs, tube worms, sea urchins, brittle stars, starfishes, hermit crabs and hydroids. Red Sea individuals have smaller and more numerous white spots than those from elsewhere in the Indo-Pacific.

### 323 Blackspotted Puffer

*Arothron stellatus* (Bloch and Schneider), 1801

Dorsal rays 11, anal rays 11, pectoral rays 19; no ridge of skin on back; snout moderately short and obtuse; nasal organ consisting of two tentacles from a short stem; head and body covered with small spinules, more evident ventrally; light brown to whitish with numerous black spots on head, body, and caudal fin except ventrally on posterior part of head and lower abdomen; largest black spots on and around pectoral fin base and gill opening. Black spots relatively smaller and more numerous on larger individuals. Reported to 90 cm. Indo-Pacific.

# Porcupinefishes & Burrfishes
## (Diodontidae)

The diodontid fishes are similar to the puffers but differ conspicuously in the prominent spines that cover the head and body except the caudal peduncle and around the mouth; the eyes are large, and there is no median suture on the dental plates; the pectoral fins are broad, the posterior edge often emarginate. Two genera occur in the Red Sea, *Chilomycterus* (burrfishes) on which the spines are relatively short, three-rooted, erect, and rigid; and *Diodon* (porcupinefishes) with long spines, most of which are two-rooted and hence can be moved. When not inflated, the spines of *Diodon* lie against the body with their sharp tips pointing posteriorly; after the body is inflated, they become fully erect. The porcupinefishes and burrfishes are nocturnal, usually hiding in small caves or beneath ledges by day. They feed mainly on invertebrates with hard shells or exoskeletons which they crush with their powerful dental plates. Four diodontid fishes are recorded from the Red Sea, two in the genus *Diodon* and two in *Chilomycterus*.

## 324 Porcupinefish

*Diodon hystrix* Linnaeus, 1758

Dorsal rays 14 to 17; anal rays 14 to 16; pectoral rays 21 to 25; spines long and erectile; about 15 rows of spines dorsally between pectoral fin bases and about 25 ventrally; spines in middle of front of head not very long, shorter than longest spines behind pectoral fins; nasal organ a short cylindrical loop of skin; median fins rounded; greenish grey dorsally with small black spots on head, body and fins, shading to white ventrally; a dusky bar passing ventrally from eye. Reaches 70 cm. Circumtropical. Feeds mainly on gastropod molluscs, crabs, hermit crabs and sea urchins. The second *Diodon* recorded from the Red Sea, *D. holocanthus* Linnaeus, was not seen by the author. It is smaller (to about 35 cm) and differs in having the spines on the front of the head longer than those posterior to the pectoral fins, two small barbels on chin, and several large dark brown blotches on back and side.

## 325 Yellowspotted Burrfish

*Chilomycterus spilostylus* Leis and Randall, 1982

Dorsal rays 12 or 13; anal rays 10 to 12; pectoral rays 20 to 22; spines on head and body short and fixed, shorter than the roots (but body still greatly inflatable); about 12 spines in a row anterior to dorsal fin, the most anterior a median one between nostrils; three spines over eye; nasal organ cylindrical, open at both ends; median fins rounded; greyish brown dorsally, each spine in a white or yellow spot, shading to whitish ventrally, the spines there in a black spot (some spines on side of body each in a yellow and black spot); fins grey without spots. Largest specimen, 34 cm. Known thus far only from the Red Sea, the Gulf of Oman, the west coast of India, Indonesia, the Philippines and the South China Sea. Collected in the depth range of 3 to over 90 m. *C. orbicularis* (Bloch) has fewer spines (about 9 anterior to dorsal fin) and a few large black spots not associated with spines.

177

# Glossary of Terms

**Adipose eyelid:** An immovable transparent outer covering or partial covering of the eye of some groups of bony fishes, such as mullets and jacks, which performs protective and streamlining functions.

**Adipose fin:** a small fleshy fin without rays found on the back behind the dorsal fin of some primitive teleost fishes such as the lizardfishes.

**Alcyonarian:** an animal of the Subclass Anthozoa (corals, sea anemones) of Phylum Coelenterata; polyps with eight tentacles; includes soft corals and gorgonians.

**Allopatric:** in reference to species with different geographical distributions; the opposite of sympatric.

**Anus:** the posterior external opening of the digestive tract from which wastes are voided; sometimes called the vent.

**Axil:** the acute angular region between a fin and the body; usually used in reference to the underside of the pectoral fin toward the base. Equivalent to the armpit of man.

**Band:** an oblique or irregular marking (compare 'bar' below).

**Bar:** an elongate colour marking of vertical orientation, the sides of which are usually more-or-less straight (although they need not be parallel).

**Barbel:** a slender tentacle-like protuberance of sensory function which is often seen on the chin of some fishes such as goatfishes and some of the croakers.

**Benthic:** referring to the benthos, the fauna and flora of the sea bottom.

**Canine:** a prominent slender sharp-pointed tooth.

**Carnivore:** a flesh-eating animal.

**Caudal fin:** the tail fin. The term tail alone generally refers to that part of a fish posterior to the anus.

**Caudal peduncle:** the part of the body between the posterior basal parts of the dorsal and anal fins and the base of the caudal fin. The usual vertical measurement is the least depth; the length measurement herein is horizontal, and the fin of reference (i.e., rear base of dorsal or anal) is designated.

**Chiton:** an animal of the Class Amphineura of Phylum Mollusca; has an elliptical body protected by eight overlapping calcareous plates; clings strongly to rocks.

**Cirrus:** a small slender flexible fleshy protuberance; the plural is cirri.

**Coelenterate:** an aquatic animal of the Phylum Coelenterata which is characterized by a central mouth usually surrounded by tentacles bearing stinging cells, and no anus; includes sea anemones, corals, and jellyfishes.

**Community:** the assemblage of animals and plants living in one habitat.

**Compressed:** laterally flattened; often used in reference to the shape of the body – in this case deeper than wide.

**Crenulate:** wavy or scalloped.

**Crustacean:** an animal of the Class Crustacea of the Phylum Arthropoda; includes crabs, lobsters, shrimps, and copepods.

**Ctenoid scales:** scales of bony fishes which have tiny tooth-like projections along the posterior margin and part of the exposed portion. Collectively these little teeth (or ctenii) impart a rough texture to the surface of the scales.

**Cycloid scales:** scales of bony fishes, the exposed surfaces and edges of which lack any small tooth-like projections; they are, therefore, smooth to the touch.

**Demersal:** living on the sea bottom.

**Depressed:** dorsoventrally flattened. The opposite in body shape of compressed.

**Depth:** a vertical measurement of the body of a fish; most often employed for the maximum height of the body excluding the fins.

**Distal:** outward from the point of attachment; the opposite of proximal.

**Dorsal:** toward the back or upper part of the body; the opposite of ventral.

**Dorsal fin:** a median fin along the back which is supported by rays. There may be two or more dorsal fins, in which case the most anterior one is designated the first.

**Double emarginate:** biconcave; used to describe the shape of the posterior edge of the caudal fin in which there are two curved indentations separated by a convexity.

**Echinoderm:** an aquatic marine animal of the Phylum Echinodermata; radially symmetrical with a skeleton composed of calcareous plates (may be reduced to spicules); many move via their numerous tube feet; includes starfishes, brittle stars, sea urchins, and sea cucumbers.

**Emarginate:** concave; used to describe the posterior border of a caudal fin which is inwardly curved.

**Endemic:** native; in reference to an animal or plant restricted to a particular area.

**Family:** a major entity in the classification of animals and plants which consists of a group of related genera. Family words end in 'idae', an example being Gobiidae for the goby family; when used as an adjective, the 'ae' is dropped, hence gobiid fish.

**Forked:** inwardly angular; used in describing the shape of a caudal fin which is divided into two equal lobes, the posterior border of each of which is relatively straight.

**Frenum:** a connecting fold of membrane serving to support or restrain a part.

**Fusiform:** spindle-shaped; used in reference to the body shape of a fish which is cylindrical or nearly so and tapers toward the ends.

**Gas bladder:** a tough-walled gas-filled sac lying in the upper part of the body cavity of many bony fishes just beneath the vertebral column, the principal function of which is to offset the weight of the heavier tissues, particularly bone. The organ is also called the air bladder or the swim bladder.

**Genus:** a group of closely related species; the first part of the scientific name of an animal or plant. The plural is genera.

**Gill arch:** the bony support for the gill filaments and gill rakers. Normally there are four pairs of gill arches in bony fishes.

**Gill membranes:** membranes along the ventral and posterior margin of the operculum (gill cover) which function in respiration; they are supported by the branchiostegal rays.

**Gill opening:** the opening posteriorly and often also ventrally on the head of fishes where the water of respiration is expelled. Bony fishes have a single such opening on each side whereas cartilaginous fishes (sharks and rays) have five to seven. The gill openings of sharks and rays are called gill slits.

**Gill rakers:** stout protuberances of the gill arch on the opposite side from the red gill filaments which function in retaining food organisms. They vary greatly in number and length and are important in the classification of fishes.

**Gorgonian:** a sessile animal of the Subclass Alcyonaria, Class Anthozoa, Phylum Coelenterata; includes sea fans and sea whips.

**Head length:** the straight-line measurement of the head taken from the front of the upper lip to the membranous posterior end of the operculum.

**Herbivore:** a plant-feeding animal.

**Heteracanthous:** successive spines alternating in position left to right.

**Illicium:** the 'fishing pole' and 'lure' of lophiiform (pediculate) fishes which is used to attract prey close to the mouth of these fishes.

**Incisiform:** chisel-like; used to describe teeth which are flattened and truncate with sharp edges like the front teeth of some mammals such as man.

**Interopercle:** one of the bones comprising the operculum; bordered anterodorsally by the preopercle and posterodorsally by the opercle and subopercle.

**Interorbital space:** the region on the top of the head between the eyes; measurements may be taken of the least width, either fleshy (to the edges of the orbits) or bony (between the edges of the frontal bones which rim the orbits).

**Invertebrate:** an animal lacking a vertebral column; includes the vast majority of animals on earth such as the corals, the worms, and the insects.

**Isthmus:** the throat region of a fish which extends forward from the ventral part of the chest and narrows anteriorly.

**Keel:** a lateral strengthening ridge posteriorly on the caudal peduncle or base of the caudal fin; typically found on swift-swimming fishes with a narrow caudal peduncle and a broadly lunate caudal fin.

**Lanceolate:** lance-shaped, hence gradually tapering to a point; used to describe a caudal fin with very long middle rays. An unusual fin shape most often seen among the gobies.

**Lateral:** referring to the side or directed toward the side; the opposite of medial.

**Lateral line:** a sensory organ of fishes which consists of a canal running along the side of the body and communicating via pores through scales to the exterior; functions in perceiving low frequency vibrations, hence provides a sense which might be termed 'touch at a distance'.

**Lateral-line scales:** the pored scales of the lateral line between the upper end of the gill opening and the base of the caudal fin. The count of this series of scales is of value in the description of fishes. Also of value at times is the number of scales above the lateral line (to the origin of the dorsal fin) and the number below the lateral line (to the origin of the anal fin).

**Leptocephalus:** the elongate, highly compressed, transparent larval stage of some primitive teleost fishes such as the tarpon, bonefish and eels.

**Lower limb:** refers either to the horizontal margin of the preopercle or to the number of gill rakers on the first gill arch below and including the one at the angle.

**Lunate:** sickle-shaped; used to describe a caudal fin which is deeply emarginate with narrow lobes.

**Maxilla:** a dermal bone of the upper jaw which lies posterior to the premaxilla. On the higher fishes the maxilla is excluded from the gape, and the premaxilla bears the teeth.

**Medial:** toward the middle or median plane of the body; opposite of lateral.

**Median fins:** the fins in the median plane, hence the dorsal, anal, and caudal fins.

**Median predorsal scales:** the number of scales running in a median row anteriorly from the origin of the dorsal fin.

**Molariform:** shaped like a molar, hence low, broad, and rounded.

**Mollusc:** an animal of the Phylum Mollusca; unsegmented with a muscular 'foot' and visceral mass; often protected by one or two shells; includes gastropods (snails and nudibranchs), pelecypods (bivalves such as clams and oysters), cephalopods (such as squids and octopuses), and amphineurans (chitons).

**Morphology:** a study of the form and structure of animals and plants.

**Nape:** the dorsal region of the head posterior to the occiput.

**Ocellus:** an eye-like marking with a ring of one colour surrounding a spot of another.

**Omnivore:** an animal which feeds on both plant and animal material.

**Opercle:** the large bone which forms the upper posterior part of the operculum; often bears one to three backward-directed spines in the higher fishes.

**Operculum:** gill cover; comprised of the following four bones; opercle, preopercle, interopercle, and subopercle.

**Orbital:** referring to the orbit or eye.

**Order:** a major unit in the classification of organisms; an assemblage of related families. The ordinal word ending in the animal kingdom is 'iformes'.

**Organism:** a living entity, whether unicellular or multicellular, animal or plant.

**Origin:** the beginning; often used for the anterior end of the dorsal or anal fin at the base. Also used in zoology to denote the more fixed attachment of a muscle.

**Oviparous:** producing ova (eggs) that hatch after leaving the body of the mother; the mode of reproduction of the great majority of bony fishes.

**Ovoviviparous:** producing eggs which hatch within the body of the mother; the mode of reproduction of most sharks and rays.

**Paired fins:** collective term for the pectoral and pelvic fins.

**Palatine:** a paired lateral bone on the roof of the mouth lying between the vomer and the upper jaw; the presence or absence of teeth on this bone is of significance in the classification of fishes.

**Papilla:** a small fleshy protuberance.

**Pectoral fin:** the fin usually found on each side of the body behind the gill opening; in primitive fishes this pair of fins is lower on the body than in more advanced forms.

**Pelagic:** pertaining to the open sea (hence not living inshore or on the bottom); oceanic.

**Pelvic fin:** one of a pair of juxtaposed fins ventrally on the body in front of the anus; varies from abdominal in position in primitive fishes such as herrings to the more anterior locations termed thoracic or jugular in advanced fishes. It is sometimes called the ventral fin.

**Pharyngeal teeth:** opposing patches of teeth which occur on the upper and lower elements of the gill arches. They vary from sharp and piercing to nodular or molariform; they may be modified into a grooved grinding apparatus (or pharyngeal mill), such as is seen in the parrotfishes.

**Plankton:** a collective term for pelagic animals and plants that drift with ocean currents; though many are motile, they are too small or swim too feebly or aimlessly to resist the sweep of the current. By contrast the animals of the nekton are independent of water movement.

**Polychaete:** an animal of Class Polychaeta of Phylum Annelida; a segmented worm with setae (bristles), which may move about freely or live permanently in a tube. Polychaete is from the Greek meaning many hairs or bristles.

**Polyp:** the sedentary form of coelenterate animals consisting of a tubular body with one external opening (the mouth) rimmed with tentacles; may be one of a colony; the soft part of a living coral.

**Premaxilla:** the more anterior bone forming the upper jaw. In the higher fishes it extends backward and bears all of the teeth of the jaw. It is this part of the upper jaw which can be protruded by many fishes.

**Preopercle:** a boomerang-shaped bone, the edges of which form the posterior and lower margins of the cheek region; it is the most anterior of the bones comprising the gill cover. The upper vertical margin is sometimes called the upper limb, and the lower horizontal edge the lower limb; the two limbs meet at the angle of the preopercle.

**Preorbital:** the first and usually the largest of the suborbital bones; located along the ventroanterior rim of the eye. Sometimes called the lachrymal bone.

**Principal caudal rays:** the caudal rays which reach the terminal border of the fin; in those fishes with branched caudal rays, the count includes the branched rays plus the uppermost and lowermost rays which are unbranched.

**Produced:** drawn out to a point; lengthened.

**Proximal:** toward the centre of the body; the opposite of distal.

**Ray:** the supporting bony elements of fins; includes spines and soft rays.

**Rhomboid:** wedge-shaped; refers to a caudal fin in which the middle rays are longest and the upper and lower portions of the terminal border of the fin are more-or-less straight; essentially the opposite of forked. It is an uncommon fin shape.

**Rounded:** refers to a caudal fin in which the terminal border is smoothly convex.

**Rudiment:** a structure so deficient in size that it does not perform its normal function; often used in reference to the small nodular gill rakers at the ends of the gill arch.

**Scute:** an external bony plate or enlarged scale.

**Segmented rays:** the soft rays of fins which bear cross striations, at least distally.

**Serrate:** notched along a free margin, like the edge of a saw.

**Seta:** a bristle or bristle-like structure; the plural is setae.

**Sexual dichromatism:** a condition wherein the two sexes of the same species are of different colour.

**Simple:** not branched.

**Snout:** the region of the head in front of the eye. Snout length is measured from the front of the upper lip to the anterior edge of the eye.

**Soft ray:** a segmented fin ray which is composed of two closely joined lateral elements. It is nearly always flexible and often branched.

**Species:** the fundamental unit in the classification of animals and plants consisting of a population of individuals which freely interbreed with one another. The word 'species' is both singular and plural.

**Spine:** an unsegmented bony process consisting of a single element which is usually rigid and sharply pointed. Those spines which support fins are never branched.

**Spinule:** a small spine. The term generally not used in reference to the small spines of fins.

**Spiracle:** an opening between the eye and the first gill slit of sharks and rays which leads to the pharyngeal cavity.

**Standard length:** the length of a fish from the front of the upper lip to the posterior end of the vertebral column (the last element of which, the hypural plate, is somewhat broadened and forms the bony support for the caudal fin rays).

**Stripe:** a horizontal straight-sided colour marking.

**Subopercle:** an elongate flat dermal bone which is one of the four comprising the operculum; lies below the opercle and forms the ventroposterior margin of the operculum.

**Suborbital depth:** the distance from the lower edge of the eye to the nearest edge of the upper lip.

**Supraorbital:** the region bordering the upper edge of the eye.

**Symbiosis:** the living together in close association by two dissimilar organisms. This term includes commensalism whereby one organism derives benefit from the association but the other does not (though it is not harmed), parasitism where the association is disadvantageous or distractive to one of the organisms, and mutualism where both organisms exist to mutual advantage.

**Sympatric:** in reference to species which live in the same major geographical area.

**Symphysis:** an articulation, generally immovable, between two bones; often used in reference to the anterior region of juncture of the two halves of the jaws.

**Synonym:** an invalid scientific name of an organism proposed after the accepted name.

**Tail:** that part of an animal posterior to the anus (disregarding the hind limbs of quadrupeds).

**Teleost:** refers to the Teleostei, the highest super-order of the rayfin bony fishes. The other super-orders are the Chondrostei (the sturgeons and paddlefishes are the living representatives) and the Holostei (the bowfin and gars are the contemporary forms). The Teleostei and Holostei may be polyphyletic (of multiple origin), so these superordinal names, though often heard, are usually omitted from recent formal classifications. The great majority of living fishes are teleosts.

**Thoracic:** referring to the chest region.

**Total length:** the length of a fish from the front of whichever jaw is most anterior to the end of the longest caudal ray.

**Truncate:** square-ended; used to describe a caudal fin with a vertically straight terminal border and angular or slightly rounded corners.

**Upper limb:** refers either to the vertical free margin of the preopercle or to the number of gill rakers on the first gill arch above the angle.

**Ventral:** toward the lower part of the body; the opposite of dorsal.

**Villiform:** like the villi of the intestine, hence with numerous small slender projections. Used to describe bands of small close-set teeth, particularly if slender. If the teeth are short, they are often termed cardiform.

**Viviparous:** producing living young which develop from nourishment directly from the mother.

**Vomer:** a median unpaired bone toward the front of the roof of the mouth, the anterior end of which often bears teeth.

**Zooplankton:** the animals of the plankton.

# Index

to common and scientific names